Macromedia Flash™ Animation & Cartooning: A Creative Guide

About the Author

Ibis Fernandez has the experience of a diverse career in the entertainment industry. In 1996, while working as the director of advertising for Ocean View Publishing, Ibis moved into part-time, freelance cel animation and video production. In January 1999, he made the final leap and became a full-time, freelance animator. As a freelance animator, he has worked on a series of animated shorts and features for TV and the Web. He has also appeared in Star Trek: Voyager and as the lead character in a film, *The Parlor Boys*. Ibis currently maintains Flashfilmmaker.com, a site dedicated to Flash animated shorts and sketches.

Macromedia Flash™
Animation & Cartooning:
A Creative Guide

Ibis Fernandez

McGraw-Hill/Osborne

New York Chicago San Francisco
Lisbon London Madrid Mexico City Milan
New Delhi San Juan Seoul Singapore Sydney Toronto

McGraw-Hill/Osborne
2600 Tenth Street
Berkeley, California 94710
U.S.A.

To arrange bulk purchase discounts for sales promotions, premiums, or fund-raisers, please contact **McGraw-Hill/Osborne** at the above address. For information on translations or book distributors outside the U.S.A., please see the International Contact Information page immediately following the index of this book.

Macromedia Flash™ Animation & Cartooning: A Creative Guide

1234567890 DOC DOC 01987654321

ISBN 0-07-213323-6

Publisher	Brandon A. Nordin
Vice President & Associate Publisher	Scott Rogers
Acquisitions Editor	Jim Schachterle
Project Editor	Patty Mon
Acquisitions Coordinator	Tim Madrid
Technical Editor	Amanda Farr
Reviewer	Jim Caldwell
Copy Editor	Marcia Baker
Proofreader	Paul Tyler
Indexer	David Heiret
Computer Designer	Melinda Moore Lytle
Illustrators	Lyssa Wald, Beth Young, Michael Mueller
Series Designer	Roberta Steele
Cover Designer	William Voss

Acknowledgments for copyrighted material appear on the last page of the book, which is an extension of this copyright page.

This book was composed with Corel VENTURA™ Publisher.

To the men and women who put their lives on the line everyday in the name of freedom so that schmoes like me can be free to make a living drawing funny pictures.

Contents at a Glance

Contents

Part III   Production

Cartooning and Animation

CHAPTER 1

Introduction to Cartooning

C artoons have been around for as long as there have been people to draw them. In the early days, cavemen would amuse themselves by drawing each other in humiliating and embarrassing situations. These images often depicted some poor slob being ferociously devoured by a pride of saber-toothed tigers or wild beasts.

These early forms of cartoons often followed the typical premise of boy meets girl, girl runs away, water buffalo chasing girl mauls boy. Unfortunately, this type of humor was never really appreciated and, crude as it might have been, it was the basis for what would someday be referred to as the fine art of cartooning.

But Mommy, Where Do Cartoons Come From?

Cartoons, as we know them, have their origin in Italy sometime during the Renaissance (between the fourteenth and seventeenth centuries). A common practice at the time was the drawing of large murals, called *frescoes,* across the walls and ceilings of buildings. This practice often required the participation of many people working together to create the final rendering. To create these large murals, full-sized preparatory drawings had to be made first on a thick, cardboard-like paper. These drawings were called *cartoni,* after the Italian name for the cardboard-like paper on which they were drawn.

The cartoons were often destroyed during the transfer from the paper to the wall surface or simply discarded afterward because they were no longer of any use. Lucky for us, a few of the original cartoons from this era were preserved. Perhaps the most well known of these are by Raphael, for the design of the wall tapestries in the Sistine Chapel in the Vatican, and by Leonardo da Vinci, for the painting of *The Virgin and Child with Saint John the Baptist and Saint Anne.*

Sometime in the 1840s, Prince Albert, who was looking to decorate the walls of the new Houses of Parliament in London with frescoes, sponsored a design competition. Some of the cartoon submissions were so absurd and ridiculous, they were published and made fun of in the English magazine, *Punch.* This important event is when the definition of the word "cartoon" literally changed to its modern-day meaning: a humorous or satirical drawing. I wouldn't be particularly surprised if the term "*punch line*" also originated from around that time.

Drawing Isn't Necessarily a Talent — It's a Skill!

The single most important factor in cartooning and animation is the ability to be able to draw. Although natural talent is always helpful, one thing to remember is the act of drawing itself isn't necessarily a talent. Drawing is a skill that can be learned and taught by virtually anyone with the desire to do so.

In much the same way a person learns to read and write, anyone can learn how to draw. The process of drawing cartoons isn't that different from the skills employed when writing. If we want to communicate a message to another person in writing, what we're doing is composing a drawing by using a series of pictures, which at one point in our lives, we had to learn to draw. Someone once showed you that the capital letter *A* was drawn using two lines in a tent formation with a third horizontal line intercepting them at the center. And the capital letter *B* is drawn using one vertical line with two arches protruding to the right side.

When illustrating, we also make a drawing using a series of pictures, which, just like the letters in the alphabet, are composed using simple basic formulas.

If you're a seasoned Web developer already working with Flash and are interested in doing animated cartoons (or even if you're not, but your interests are in learning how to draw and animate), then I highly recommend Part I of this book.

If you're already a cartoonist or an animator, but your interests lie in bringing your talent to the Web using Macromedia Flash and learning the software, then by all means feel free to jump ahead to Chapter 6 where the Flash part of the book actually begins.

Types of Cartoons

Cartooning is an art form much like any other. Part of it extends from creative inspiration but, without context, the idea is lost. Cartoonists usually work from a variety of sources and strive to develop their own unique styles. The media used to create cartoons are as varied as the market itself and, depending on the cartoon's purpose, its use, and its format, they're classified according to the following types.

Editorial Cartoons

Editorial cartoons are often also called *political cartoons*. They serve to convey the artist's political opinion or to further illustrate viewpoints in editorial articles.

Editorial and political cartoons are known to have played a vital role in almost every major political event in recorded history. Whether used for good or evil, they serve as a visual commentary on current events and can play an important part in swaying public opinion, as was proven by the Nazis in Germany during World War II.

For the most part, political cartoons make use of *caricature,* a deliberate exaggeration or distortion of people's features.

Gags

A *gag* is a single-panel cartoon also known as a *funny*. In many cases, the drawing itself is funny enough to bring a chuckle or two from the viewer, but often a funny one-liner, a caption, or a punch line accompanies the gag for the full effect to be achieved.

Illustrative Cartoons

Illustrative cartoons are used in conjunction with advertising as well as various forms of literature, such as children's books or *spot drawings,* which are common in periodicals like *The Wall Street Journal*. Companies often either license established cartoon characters to use in their adverting or commission specific characters to be created for the same purpose. A good example of this is the use of the cartoon characters from the popular comic strip *Dilbert* for Office Depot's advertising, which is licensed via a syndicate. Domino's Pizza at one point commissioned the creation of a character named "The Noid" for use in their marketing campaigns. The 7 UP people also employed the same procedure when they used the "Spot" character as their spokesperson.

Comic Strips and Comic Books

Basically, comic strips and comic books are just sequences that tell a story. Rightfully so, they are most often referred to by the term *sequential art*. A comic strip or comic doesn't always have to be humorous. Normally, it follows the lives of certain recurring characters and the reader becomes familiar with the comic series or characters. Cartoonists often make use of that familiarity to help them create humorous moments.

Character dialogue in a comic is presented in the form of balloons, which point to the character delivering the comment.

A comic can also present itself either as a self-contained little story, such as the ones seen in comic strips like *B.C.* and *Hagar the Horrible,* or as part of a continuing story line, such as the *Phantom* or *Spiderman*.

Animated Cartoons

Animation is the process of recording and playing back a sequence of stills to achieve the illusion of continuous motion.

Animation toys and devices, such as flipbooks and animation wheels, have been in use for centuries, but not until the creation of the motion picture in the early twentieth century did animation emerge as a cartoon genre.

In recent years, the Internet has provided cartoonists with a medium to publish and distribute their work unlike anything ever imagined. The Web has also made it easier for cartoonists to self-syndicate their work on a global level. With the advent of Macromedia Flash, the Web has become a hotbed for animated content, opening a whole new market for both cartoonists and Web developers.

Basic Cartooning Equipment

Among the biggest perks of being a cartoonist is the sweet, low overhead involved. Cartoonists can kick-start an entire career for about 20 bucks and still have enough money for chili-fries and a Coke on their way home from the office supply store.

One of the most frequently asked questions by any aspiring cartoonist is, "What do you use to draw with?" The answer is always something along the lines of "Whatever floats your boat." Basically what this means is that if by wearing the same shoes a basketball player like Michael Jordan wears could make you play like him, then the whole world would be composed of high-flying NBA players. The fact of the matter is, when it comes to cartooning, all you really need is something to draw with, something to draw on, and a bit of imagination.

Here are some points to keep in mind about supplies needed to complete this section of the book.

Pencils

To get started, you need some good, reliable pencils. You'll do a lot of erasing and cleaning up, so it's a good idea to buy pencils that don't smear much (or as little as possible) and that can easily be erased without leaving behind many trails.

Inking Tools

The most common inking pens among cartoonists are the *nibbed dip pens,* which are made up of two separate components: the handle and the nib. The handle is just a piece of wood or plastic designed to hold your nibs.

Nibs come in various shapes and sizes. They are used to ink your work to produce a more stylized and professional look. You need a bottle of ink to go along with your dip pen. The most common type of ink used is called *India* ink and can be purchased at any hobby shop or office supply store.

NOTE

If you are going to use dip pens, be sure you keep your nibs clean after every use and that you are the only person who uses them. Nibs tend to bend and conform to your own particular way of inking. So if a friend decides to use your pens for inking their own work, you can pretty much consider them ruined. Bent or rusty nibs will damage your artwork and tear up your paper.

Not all cartoonists use dip pens. Some use brushes, felt-tip pens, or magic markers, while others use technical pens and basically any kind of ink-based stylus that gives you the desired line work you're aiming for in your finished art work. In the past, I have found myself inking with anything from cotton swabs to toothbrushes. It's all a matter of what type of look you are going for.

Depending on which cartoon I'm working on, I either use the traditional dip pen to ink my line work or I use my favorite little inking tool, which is the dual-tip Sharpie permanent marker. The Sharpie twin-tip marker has a fine point on one side, which is great for inking outlines, and a thicker tip on the other side that allows for quick area fills.

Paper

The type of paper doesn't matter much either. You have to get something strong enough to withstand a lot of erasing, and when ink's applied to it, you need paper that won't bleed or ooze into the fibers or tear easily. So, be aware of this before you buy your paper. Because the purpose of this book is, ultimately, to have you animating in Flash, I won't place much emphasis on cartooning for traditional publishing. Instead, the focus is on drawing with the idea that you'll be transferring to and publishing your work via Macromedia Flash. Some things to remember as you purchase your paper:

► You'll be doing a lot of drawings, and those drawings will be of little use to you after you scan or capture them into your computer. Regular 8 1/2 by 11-inch paper is perfect for this purpose because it can easily be fitted onto most standard scanners. But some types of paper—such as those one used for high-volume copying—are of poor quality, and might tear and smear easily.

► Does the price of the paper really say anything about its quality? Just how much does the quality matter to you (when you're done with it, the paper's going to end up in the garbage bin anyway)?

► Will the drawings I make with this paper fit into my scanner? Although computer tech issues aren't covered in this part of the book, the size of the paper you choose must let you easily transfer your drawing using your scanner or capture device.

Also, remember, scanners aren't the only way to transfer images into your computer. Digital cameras and camcorders are actually a faster, more convenient way to make captures for animation. When used correctly, a camera hooked up to your computer is a far more powerful and efficient tool than a scanner. When using a video or digital camera for capturing the images, you're less restricted in your choice of paper sizes. This is covered later in the book.

A Nice Light Box or Animation Disk

Light boxes aren't always necessary, especially if you're just doing basic cartooning. If your goal is to animate your toons, though, and I suspect it is, then beginning to think about acquiring a light box is a good idea. Light boxes are extremely useful for cleaning up drawings and creating cel animation–type sequences before importing them to Flash for further manipulation.

There is also no need to go out and spend a wad of money on an animation disk or light box. If you'd like to learn to create your own animation disks or light boxes, just surf on over to www.flashfilmmaker.com/how-to/tools.

Summary

The art of cartooning was originated in Italy during the Renaissance. The name cartoon was derived from the Italian word for the thick cardboard-like paper used to draw them on. Drawing a cartoon was the first step in the process of getting a wall or ceiling tapestry painted.

In the 1840s, Prince Albert hosted a contest to see who could draw the greatest cartoons, which would be used to paint the murals of the Houses of Parliament in London. Some of the submissions were so ridiculous that the English magazine, *Punch,* published and ridiculed the illustrations. It was from this moment on that the word cartoon became synonymous with being a humorous satirical drawing.

The act of drawing is a skill like any other. While some may be able to learn it and develop it into a natural talent, any person is capable of learning it. The process is not that different from the process involved in learning how to write. The most common types of cartoons are satirical, illustrative, comical, editorial, and animated. Cartoons in any form have the ability to reach people like no other medium can. They can strongly affect public opinion towards a product or service or towards our celebrities and political leaders, or they may simply entertain us by providing a familiar set of faces whose quirky lives we follow day in and day out when we sit to read the newspaper.

CHAPTER 2

The Cartoon Head

The *head* is probably the most important overall feature of a cartoon character. Wherever the head is located, this is the one area where, by default, your focus is concentrated. The cartoon head also plays an important role in determining the character's size. For example, a tall cartoon character may be measured as being seven heads tall, whereas a short and chunky character may be measured as being only four heads tall. These are measurements based on their own head and not a predetermined head in general.

Head Construction

Although cartoon heads can be created from almost any shape imaginable, you can draw them in two basic approaches.

Traditional Head Construction

The *traditional head construction* for cartoon characters is based on a single circular mass. The shape is divided at the center by two guidelines, which are perpendicular to each other. These lines are also known as *axis lines*. The point at which these two lines meet determines the center of the face, as shown in Figure 2-1.

The *horizontal axis line* acts as a base for the eyes to rest on. This guide is also used to determine the head's direction or position. Depending on the direction implied by the horizontal axis, the head of the character will rotate in a vertical direction.

The *vertical axis line* is used for placing the nose on the character, as well as for determining the head's rotation along a horizontal level (see Figure 2-2).

A good idea is to think of the mass as a three-dimensional shape that can be rotated 360 degrees in any direction. When the figure is rotated, the angle of the axis lines drawn on the surface of that shape will change to reflect the new direction of the head.

To keep your cartoon characters looking consistent from all angles, you simply need to place the features, such as eyes, nose, mouth, hair, and so on, along the axis

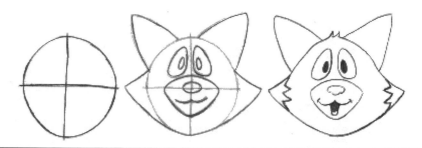

Figure 2-1   *Example of the head axis model*

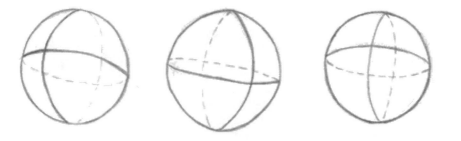

Figure 2-2   *Axis lines help to indicate the position of a shape in relation to its environment.*

lines and keep the angles relative to the direction of the head at all times. In doing so, you can effectively create an unlimited number of head poses, while retaining the character's original design (see Figure 2-3).

Modern Head Construction

The modern head is divided into two sections: the skull and the jaw. The *skull* is basically the same circular shape used to construct the traditional head. The same rules as for the traditional head also apply to the skull except, in this case, the mouth isn't placed directly onto it. The mouth is placed on the jaw section. Think of the *jaw* as a prosthetic extension of the skull where the character's mouth will rest. The jaw is like a physical object glued to the skull.

   If the skull and the jaw were two tangible items, which you could actually pick up and hold in your hands, you could take that skull and place it directly onto the jaw, where it would rest nice and snugly. When the two objects come together, the modern head construction is complete. As the skull rotates and turns, so does the jaw, as shown in Figure 2-4.

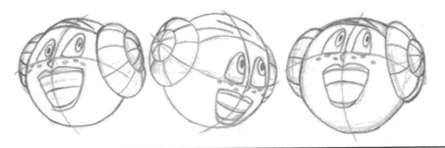

Figure 2-3   *The features of the character are placed along the axis lines and drawn in the perspective indicated by these lines.*

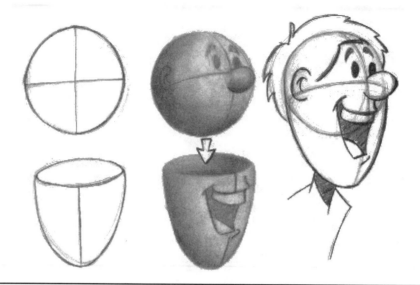

Figure 2-4   *The cartoon skull and jaw construction*

By using the skull and jaw construction, you can create more advanced cartoon heads with great ease. Even though the drawing itself will be two-dimensional, 3-D and perspective drawing tend to play a major role in the creation of visually appealing characters. As we move into animation, you'll see this technique used much more often.

The Male Head (Front View)

Let's take a moment to study the general male head. No matter how great an artist you are, always start by drawing a general outline of the figure.

1. Draw a skull and jaw construction to use as a guide. Don't worry about inking your drawings now, but be sure when you draw, you draw light enough to erase those outlines easily during cleanup.

2. Add ears and a neck to your head.

3. Now you're ready for some hair. Be sure to indicate the slope of the forehead.

4. Add the nose, eyes, eyebrows, and mouth. As you draw your mouth, think about how that expression will affect the shape of the cheeks, and then modify them as needed.

5. Finish this drawing by enhancing your line work, filling in the hair, and drawing a slight shadow just below the chin.

The Male Head (Side View)

Now let's draw the same character's *profile,* or side view.

1. Once again, start your drawing from a basic modern head construction outline. Because this is a profile shot, draw your axis lines and head construction fully rotated to the side. Adjust the tilt of the head accordingly.

2. This time, the ear is placed on the inside area of the head. The neck may either protrude directly from the skull or it may be attached directly to the jaw, just slightly behind the chin of the character.

3. Now you should add the hair. Once again, be sure to indicate the slope of the forehead. In this view, you can see a slight indentation added, where the curve should be.

4. Add the nose, eyes, eyebrows, and mouth. In this case, we're only using one eye and one eyebrow. You're now drawing the mouth from a profile view. The nose creates an automatic bond with the upper lip. In addition, as the upper lip

is formed, in most cases, it overlaps the lower lip. Draw a curved line slightly behind the corner of the mouth. As the mouth moves, this line indicates changes to the cheeks as the mouth changes positions. Depending on whether the mouth is open or shut, the chin must also be modified accordingly.

5. Finish this drawing by enhancing your line work, filling in the hair, and drawing a slight shadow just below the chin.

The Female Head (Front View)

Many cartoonists have trouble drawing the opposite sex. A major contributor to this problem is that females are often left out, for some reason, from most art instruction books. Even in classes and workshops, the male figure is most often used to teach people to draw. The role of females in cartoons is just as important as in real life and learning how to draw female characters can add great value to your work.

1. A woman's head shares the same basic structure as a man's head, however slight the modifications to the basic outline that must be made prior to drawing

her facial features. Her chin will be slightly less pronounced than the male chin, and her jaw will be narrower.

2. Draw the ears and neck. The female ear will be slightly higher than the man's to make her neck appear longer and sexier.

3. Add the hair, eyes, and mouth, and then indicate a nose. To pull off this drawing, you need to exaggerate common female stereotypes, such as fuller lips, eyes and eyelashes, and hair. Following the same stereotype, a female's nose and neck should be minimized to give her a more vulnerable appearance.

4. Finish your drawing by accentuating your line work and filling in the rest of the details. Don't forget that little shadow underneath the chin. Decorate your female head with feminine accessories, such as a pearl necklace and earrings.

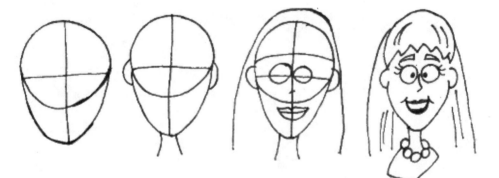

The Female Head (Side View)

Let's now examine the female head as drawn from a side view. Try to get into the routine of drawing things from a variety of different angles. It will help you avoid favoring particular angles and poses, which after a while become monotonous and boring. In animation, you also have the task of animating characters as they change from one pose to another.

1. When viewed from the side, the female's skull appears slightly larger than the male's. Don't take this the wrong way, guys, but the fact is, the majority of all cartoon females are smarter than men, and it usually shows.

2. Whether inverted or not, the forehead has a rather larger slope, which is mainly to accentuate the nose and often as a statement of her intelligence or lack of it. As previously stated, a female's nose is much smaller and perkier than a man's.

The ear is basically the same size; however, the less detail the better. A simple arch will do just fine.

3. The neck is longer and more slender. It may be attached directly to the jaw, as you did earlier for the male head but, most often, the neck protrudes directly from the base of the skull. The upper lip also protrudes farther than the male's. This is to accommodate the larger lips.

4. The size of the hair and eyes is exaggerated.

5. Enhance all details and clean up your artwork by erasing your outlines.

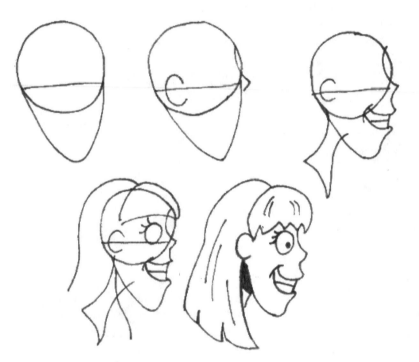

Heads That Defy Logic

A third, less conventional, yet highly regarded method of creating character heads also exists. This method requires the use of odd shapes as a guide. In most cases, these heads can still be broken down to a basic skull and jaw construction, but the method of getting these drawings down the first time around is based on the use of odd shapes as a starting point.

Blobs

The *blob* technique is probably the most common among this group. Blobs are also known as *sloppy circles* and, as the name implies, are nothing more than irregular circles. The shapes of these circles are modified to accentuate certain particular features, such as pudgy cheeks, and varied cranium and chin sizes. Here are some samples of heads created using blobs.

Rectangles

Squares and *rectangular-shaped* heads are great for villains. Nothing communicates "bad guy" better than a jagged-edged face. A vertical rectangle shape is also great for robots and tough-looking good guys. Animals, such as horses, camels, and even dogs, can have a head based on a rectangular shape.

Triangles

The *triangular* shape is great for females. It allows for the creation of characters with tiny chins and large craniums. This makes any female character look conceited and sneaky, like she's always plotting something. For the male figure based on this shape, you can have either the traditional rat-faced villain with great smarts or a hero who looks like a dimwit.

Pear Shaped

The *pear-shaped* head is extremely common. This shape is based on the modern head construction, which uses a skull and a jaw, but in a pear-shaped head, the skull and jaw are altered to different sizes, depending on the look desired. You can have a character whose skull is bigger than his jaw or a character whose jaw is larger than his skull. Starting an illustration based on the pear shape is an easy way to skip the usual skull and jaw construction, and to jump directly into the basic facial structure desired for these types of heads.

Diamond

The *diamond* shape lends itself better to the drawing of the female head. It allows for an almost-perfect chin and cheekbone combination, which in most cultures is viewed as a characteristic of beauty. Extremely jagged features and such—like an overly pointed nose or chin—are always a great recipe for a good villain.

The Half Moon

The *half moon* belongs to the circle fraction family. The half moon is a head created using half a circle as a starting point. A half moon can also be used as a simplified pear shape, where one of the ends composes the general skull area, while the rest of it acts as a jaw. In most cases, however, this shape is used in its entirety as a modified skull construction.

Circle Fractions

Circle fraction heads are just what their name implies. They are heads created using fractions of a circle. A shape used as a guide can be a quarter of a circle, a half moon, three fourths, and so on.

Head Proportions

The basic anatomy of the head is measured at being approximately five eyes wide. When the face is at rest with its mouth in a closed position, the eyes are directly on the center of the face, with only one-eye distance between them. The top of the ears is at the same level as the eyebrows. The top of the nose begins at the center of the face and, if measured vertically, extends down no farther than one fourth the size of the entire face. The mouth is then placed directly between the nose and the tip of the chin.

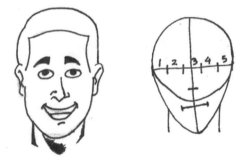

Basic anatomy is boring and plain, which is why distorting and exaggerating these proportions is the heart of cartooning. For the most part, cartoon characters have their eyes positioned toward the top of their heads, unless they're babies or form part of the cute category, which we explore later under character types.

1. Begin by drawing an original character head. You can copy mine, but I recommend you practice using your own designs. Draw your head by following the basic

anatomical guidelines we just covered. Remember, if your character is female, the jaw will be narrower and the chin less pronounced than a man's.

2. Make a second drawing of the same character. However, this time make the skull seven eyes wide. Keep the eyes at the same location and distance from each other. Add the rest of the features and modify them as necessary. The larger skull appearance makes the character look smarter, more like a nerd.

3. Now let's draw the character with the same proportions as the previous one, but, this time, enlarge the eyes, making the skull only three eyes wide. This guy looks like he's in need of some serious therapy or maybe some herbal tea.

4. Next, draw the character with a skull that's four eyes wide, using his original eyes (from the first drawing) as a measuring tool. In other words, he will have a smaller skull. Don't give him normal eyes, though. Instead, give him flesh-embedded eyes and a unabrow. Keep the rest of the features the same and modify the jaw to fit the smaller skull.

5. Make one last drawing of the same character. Draw his head at the normal five-eye proportions but, this time, keep his jaw equally wide, while squishing its length to half the original size. Don't put eyes on him. Instead, use big old, thick glasses whose lenses take up the entire width of his face. Then make him bald and add the rest of the features. Now you've got yourself one creepy looking dude.

Create an entire community of zany characters by taking a single character and distorting his appearance. Keep this exercise in mind, as we discuss the development of a cartoon formula later in the book.

▶ After you finish drawing each head, study it for several minutes and see if you can describe its personality as implied by its stereotypical features. How would that character interact with the other characters?

▶ Would the character be a good guy or a bad guy? Practice changing just one feature at a time, such as the hair, while keeping the rest of the features consistent.

▶ How would that character look if he were tall and lanky or short and chubby?

▶ How would his voice sound like if he were able to speak? Would he stutter or speak with a slur?

Facial Features

The goal of every cartoonist is to draw compelling and memorable characters with whom the audience immediately identifies, before they even say a word. Although this is often a task that takes years of trial and error to perfect, a good place to focus your efforts is in the drawing of the character's head; more specifically, in drawing its features. Facial features express much of a cartoon's personality without the need for explanations.

The Eyes

The eyes, of course, play an important role in the way a character expresses emotion, but I won't give you some poetic essay on the whole "windows to the soul" thing—at least not yet—because for cartoons, they're not. By manipulating the eyes, you can efficiently enhance emotions and moods, such as anger, frustration, boredom, sadness, and contempt. But the eyes aren't necessarily an essential part of the face to express those feelings. Many successful cartoon characters have managed to get by without eyes. Aside from *Mr. Magoo*, who was blind and always had his eyes shut, *Andy Capp* and *Beetle Bailey* are two of the most memorable cartoon characters whose eyes you've never seen. Hiding the eyes is a fairly common practice. Well-developed characters, like Hanna-Barbera's *Johnny Bravo,* whose eyes are constantly hidden from view behind a tiny pair of shades, do have limited personality traits, but they make up for it with charisma and body language.

The Nose and the Ears

The human nose and ears are made up of a soft bonelike substance called *cartilage*. Although cartilage is neither a bone nor a muscle, it does grow and regenerate at a steady pace throughout a person's entire lifetime. Cartoonists logically exploit this medical fact as an effective way to transmit the idea of a character's age to their audience. Just as in the real world, the older a character is, the larger his nose and ears are.

The nose can also be a powerful tool for shaping a character's personality type or function in life. If a nose is pointy and has a hairy mole in it, then this character automatically registers as evil to the viewer. If the nose is short and pudgy, this is most likely a cute character. Sometimes a character, such as a butler, is exceedingly stuck-up or smug. He has a type of nose that always seems to point upward, no matter how his face is tilted. Having large nostrils can be used to imply a keener sense of smell. Then, of course, there's Bob Cescas's trademark style. His characters have no nose at all and are just flat-out disturbing. Look at this character, seen at various stages of her life, and notice how the role of the nose and ears change to reflect her age.

The Mouth

The mouth is the most expressive feature of a cartoon character. In cartooning, the mouth, not the eyes, is the window to the soul. Mouth positions are generated by the character's emotion and state of mind, and the mouth's action or poses enhance the rest of the facial features, however they may be laid out across the face. Practice generating various emotions on a character's face by placing the mouth as your center of focus and using the other features to enhance that expression.

Facial Hair

Beards and mustaches can give a character—literally—a 180-degree transformation. Look at this character and notice how, as we change his facial hair to different styles, we also dramatically alter his appearance, creating an entire entourage of characters ready to populate a small town somewhere.

Expressions

In animation, your characters are the actors in your production. They need to convey or express their emotions effectively. When you design your characters, it's important to take the time to explore your characters' range of expressions before truly committing yourself to them. Find out early what works and what doesn't. If certain poses don't work for you, then what must be done to achieve the desired result?

My crowning achievement as a cartoonist was the day I realized I'd finally discovered my very own unique style. My comic strip, *Braindead,* uses a technique I developed over the course of many years of practice and experimentation. Because the construction of these characters' heads isn't based on average drawing principles, exploring my characters' range of emotions was somewhat of a challenge for me. Knowing I'd conquered it was one of the greatest feelings I've ever had in my quest to develop my own unique style.

Look at my cartoon counterpart, *Ibis,* as he displays several convincing expressions for you. See if you can name the emotion or state of mind being played out and try to re-create those emotions using your own characters.

Summary

In this chapter, we discussed the cartoon head and its construction using basic shapes. We also covered facial features and how to use and modify them to suit your unique character's personality, age, and demeanor. Here are some key points to remember:

▶   Drawing your cartoon characters from basic shapes is not necessarily a cookie-cutter approach. Your own drawing style should take precedence in their creation. By using basic shapes as a starting point or conforming your own style to constructions based on predetermined shapes, you are streamlining the process of drawing your characters, allowing you to render your characters in ways that will be more appealing to the public.

▶   Axis lines help determine the tilt and rotation of a shape. They are imaginary lines that will aid you in the placement of features onto a shape.

► Get into the habit of drawing females. They are an integral part of storytelling just as much as male characters are. In many cases, females are drawn using the same constructions as males, but pay particularly close attention to traditional stereotypes often associated with females. Female features are often less pronounced than those of a male.

► Learn to draw your characters from a variety of angles and try not to favor a particular pose. Keep your drawing interesting by attacking a pose from various angles.

CHAPTER
3

The Character Body

J ust as the head has its basic formulas, the body of a cartoon character must also be created using similar construction methods. When you design a body for your characters, make sure you pay close attention to its proportions and weight. Remember, our goal is ultimately to design character bodies that lend themselves well to animation and, more importantly, to Flash animation.

Understanding the basic anatomy and structure of people in general plays an essential role in whether your characters are believable when you present them to the public. Poorly designed characters have a harder time holding a person's attention than those that display realistic characteristics. This bit of realism can prove the determining factor in whether your character is totally accepted by your audience or totally rejected.

Body Types

William H. Sheldon, a psychologist, introduced his theories of Somatypes and how the human body can be categorized into various physical types in a work titled *The Varieties of Human Physique*. The book was published in the year 1940, and the following year Sheldon published a second book, *The Varieties of Human Temperament: A Psychology of Constitutional Differences*.

According to Sheldon's theory of *Somatypes,* three basic body types exist and, depending on what category a person may fall under, certain personality traits or psychological characteristics may be associated with that person.

Today, Sheldon's theories are a central focus among physical fitness and body-building literature. In fact Arnold Schwarzenegger's book, *The Encyclopedia of Modern Bodybuilding,* first turned me on to this concept.

The Ectomorphic Body Type

The *ectomorphic* body type is described as your basic beanpole person. This person has such a high metabolism rate that no matter how much he eats or how much muscle he attempts to put on, his body will use up most of the nutrients fast, leaving very little to be used for growing or storing in the form of fat.

All ectomorphic people share these basic characteristics:

► They have trouble gaining weight.

► Their muscle growth and regeneration take longer.

► They possess a delicate build.

► They are thin.

► They have a flat chest.

► Their muscle definition may be noticeable.

► They appear to have larger brains or skull mass.

► Their arms appear longer.

Endomorphic People

The *endomorphic* body type is the complete opposite of the ectomorph. An over-developed digestive system combined with a lower metabolism will allow his body to use up more of the nutrients he consumes. The results are the appearance of roundedness or softness. Unfortunately, either way, this type of person can't do much to keep from being—by traditional standards—considered overweight.

Endomorphs generally possess the following:

► They have an underdeveloped muscular structure.

► They have a softer body quality.

► They can easily increase their muscle mass.

► They have round-shaped features.

► They will gain large amounts of fat extremely fast and will have trouble losing it.

Mesomorphic People

The *mesomorphic* body type is, in theory, the ideal body type. This person's body is harder in nature and possesses a well-developed muscular structure.

The mesomorphs share these common features:

- ▶ They have an overly mature appearance.
- ▶ They have an upright posture.
- ▶ They have thicker skin.
- ▶ They can either gain or lose weight at will, fast and efficiently.
- ▶ They can grow muscle mass quickly.

The Subcategories

Of course, not every body fits directly within the basic three categories. Instead, many bodies have the combined body qualities of two different types. The average Joe weighs in at approximately 165 to 175 pounds, while his height is somewhere around 5'8" to 6' tall. His body type falls in a category somewhere in the middle of the ectomorph and the mesomorph. This subcategory is called the *ecto-mesomorph*. Likewise, if his body type fell in between being a mesomorph and endomorph, he would be referred to as having an *endo-mesomorphic* body type.

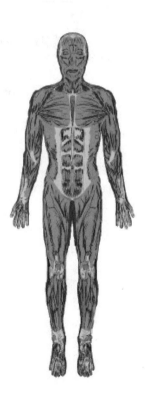

Shown here is a basic anatomy of an ecto-mesomorphic body type, which is considered the average person.

Cartoon Anatomy

The cartoon anatomy is an exaggerated, yet simplified, representation of the real anatomy. Depending on the style of the character and its design, you need to become familiar with how that character is put together.

The way a specific character is constructed dictates how he will carry out certain actions. For example, if a character has large, massive legs and tiny arms, such as a Tyrannosaurus rex, he will have great difficulty reaching for things with his hands. Most likely, he won't be able to reach his mouth, so he'll also have to find a way to eat without using his arms.

The Tyrannosaurus rex will have strong and massive legs that allow him to run faster and take longer strides as he walks. Because he has such a huge lower body, a small upper body, and an enormous head, the Tyrannosaurus rex tends to be extremely clumsy in his movements. He must also rely constantly on his enormous tail to keep himself balanced. This, too, affects his posture.

A common technique used among actors when creating personality traits for the characters they are portraying is to put themselves in the role of members of the animal kingdom. In doing this, actors can generate unforgettable and unique personality traits for their characters. Using the same technique, cartoonists can also give their characters interesting personality traits and idiosyncrasies, but they can also create genuinely unique physical characteristics. This technique is explored further in Chapter 4.

Look at this nightclub bouncer. His body was designed in parallel to the Tyrannosaurus rex. Can you imagine this guy walking up to you and demanding to see your ID card? How would he go about kicking someone out of a club? These questions can be substance enough for some hilarious situations.

On the other hand, when we take this bouncer and design him in parallel to another animal, such as a gorilla, his entire attitude changes. He now has larger arms and a more intimidating appearance. And he would have a completely different approach in the way he moves and behaves.

A simplified skeletal system acts as a foundation for us to attach the body parts and features easily, as well as to draw our characters in a wide variety of poses. Stick figures, such as the ones shown here, are perfect for the job.

Notice how in drawing these stick figures we allow ourselves the ability to place the arms and legs accurately, in a manner that will be more convincingly real.

A common mistake is to draw your stick figures without a chest and shoulder or hip area. In doing this, you not only do your characters a great disservice, you also rob yourself from being able to pose and create realistic character movement.

Drawing stick figures like this is wrong.

    Practice drawing various skeletons in a variety of poses. Don't worry if your drawings don't come out all right the first few times around. Everything comes with practice. Draw your skeletons at various stages of actions, such as running, jumping in the air, sneaking up to something, throwing a ball, and carrying some weight around, such as a large bag of rice.

    You can copy my drawings; but I strongly urge you to draw your own. The skeleton is one of those structures that will need to be erased later on, so draw it lightly and loosely.

    Try some odd character skeletons. What would a bird's skeleton look like? How about a gorilla or a monkey? If a person were a hunchback, how would you draw his skeleton? Practice drawing a variety of skeletons in various poses. There's no such thing as too much practice.

The Center of Gravity

Among the most noticeable body structure characteristics of the male and female figure is their center of gravity. Just like the Tyrannosaurus rex relies on his tail for balance, people must also maintain a center of gravity, constantly aligned to keep themselves from falling over. To maintain this center of balance, people must rely on their bodies and limbs to constantly work together as a unit.

Because of this, certain guidelines must be considered when drawing any type of character, whether it's a stationary pose or an act of motion. Maintaining the balanced center of gravity gives the illusion of physics and gives the character a more vulnerable quality. If that center of balance is disturbed at any point, by the laws of cause and effect, then that character must react accordingly.

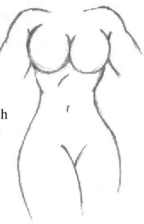

A female's center of gravity lies in the hip area, which is much broader than a male's. If, at any time, a woman's hips become off-balance, she could fall.

Any time a female performs an action where she is required to remain in a standing position—such as walking, running, jogging, or skipping—she must maintain her hips in the center of all action. If her hips become unbalanced, gravity will cause her to either fall down or react accordingly to keep herself upright.

A male's center of gravity lies in the chest and shoulder area. This area tends to be wider and more massive than a female's body structure. Unlike a female, a man is perfectly capable of throwing his hips around in any direction with little effect on his balance. Of course, this doesn't explain some of Earth's greatest mysteries like the Bermuda Triangle, but it does point a big old fat finger at another strange anomaly known as Ricky Martin.

One of the reasons females move more gracefully than males do is because their center of gravity is closer to the ground. Males, on the other hand, must keep the chest area centered at all times to remain balanced.

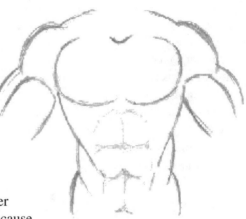

A basic principle applied to all forms of martial arts is working with a person's center of gravity. By concentrating on an opponent's chest (if he's male) or on an opponent's hips (if she's female) and causing that area of the body to become off-balance, you can easily take the upper hand in a combat situation. Now, just because I said this, I don't mean you should go around knocking people over. Just stay with me on this one and no one has to get hurt.

When a man's chest becomes off-balance, he reacts with his legs and arms in an attempt to regain his balance. In these images, thrusting pressure acts against a male and a female's left shoulder. Their reaction is based on how far off their center of gravity was affected by the thrust.

With the male figure's chest and shoulder area out of balance, he struggles desperately to find an equal or greater opposing force to maintain himself on his feet. He reaches with his arms to generate an equal amount of weight on the opposite side of the action. When that doesn't work or if it isn't enough, he lifts his opposing leg—in this case the right leg—and throws it in the direction against the antagonistic action. The female is virtually unaffected by this action.

On the other hand, when we apply that same kind of force to a male's hips, his chest would still most likely remain balanced and, thus, no major reaction is triggered. When a woman's hips are knocked off-balance, though, she will most likely fall. She, too, will react with her limbs in a desperate attempt to remain on her feet.

A female's center of gravity, being so much closer to the ground, requires a much faster reaction on her part if she is to maintain her footing. Her arms aren't always enough to keep her balanced, so she must also rely on the use of her entire upper body. For a female to maintain her balance, she'll usually bend her knees to a certain degree, while thrusting her arms and upper body weight in the opposite direction of the force being applied. The male, in this event, is unaffected.

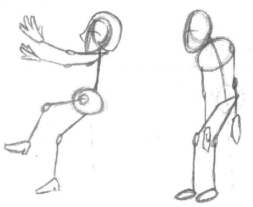

Lines of Action

Knowing where your line of action is should be the first step in any type of character drawing. A good idea is always to think about your line of action before attempting to draw your characters. In fact, you should draw your line on the paper and use it as a visual reference.

The *line of action* is an imaginary line that extends through the main action of a figure. When you draw your characters, be sure to plan your figures and details first, and then draw them in a way that they accentuate this line.

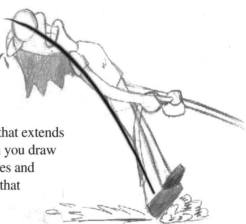

A character following an awkward or poorly thought-out line of action can easily ruin your scene composition and completely destroy any shred of believability you might have otherwise accomplished. A line of action represents active forces acting either with or against the figure in motion. When used in context, drawing characters with their center of gravity off-balance is quite safe but, in reality, the line of action allows the forces of nature to balance each other out and enables the cartoonist to create new and interesting dynamic poses and motion flow.

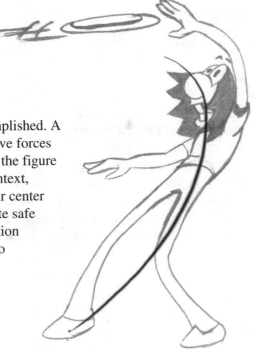

Notice how much harder actually believing this image is. For one, the center of gravity is way off-balance. Perhaps if his left leg had been more forward to support his weight, I could have managed to save this drawing. As I mentioned earlier, it's also quite possible to have a person's center of gravity off-balance when an equal amount of pressure is being applied against a character, such as pushing a car, pulling on a rope, or being affected by forces of nature, such as the wind during a storm or water currents. In this case, as you can see from the flag and the direction of his hair, no wind is blowing, so the illusion is totally ruined. Take a moment to draw a character following the action attempted in this image. What could have I done in terms of action and posture to have carried off my idea effectively?

Body Language

Being animated is not just the capability to move. An animated character is one that's full of life, even when he's not moving at all. A well-drawn dynamic pose can be held for long periods of time and still maintain a certain living quality within that character.

Talking heads are boring; they only show a lack of effort on the cartoonist's part. They have a harder time maintaining an audience's attention. How can you possibly ask your audience to suspend disbelief when all your characters do is move their mouths and look at each other as they deliver the dialogue? Can you honestly interpret what these characters are trying to say just by looking at them?

Characters who use their bodies as a communication tool are more eye-catching and get their point across more accurately. If we incorporate body language into our characters, they're no longer only talking heads, and although we still don't know the actual words they are saying, we can still get a clearer picture of the ideas, the mood, and the energy they're attempting to carry across.

As characters are influenced by various forces—whether they're internal or external—they tend to use their entire bodies to display their emotions and physical comforts or discomforts visually. These are known as *expressions*.

When something is sour to the taste, they react by cringing their faces and puckering their lips tightly. They may even shiver a bit, depending on the potency of that sourness. When a foul smell is in the air, they quickly clench their nostrils with one hand, while waving their other arm around in a futile attempt to get rid of that smell. These are all expressions.

Every cartoon character has its own unique way of expressing certain reactions; however, they're all exaggerations of real-life expressions. When a person is startled at the office by a coworker, he jumps up in a surprised manner and displays all the usual symptoms of shock and amazement. People don't physically levitate in the air, while their jaws drop halfway to the ground and their tongues grow about a foot long and wave around like crazy. That's only something a cartoon would do.

Limiting your character's expression simply to its face is a serious mistake. Always try to use the entire body to accentuate each and every expression.

Shoulders and Hips

Aside from the general purpose of maintaining a properly balanced character, the shoulders and hips play a strong role in a character's personality type and mannerisms. The way a character stands or walks along a given path can be modified by a simple tilt of the hip and shoulders. When standing in a neutral position, a character facing forward can be quite plain and boring to watch. Just by adjusting the tilt of the hip and shoulders in various directions, you can create much more interesting and dynamic posture effects, even at a standing position.

If your hips and shoulders tilt in the same direction, the figure looks a bit odd, but this can sometimes be a desired look for large, clumsy characters, such as an abominable snowman or a sumo wrestler.

If you make a hip-and-shoulder tilt a permanent fixture on the character, it can cause him to walk with a limp, as in a hunchback. Unless this is the effect you want, it's advisable to tilt the hip and shoulders, depending on the direction and shifting of the weight, as the character changes from one pose to another. This will ensure a consistent feel for body mechanics and weight distribution, and instill an overall sense of physics within your character that will effectively register with your audience.

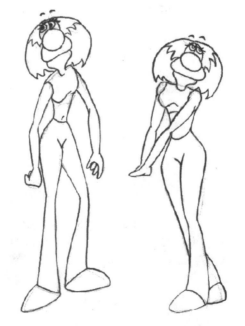

Summary

Under Sheldon's theories of Somatypes, the human body is classified through a system that measures the degree of certain physical attributes and the degree by which they are apparent on a person. At the very extreme, there are three basic body types: ectomorphic, endomorphic, and mesomorphic. An ectomorph is an extremely skinny person, an endomorph is the highly overweight person, and a mesomorph is the perfect blend of muscle and mass. A large number of body types are actually hybrids falling under the category of ecto-mesomorphic and endo-mesomorphic body types. By adhering to the following principles, you can draw believable characters that can be used in any number of positions:

▶ The cartoon anatomy is a simplified, yet exaggerated, version of real-life anatomy. Many cartoon characters share the physical characteristics and emotional qualities of species other than their own.

▶ The cartoon skeletal system can be defined by the simple use of a stick figure. Stick figures used for character construction purposes must be anatomically accurate by containing a collarbone area from which hang the shoulders and arms. A cartoon skeleton must also be drawn with a hip area to place and pose the legs accurately in any given direction.

▶ A male figure's center of gravity lies in the chest and shoulder region where this mass is far wider than a female's. The female's hips are broader than a male's, so the hip area is the female's center of gravity. If the center of gravity becomes offset, either by force or by her own initiative, she must react with the rest of her body accordingly to maintain her balance.

▶ The line of action is an imaginary line that extends through the character's figure. This line represents the flow of the character's movement and direction of the action being played out. Draw your characters in a way that accentuates this line while, at the same time, retaining the scene's composition.

▶ When a character communicates, make use of its entire body to illustrate even further the dialogue being delivered. Don't create talking heads; they are boring and do nothing for you, aside from getting you lynched by a posse of ornery, unsatisfied viewers.

▶ Find your character's range of expressions, and remember, an expression isn't only limited to the face. The entire body performing an expression will always register better than a simple twitch of the face, a grunt, or a roll of the eyes.

CHAPTER
4

Character Types

Character typecasting is a well-known and adopted method of cartooning used by virtually every selling cartoonist in the world. Viewers have already developed certain expectations of what a character should be when watching any genre of cartooning. They expect children to be adorable even if they're obnoxious brats. They expect old people to be easily irritable with bad hearing, and they expect bad guys to be mean and ruthless, as pictured in this scene from *Boids of a Feather* (copyright of Suzan Ponte-Crowell and Glen Crowell).

Many cartoonists occasionally enjoy taking part in some underground, perhaps even cutting-edge cartoons. This is fun and enables you to break free from the mold, avoiding stereotypes and creating something completely new. The trouble is, this type of cartooning has rarely been known to emerge from the underground because of its limited appeal. The majority of commerce does take place in the *mainstream,* a place where cartoon stereotypes are freely accepted and even welcomed.

If your goal is to draw characters the majority of your targeted viewing audience can identify with and relate to, then it's important to build characters that contain certain basic, expected attributes. In the following pages, you find a collection of many of the basic character types. Feel free to turn to these pages at any time when designing your own cartoon characters.

Character Types

Characters are designed with three things in mind: personality, physicality, and attitude. The personality of the characters dictates how those characters interact with others. The characters' physicality determines their ability to move about and how others perceive them. Their attitudes mark the way they react to and carry themselves in any given situation.

Think of this chapter as a cartoonist cheat sheet. If, at any time, you get stuck trying to create that perfect character for your production, turn to these pages and start mixing and matching the features. If your characters don't fall within the basic character types described here, you can combine the characteristics of two or more of the characters until you find the perfect one to fit your needs.

The Wise Guy

The *wise guy,* as shown in Figure 4-1, is usually a welcome character type to any production. He's always setting someone up for a practical joke or playing the role of a con artist. Bugs Bunny and Daffy Duck are among my all-time favorite wise guys.

Wise guys' physical qualities include

- ▶ Constant aggressive posture
- ▶ Slim neck
- ▶ Big mouth with teeth showing
- ▶ Long nose
- ▶ Pear-shaped torso

Figure 4-1   *Your average wise guy is tall and lanky, and he's a good trickster.*

The Kid

The *kid* is impulsive. She must always get her way. Often, the kid is a mischievous brat, but she can also be cute and naïve (Figure 4-2).

Keep the following physical characteristics in mind when drawing the kid:

- ► Large head
- ► High forehead
- ► Arched back
- ► Small arms
- ► Small hands
- ► Small feet

- ► Chubby legs
- ► Pudgy stomach
- ► Small neck or no neck
- ► Buttocks are also the lower thigh
- ► Slim shoulder length unless he or she's a thug

Figure 4-2   *Kids are a modified version of the cute character.*

The Genius

The *genius* is often a loner, who relies solely on his intellect. He can outwit the biggest of bullies. The genius often plays the role of the nerdy kid next door or even a mad junior scientist in the making, as shown in Figure 4-3.

The genius has the following attributes:

- Large skull
- Large head in comparison to the body
- Short torso

- Weak legs
- Stiff attire
- Young face
- Large eyes or eyeglasses

Figure 4-3 *Geniuses aren't mad scientists, although they aren't far from it.*

The Chubby Character

The *chubby* character is often a friendly individual, as shown in Figure 4-4. He likes to laugh and get what he can out of life. He's usually lovable, whether he's playing the protagonist or an antagonistic role. In the case of a supervillain, his body mass is portrayed as grotesquely as possible.

Here a few more features which are desirable in a chubby character:

- ▶ Large stomach
- ▶ Short legs
- ▶ Protruding rump
- ▶ No neck

- ▶ Somewhat large head
- ▶ Skinny arms make him more of a nerd. Thicker arms make him more of a thug.

Figure 4-4   *This is Wayne Gamble, who likes to dance and blow up things.*

The Wimp

The *wimp* is a character too fragile to defend himself physically or mentally. He lets others boss him around. The wimp type is often a lackey or a scapegoat for other characters. His character is a classic, very successful type (see Figure 4-5). His boss hates him, his wife never lets him get his way—even his kids control his life.

Wimp characteristics include

- ▶ Big nose
- ▶ Bags under his eyes
- ▶ Weak chin
- ▶ Caved-in chest
- ▶ Large feet

- ▶ Messed-up hair
- ▶ Slouching shoulders
- ▶ Curved posture
- ▶ Skinny legs

Figure 4-5 *This poor guy never gets a break.*

The Dimwit

The *dimwit* has a limited attention span and is very slow minded. People tend to get hurt around him and, whether he realizes it or not, he's often the cause of many headaches for any character he interacts with (see Figure 4-6). The worst part is the dimwit doesn't realize how stupid he is.

Dimwits are characterized by

▶ Small forehead

▶ Droopy eyes

▶ Large nose

▶ Small or no chin

▶ Slouching posture

▶ Low beltline

▶ Large feet

▶ Thin legs

▶ Large hands

▶ Lanky arms

▶ Head hangs forward

Figure 4-6   *Guys like this never mean any harm, but they do a great job of spoiling your day.*

The Jock

The *jock* is often a dim bulb as far as brains go, but what he lacks for brains, he makes up with brawn, as shown in Figure 4-7. The jock is rarely the lead character and often is a sidekick to a wise guy character or villain.

Jock characteristics include

- Square-shaped head
- Broad shoulders
- Mesomorphic body
- Small waist
- Large hands

- Very strong
- Thin legs
- Strong jaw
- Thick neck

Figure 4-7   *Jocks can easily be used as bullies, as well as heroes, but their lack of intelligence prevents them from being successful bullies.*

The Short Guy

The *short guy* tends to have an equally short temper. He is normally depicted as somebody's grouchy boss. When paired with a female, the female is almost always taller and gets to boss him around. The short guy (Figure 4-8) lends himself to many memorable character possibilities—from grouchy old Mr. Spacely in *The Jetsons* to the adorable mayor in the *Powerpuff Girls*.

Things that should be present in a short character include

▶ Short arms   ▶ Thick body structure

▶ Large head   ▶ Large hands

▶ No neck   ▶ Usually chubby

▶ Short legs

Figure 4-8 *The typical short guy*

The Bully

The *bully,* as shown in Figure 4-9, is a mean character who finds no greater pleasure than pounding some poor soul into the ground. Although bullies are often villains, they rarely are the main antagonists. In fact, bullies are usually wimps on the inside and tend to be someone else's lackey.

Bullies are physically characterized by

▶ No neck

▶ Large jaw

▶ Body is one large mass

▶ Thick arms and wrist

▶ Massive shoulder width

▶ Body doesn't taper (no waistline)

▶ Skinny and weak legs

▶ Often have excessive body hair, except in the case of a child bully

Figure 4-9   *Bullies are overgrown and insecure kids. They are hardly ever as tough as they appear.*

The Old Geezer

Grouchy and senile—man, what a combination! *Old geezers* are mean, ornery, outspoken, hard of hearing, forgetful, loud, and sometimes even smelly. These guys have been around for a long, long time and have accumulated a large amount of wisdom. They want to share it with you whether or not you want to hear it. Figure 4-10 shows a classic old geezer.

"When I was your age, we were so poor we couldn't afford to buy legs! We had to walk ten miles to school, on our hands, over ten feet of snow backwards! Who are you and what did you do with my pudding?"

Old folks are characterized by

- ► Big hands
- ► Bald-headed
- ► No neck
- ► Slouched shoulders; they can even be humpbacked sometimes
- ► Large feet

- ► Weak knees, always bent
- ► Large chin
- ► No teeth (if you must draw teeth, only draw the bottom ones or just draw the gums)
- ► Large noses and ears

Figure 4-10   *Old people are often senile, lending themselves quite easily for some great comedic moments.*

The Goofy Klutz

Goofy klutzes are flat-out goofy. They do things completely opposite from the norm and often defy the laws of nature, simply because of their ignorance, as seen in Figure 4-11.

Things to look for in a goofy character include

- ▶ Knees always bent
- ▶ Skinny body construction
- ▶ Long thin arms
- ▶ Always slouching
- ▶ Big ears

- ▶ Large heads
- ▶ Large buck teeth
- ▶ No chin
- ▶ Large hands
- ▶ Freckles optional, but often helpful

Figure 4-11   *These people are awkward and quite determined to know everything about you—they even court you. People get hurt around klutzes.*

The Mad Scientist

The *mad scientist* or *mad inventor* comes in two flavors: short and chubby or tall and lanky (see Figure 4-12). These guys are flat-out cuckoo. They spend their lives searching out the mysteries of the universe and plotting to take over the world. Mad scientists always make great adversaries and tend to have the coolest of toys.

The Idiot Thug

The *idiot thug* is an enormous bully with a mental capacity slightly below chicken broth. These guys can be some mean, yet lovable, villains, as shown in Figure 4-13. The idiot thug doesn't know his own strength and he often does things just to please his partner in crime, often played by a wisecracking skinny or shorter character.

The Trendy Chic

Like, her name is Buffy and stuff. And she, like, lives in the best gosh darn neighborhood in town away from all those winos and dresses with, like, the most modern of attire and stuff. She only eats vegetables and no animal by-products cause she's a vegan and not a vegetarian, and like yeah, as shown in like Figure 4-14. Yeah, Team!

Trendy chics are extremely annoying and add plenty of humorous qualities to any big sister, annoying girlfriend, gossipy neighbor, or wife. If your main character is a young kid, consider the idea of giving him a trendy chic for an older sister. This is always a winning combination.

Figure 4-12   *Short mad scientists are normally more humorous and lovable. Tall mad scientists are usually more dramatic and maniacal.*

Figure 4-13   *This bully is strong and clumsy. Despite being a villain, his appearance (and sometimes his actions) makes him lovable.*

Figure 4-14   *These people tend to be extremely hyper and obnoxious. They believe they're perfect in every way.*

The Socialite

The *socialite* lives to impress her acquaintances (the socialite doesn't have real friends and often dons the most elegant attire. They are snobbish, arrogant, and self-centered, as seen in Figure 4-15. Among the most well-known and loved socialite characters are Frazier and Niles Crane from the TV sitcom *Frazier* and Cruella De Vil from *101 Dalmatians*.

The Leading Man

The *leading man* has broad shoulders and a slim waistline. He has a strong jaw, thick neck, slim legs, and remarkably great hair, all of which defy the laws of nature!

Two types of leading men exist, however, and they both share the same physical qualities.

Dick Tracy was a classic leading man. In the olden days, this strong and handsome character was the hero of the story. He was strong, intellectual, and always got the dame. Now, this character is portrayed more often as a laughingstock and, although he's still the hero of the story, we no longer accept him as the classic hero type

Figure 4-15 *Socialites are always thinking up ways to show off their wealth and talk about themselves.*

(see Figure 4-16). Instead, cartoonists and animators are portraying this type of character as a self-centered, arrogant, egotistical snob with a low IQ.

While in the old days, classic leading men were like Superman—who lived to defend the world against evil supervillains—and Batman—who successfully protected the citizens of Gotham City from harm—the modern-day version of the same characters are those like *The Tick, The Justice Friends* in the show *Dexter's Laboratory,* and the short-lived Web series, *Super Hero Roommate,* whose challenges and struggles are mainly centered around being able to get by in their everyday lives.

A typical plot for a story featuring these character types revolves around how they are going to pay the rent because they have no real job skills. They go through challenges, such as figuring out how to use those little keys to open a sardine can or dealing with the fact that they're middle-aged men running around in tights and living in their parents' basement.

Figure 4-16 *Krut is the world's greatest starship pilot, engineer, and everything else, at least in his own little world.*

The Cute Character

The *cute* character is a construction process all its own. It applies to babies, cute children, and cute animals (see Figure 4-17). Innocence, naïveté, and insecurity are all characteristics of a cute character.

The cute characters have

▶ Large heads, roughly one-third of their entire body size

▶ Eyes that lie on the center of the head

▶ Short chubby arms and legs

▶ The same curve that forms the buttocks is used to form the upper thigh

▶ Pudgy tummy that sticks out

▶ Small feet, small chin

▶ Tiny button nose and big old round cheeks

▶ Big eyes (this only applies to cute animal characters)

▶ The smaller the eyes, the better (this applies to cute human characters)

Figure 4-17 *A basic cute animal. A basic cute person.*

Attitude

A little attitude can go a long way. *Attitude* is the manner in which a character walks, talks, and reacts to things. (Image from *Boids of a Feather*, copyright of Suzan Ponte-Crowell and Glen Crowell).

When a kid gets aggravated, will he react by throwing a tantrum or by getting even? When a wise guy is determined to do something, how does he carry himself

to complete his mission? If a dumb thug kills a puppy by petting him, will he cry and be sad or go out and search for another puppy to pet?

Attitude is displayed both physically and verbally. Always choose poses and movements that enhance the character's attitude.

Animal Characters

The head of an animal character is as easy to draw as a human character. They use your typical skull and jaw construction, with this difference: while the jaw of a man lies beneath the skull, an animal's jaw stretches out to the front, almost parallel to the floor.

The jaw of an animal is also more diverse than that of a human. While a dog's jaw can be constructed using the same shape as a human jaw, a cat's jaw is often shaped like a diamond. A horse, for example, has a more

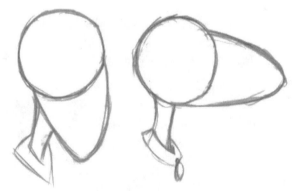

rectangular jaw, while a bird's jaw is triangular to form the beak. Consider these other animal constructions.

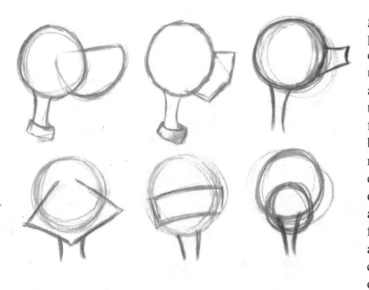

Animals make a great addition to a production and you can choose from an unlimited number of animals. If you can't think of a good animal for your cartoon, begin by drawing a random animal head construction, such as a diamond for the skull and a giant half moon for the jaw. Then start adding features to create your own original animals.

Dogs

Dogs are nearly the most popular cartoon animal because they're extremely easy to draw and register well with your audience.

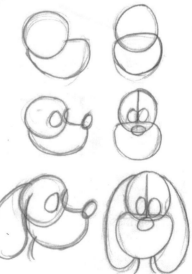

1. To draw a typical dog, start with an average animal skull and jaw construction.

2. Draw the eyes and the nose.

3. Indicate the slope of the forehead. Add the ears, neck, and mouth. Now add the ears.

4. Finish your drawing by indicating fluffy fur and modifying the cheeks to accommodate the size of the smile.

Cats

Cats are the first characters that break the mold. Cats require you to modify the jaw area into a more oval- or diamond-shaped area to accentuate the cheeks. A cat has no chin, and the mouth and snout are drawn along the center of the figure.

1. To draw a cat, begin with a skull and jaw construction.

2. Add the eyes and ears.

3. The slope of the forehead also becomes part of the cheeks.

4. Then add a neck and details.

Birds

The secret to drawing birds is their beaks. The rest of the bird construction can remain constant, but you can dramatically alter the look of a bird simply by changing its beak. Copy the head constructions pictured here and practice filling in the rest of the needed details. Notice the only thing different is the beak.

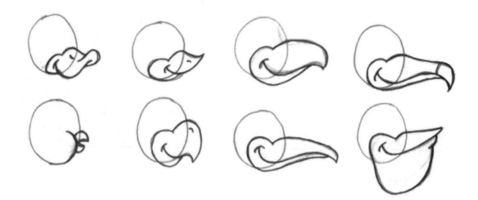

Noses

You can choose from many varieties of noses. The following illustration shows you a few of the most common types.

Smiling Animals

Animals have three basic smiles: normal, zany, and subdued. These three smiles work with virtually any animal: dogs, cats, birds, whatever.

Normal

A normal smile for an animal is placed inside the head figure and doesn't touch the outside lines. The smile begins slightly above the snout's edge and slopes upward into the skull area where it creates a crease in the cheek.

Zany

In the zany smile, the animal's smile begins at the tip of the nose and forms the snout as it curves inward—into the cheek—creating the crease in the cheek. The lower lip then attaches to the snout.

Subdued

The subdued smile floats within the jaw (snout) of the figure. This smile is relatively small.

Anthropomorphizing Animals

I previously mentioned giving human characters animal qualities and characteristics to make them more appealing in both their physicality and behavior. When this is reversed in a technique known as anthropomorphizing, the same effect can be achieved with everyday animals.

Anthropomorphizing is the act of giving nonhumans human traits. A good example of this is the teapot and the candlestick in Disney's *Beauty and the Beast* and many of the cat and mouse teams, such as *Tom and Jerry.* (Images below and right, from *Boids of a Feather,* are a copyright of Suzan Ponte-Crowell and Glen Crowell).

When you anthropomorphize animals, remember they are still animals. If you make them too human, they lose their appeal. An animal can take on the form of any character type. Explore all your options before committing to a final design. If your character is a cat, will he be a tall and lanky wise guy or a fat bully type like *Heathcliff* or *Garfield*?

Humanlike animals tend to have a role in their society, perhaps even a profession. Their physical characteristics and mannerisms must visually express what that character is all about.

Summary

▶ Characters are designed so their physical appearance visually interprets their attitudes and personalities.

▶ Anthropomorphizing is a popular technique that gives nonhuman characters human qualities.

▶ To draw certain animals, you often need to modify the typical skull and jaw construction further.

▶ The majority of all birds can be created using the same basic construction with the difference in the beak. By altering the beak, you can dramatically change the appearance of a bird.

▶ You can draw a smile on an animal in three basic ways: zany, subdued, and normal. These three basic mouth positions can be applied across virtually all animal characters. In some cases, they can even apply to people.

▶ Several standard nose types are used on animal characters. These noses tend to work well for all animals, except birds, which have bills.

Character Development:
The Finishing Touches

Many people have a lot of trouble drawing little things like hands and feet. They also have a problem effectively using props to enhance character design. One of the ways people cope with being unable to draw certain features is to hide them 90 percent of the time. Cheating your audience by relying on your bag of visual tricks and illusions is perfectly acceptable to some degree, but to hide them or shy away from drawing hands, feet, or lip action is less effective. Those pesky hands alone are a constant source of headaches for many cartoonists. This chapter discusses the tricks of the trade to effectively create hands, feet, and mouth action.

The Three-Fingered Hand, a Casualty of War

As a product evolves and makes its way into a mainstream consumership, competing entities look to find ways to create their product faster and more economically. This is an inevitable trend and, in the world of animation, this type of competition resulted in an entirely unique form of drawing. Animated cartoons must be produced fast, with as little financial drain as possible, and they must retain a quality that allows them to compete against rivaling products. Yes, a cartoon is a product or a franchise and must be treated as such.

The low-budget constraints and the need to produce high-quality cartoons on a monthly or sometimes weekly basis eventually forced cartoonists and animators to take many shortcuts and to develop various ways of manipulating the eye to perceive those shortcuts as being perfectly normal. For example, consider the three-fingered hand.

The three-fingered hand was developed for the simple purpose of increasing productivity. Why waste an extra 15 to 20 seconds drawing a hand with four fingers when a hand with only three fingers looks fine? It's not that animators are lazy; it's just that in looking at the large piles of drawings animators had to finish in one day and considering the art, certain liberties had to be taken to keep up with the high demands. The four-fingered hand was never entirely replaced, but the influence of the three-fingered cartoons is evident. Even in cartoons where the characters do use the three-fingered hand, females are often depicted with four fingers. This is because females, in general, are drawn more realistically than their male counterparts.

Many people do find drawing the hand itself is one of the most difficult things in animation. It shouldn't be, though, and drawing hands shouldn't be considered a chore. Like any type of drawing, you must always examine the basic construction of the object. Knowing the basic elements that make it up is the key to being able to draw it. As I said previously, drawing isn't a talent, but a skill that's learned, just the way the art of writing is learned. The entire alphabet is composed of basic figures— a line here, an angle there, a circle, a little tail, and so forth. The repetition, and the constant exposure to the basic shapes and how they fit together, eventually helped you learn to draw all the letters from *A* to *Z*. Later in life, you learned to write in cursive, which is where most differences in style become evident. The more you wrote, the better your penmanship became, and soon you mastered all the letters in the alphabet and even defined your own style of drawing letters. This was your handwriting and yours alone. No one can replicate your handwriting, at least not without properly studying it, because it's something you yourself came to develop over the years.

This is the same as being able to draw cartoons. Everything that can be drawn is based on shapes, lines, angles, and figures. And the best way to master the art of drawing cartoons is repetition and more repetition. Your goal should always be to reach that point where drawing an eye, a face, a hand, or an entire body is as natural as drawing any of the letters in the alphabet.

The Basic Cartoon Hand

In its most primitive state, the hand itself is drawn from a construction that resembles a flower with five petals.

1. Start by drawing a basic round shape.

2. Add the ovals around it that make up the flower.

3. Erase all unnecessary lines and trim off a piece of one of the petals to form the wrist.

4. Add fingernails to the drawing and voila! You just drew a basic cartoon hand.

The petals on the flower construction needn't be evenly spaced out. In fact, you can arrange the fingers in any manner that results in a design more suitable for your character. Look at the following section for another variation based on the same principle.

The Complex Hand

Don't let the name fool you. The complex hand is no more complicated to draw than the basic hand. The reason it's complex is because it looks more realistic in its use of joint structure and finger placement. In real anatomy, all the fingers of the hand are composed of three bones, including the thumb, which is often thought of as having only two bones. In the thumb, that third bone is hidden inside the palm area and only a small portion of it protrudes outward; nevertheless, that bone is quite visible and is covered by a huge muscle mass, which enables us to fold our thumbs inward.

Remember, though, cartoon hands aren't supposed to look realistic. They are simplified and exaggerated versions of the real thing. In the construction of the cartoon hand, you take away one bone from each finger, including the thumb, and draw them as only having two. In other words, all fingers in a cartoon hand are made up of only two bones and not three.

To draw a complex hand, follow these steps:

1. Start with a rectangular shape with smooth corners, as opposed to starting with a complete circle. This is your general palm area and you should lightly suggest a wrist at the bottom of the shape. The palm of the hand is much wider than the wrist, so be sure to take that into account when drawing.

2. Spread three fingers, just as you did on the flower, except this time, all fingers are in more of a row formation at the top of the palm. Most cartoonists draw the fingers with the index finger as the longest, with the rest of the fingers diminishing in size as they get further down to the little finger. The thumb is a short little stub that protrudes directly from the side of the palm.

    Draw a curve inside the palm to indicate this base and to indicate that little chunk of webbed skin we all have between the thumb and the index finger.

3. Erase any overlapping lines and enhance the permanent ones. This is one of the most common hand constructions used in cartooning today. Pay particular close attention to that webbed space between the thumb and the index finger. While this is just a little line, it offers a major enhancement.

The Female Hand

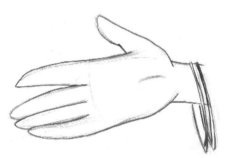

Female characters are often drawn with far more detail than men. Naturally, their hands also tend to be far more detailed than a male character's. For the most part, female hands are drawn using four fingers instead of three.

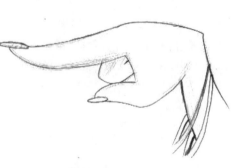

Another aspect of female hands is the fingers that taper at the tips.

Remember, if you're going to use a three-fingered female, be sure to draw her both ways first and see which way works best for you. Sometimes, three-fingered hands can be played off well if the style of the character allows it.

Yet Another Technique for Drawing the Hand

Here's another way to go about drawing the hand.

1. First, begin by drawing what looks like a mitten.

2. Add a thumb and split the main finger area into two separate fingers. Draw the base of the palm and clean up your drawing as you go.

3. Add a third little finger and that should be it. Clean up your drawing and erase any unnecessary lines.

4. Cartoon hands aren't always drawn with the index finger as the longest. In certain occasions, such as when the hand is displayed flat so the fingers are stacked up next to each other, it's better to draw the middle finger as the largest.

Study these hands in various poses. Practice drawing them and see how many other poses you can come up with. Many people don't realize this, but one of the most valuable tools for drawing dynamic hand poses is for them to use their own hands as a model. I'm amazed at the number of people who draw hands and never think to look at their own hands as a guide.

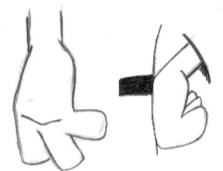

Bird Hands? Yes, Bird Hands!

When it comes to anthropomorphizing birds, there's a special way of drawing their hands. Well, obviously, birds can't have hands unless they're some kind of mutant freaks; in which case, I guess they can. What I'm getting at is a bird's wings have to give the impression of being hands. To do this, you accentuate certain features on its wings and even add an opposable feather to act as a thumb. The construction goes something like this:

1. Start by drawing a basic palm and wrist construction, but stop at the wrist. Go ahead and draw the rest of the arm.

2. Add a thumb, and then add the fingers. These fingers must be chubby and tapered, and made to look like feathers (because they are).

3. Add the rest of the feathers, going slightly away from the hand part. This creates a subtle distinction between the section of the wing that can grab things and the rest of the wing.

Here're two bird sketches with their hands/wings in action.

Getting to Know Your Characters

Getting to know your characters is the first step in creating a successful cartoon series, film, or any kind of presentation involving characters. You can't just throw images at random and expect them to magically develop a personality. Your characters must belong and they must have unique personality traits, which then enable them to interact and play off each other in various situations.

As you design your characters, ask yourself, "Where does this person come from and what's their purpose in life?"

- ▶ Does this character have any special weaknesses or bad habits?

- ▶ How does this person feel about secondhand smoke?

- ▶ How does this character feel about nudity?

- ▶ What does this character look like in the buff?

- ▶ Does this person have any embarrassing tattoos on their body?

- ▶ How often does this guy shower?

- ▶ Is this girl a cheerleader?

As a character designer, you must be able to describe every little detail about your character if you're asked. The more questions you ask yourself about your characters, the more you know about them and the better their personalities can come across to your target audience.

Because you need to know so much about your characters, this enables you to be a better storyteller. You waste less time trying to determine how to play off certain situations and you spend more time being creative and letting the situations literally create themselves. This is because you can always bring certain aspects of your characters' personal and private lives out in the open, which, in turn, creates conflict within those characters, and conflict is what stories are made of.

Susan Randall came in late last night from her date with Bobby, the captain of the football team. Susan sneaked into the house, but was discovered by her cunning younger brother, Elwood, who threatened to tell if Susan didn't cough up $20. Well, wait a minute, maybe that's not the direction we want to go with that story, so we create a counterconflict by introducing the information that Susan knows Elwood likes to wear his mother's clothes! Susan threatens to tell, and she not only ends up with $50, but Elwood also promises not to tell her parents about her late date. A nice little solution to a conflict, which would have taken longer to figure out if you hadn't known as much about your characters as you did.

Begin to know your characters from the second they start taking form on paper. Try to make yourself aware of the little things, such as:

▶ Do they stutter?

▶ Do they limp when they walk and, if so, why?

▶ Do they have a tick?

▶ Do they have any fetishes?

▶ Do they have a lazy eye?

▶ Do they have any girlfriends or boyfriends?

▶ What do they want to be when they grow up?

▶ Do they have a job?

▶ If so, what do they do, and how much do they get paid?

In short, it's better to know your characters too well than not to know them at all. Many cartoonists and writers choose to write a bible, which describes the characters in detail. This is a step I normally take only when the product is being submitted to a major studio or is part of a proposal of some kind. In most cases, getting to know your characters is a process that takes place exclusively inside your head.

Develop a Consistent Art Style

Creating a cartoon is a lot like chemistry: to build a believable world where viewers can immerse themselves and suspend disbelief, our visual interpretation of that world must be comprised of a certain unique style and characteristics that bond our characters to each other, as well as to their environment. A perfect blend of character types, environment, and drawing style must be achieved for a cartoon to appeal to its audience.

The characters you use in a cartoon must belong to that world and they must instill that sense of belonging within the viewer. In the following illustration, I placed three different characters. Can you guess which one doesn't belong with the others?

As you can see, it's the third character who's the odd man out. Not because he's a man, but because his *formula* doesn't match that of the two ladies.

Notice how the outlines of the nurse and the pregnant woman have varying widths and sizes, while Wayne Gamble, character number 3, is drawn with lines that are the same constant size.

In terms of construction, the women are created using multiple basic shapes. The eyes, face, torso, hands, legs, and color used to paint them are all designed to bear a certain resemblance to each other. The man, on the other hand, is constructed using odd shapes that don't conform to the formula used to construct the women. The colors used on the man are also brighter and much louder than the simple pastel/watercolor-like tints used on the women.

Let's suppose, though, that I did want to have Wayne Gamble appear in the same cartoon as these two women. My job is now to redesign the Wayne Gamble character to conform as closely as possible to the Nurse Betty formula. The resulting design is shown here. Now Wayne Gamble won't look so out of place if he ever makes a cameo appearance in that particular series.

So What the Heck Is a Formula?

A cartoon's formula is the basic set of design principles created by the character designer and implemented throughout all the characters in a cartoon. Take a look at Fox's hit TV show *The Simpsons*. Notice how all the characters seem, somehow, to belong with each other. This is because all the characters from *The Simpsons* were drawn using the same basic construction principles. Believe it or not, Homer Simpson's design, not Bart Simpson's design, lays the foundation for virtually all characters in that series.

If you can draw a thin Homer Simpson with tall blue hair, eyelashes, and female curves, you can draw his wife, Marge Simpson. If you can draw a shorter Homer with spikes on his head for hair, and put some shorts and tennis shoes on him, then you've drawn Bart Simpson, his son. If you give Homer a mustache, some hair, and make him a bit thinner, you create Ned Flanders, his neighbor. If you put a white face on Homer and a big red nose and green hair, then you have Krusty the Clown. Keep doing this until you have an entire town full of characters, which is what is basically done when a certain formula is chosen to be the formula for that cartoon.

To define a formula for your cartoon, you must decide what your main character looks like and how that character is drawn. You must then break up the character once again into its most primitive shape and see how that character can be reconstructed in as few steps as possible. For this, we'll use the characters from my comic strip *Braindead* as an example.

I've never been creative as far as coming up with character names. My main character is, of course, a cartoon version of myself. When drawing my cartoon counterpart and analyzing his construction, I easily determined that among his most noticeable features was that huge round nose. This would be a normal nose to have in his world, so this big round nose is considered average in his world. Great! All characters will have a huge round nose.

The next thing was that his eyes seemed to rest directly on top of his head and behind the nose. Great! Here's another unique feature to carry across throughout the rest of the characters.

Hmmm, what do we have here? The upper lip, the nose, and the eyes also seem to be some kind of solid construction. His skull looks like it isn't attached to the rest of his body. You never do see the back of the head because of the hair.

He has no forehead, so the eyebrows have to rest in the air. Okay, that doesn't seem to be a difficult formula to apply to the rest of the characters. Pretty generic.

What about the body? Well, aside from large, three-fingered hands, the rest of the body seems rather simple to construct—just a basic two-circle construction, and the arms and legs are pretty generic.

This cartoon has absolutely no resemblance to any living creature, except that he's bipedal and wears human clothing.

Cartoon Ibis was a great design, I thought, and so I began creating the rest of the world around him. Because this character is a cartoon version of myself, I figured it would only be fitting if I created cartoon versions of my closest friends as well and have them play an integral role in the life of this character. Not only did I have a nice character design and specific formula to work from, but because the characters themselves were based on real people, I could already see a million possible gags and story ideas to write about.

Create Model Sheets

Creating Model Sheets is helpful in a variety of ways. In creating Model Sheets, you can help determine absolute rules of the character's design. You lay down the law as to how your character should be drawn as he stands still, as he walks, how he looks when he gets angry, and every other possible movement and expression. If the piece is to be animated by a team of animators, they must all know what the character looks like to keep the artwork consistent (see Figure 5-1).

Character Model Sheets used in this way are most common among the larger production studios, where they don't expect you to know anything about the character you're supposed to be drawing, so they give you these as a reference.

For the rest of us—the one-man studios and other independent animators—the Model Sheets are also valuable because they help act as a way to document and

Figure 5-1   *Character Model Sheets allow artists to keep artwork consistent.*

register characters and declare them as property. A Model Sheet contains the date, the company or artist's info, and the necessary Copyright tag.

This is a convenient way to register your characters and declare them as your property. Not only will the people who get their hands on your work be informed that the product itself has been declared as your property, but they will also be able to see your company information, should they decide they want to contact you and offer you a licensing deal. The following Model Sheets are my character designs for a film I named *The Adventures of Krut and Mojo.*

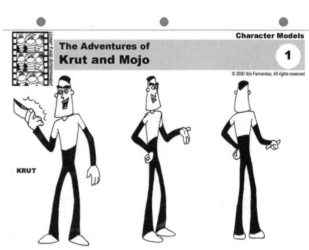

When there are more sheets for a character, be sure to number them accordingly. As you can see here, this is only the first sheet, which displays Krut in three principal angles: front, forty-five degree angle, and backside.

This is my design for the character named Mojo. Notice how the name of the series the character belongs to is prominently displayed on the sheet.

Locke Siebenhouesen is a character created after a local radio D.J. For tax purposes, even if you're a studio of one, establishing yourself as a production company helps. Make sure your company logo or branding is prominently displayed on your sheet.

The Copyright tag can be under either your name or your production company's name. Notice how I also made room at the top of the sheet for punching holes. This enables me to archive a paper copy of my characters easily in a three-ring binder and to reference my characters back and forth throughout the production process.

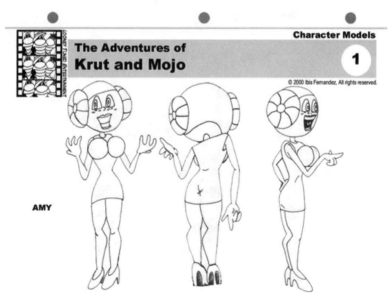

The name of the character is displayed on the sheet. If there are any special instructions, those can be drawn directly on the paper.

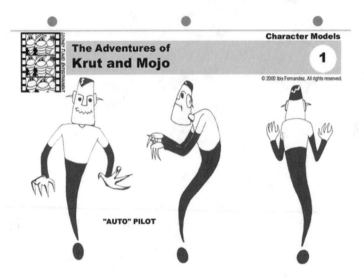

Have your characters perform various actions throughout their poses. This is both to have them look interesting and to document the way they look as their behaviors and mannerisms are played out.

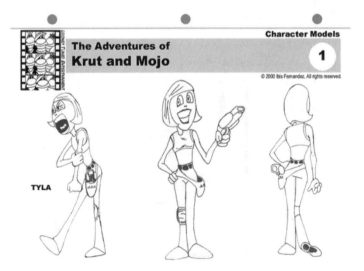

Even if your characters are only one foot tall, make use of the entire sheet to showcase them, as shown here.

A size comparison chart helps to establish the characters' size and how they should be presented when they appear in the same scene. A color chart defines how the characters will be colored. This allows for a consistent color in your characters throughout your presentation.

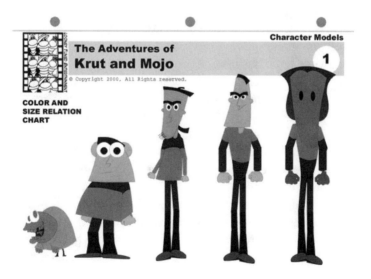

This type of color and size chart goes a bit beyond your average Model Sheet. It also shows how the character is drawn and put together within Flash.

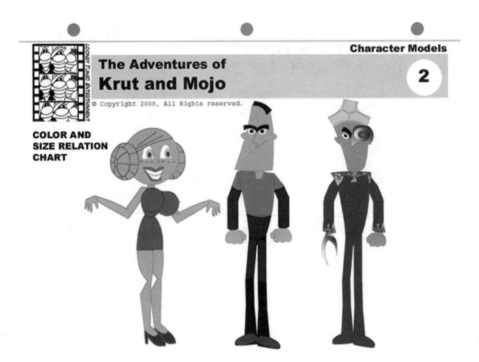

You can go about registering your characters in many ways. For people who create products of an electronic nature, such as screenplays, Flash animation, digital photography, software programming, Web site development, graphic design, and so forth, registering your work has never been easier. Online registration is an option that wasn't available until recently and it's a highly effective and convenient way to register, without the hassles of converting your work to paper. Through electronic time-stamping services, such as that offered by **firstuse.com**, you can now package all your files in a ZIP or executable format and have that file digitally fingerprinted. You then simply store your file on disk and put it away for safekeeping. Your file now hosts a special encryption that allows the date of its registration to be verified when scanned through the service.

So take all your Model Sheets. Write a description of the series or feature. Package all your images and scripts if you have them in a ZIP file or self-extracting executable and have this fingerprinted as soon as possible. The sooner you get into the habit of registering your work, the better. As an independent animator, you'll also have a greater piece of mind when it's time to publish your work on the Web, where virtually anyone in the world can gain access to it.

Summary

- ▶ Learn to detect which areas of the cartoon give you the most trouble and attack them head-on. For example, this could be in the form of a hand, which most people have trouble drawing. If you stop drawing people with their hands crossed or with their hands behind their back, and concentrate on drawing those hands, the quality of your work will be elevated to a higher level.

- ▶ Birds don't have real hands; instead, their wings are drawn in a manner that suggests a hand.

- ▶ Because of the large number of drawings an animator has to complete, the time requirements, and the under-budget conditions, many shortcuts and visual effects were developed to help increase productivity. Among these was the infamous three-fingered hand.

- ▶ At its most basic level, the hand is drawn in the form of a flower with five petals. A complex hand is a hand drawn in a more realistic manner.

- ▶ Get to know your characters from the moment they take form. Advanced knowledge about how often your characters shower and what they like to eat for breakfast can help you better understand how they interact with other characters.

- ▶ A cartoon's formula is the basic construction principles carried out through the entire cast of characters.

TIP

If you want your villains to stand out more, draw them using a totally opposite formula from the one you use for your main characters. Think humans versus Smurfs, two contradicting formulas that work within a single cartoon. If all your good characters have smooth, round features, draw your villains with jagged and angular features. The contrast always adds a dramatic flare to the composition.

- ▶ Registering your characters can be as simple as putting your Model Sheets in a ZIP file and having them electronically time-stamped.

Flash

CHAPTER
6

Flash: What It Is and What It's Not

Now that we've covered all you need to know about drawing and cartooning your own characters, it's time to move on to the second phase. Your purpose now is to learn a little about the software you will be using, and to draw and compose your graphics in Flash using its many tools. Before you do, though, let's go over a few important details to help you understand what Flash is and what it isn't. Perhaps understanding the technology behind Flash can also help you in the creation of your *shocked* cartoons.

Macromedia Flash is a tremendously powerful and versatile tool with the capabilities to be used for developing rich media content that can be streamed over the Web, through low-bandwidth restrictions. The vector-based Shockwave Flash (.swf) format not only allows for the creation of extremely small file-sized graphics, but the software package itself can be used to create high-quality animated movies, Web sites, and interactive games.

What Flash Is

For the creation of production-quality content, Flash is a heavily packed animation program that not only allows for the art to be rendered and sequenced, but also for the creation of an entire project within the software itself without ever having to depend on plug-ins or third-party tools. Traditionally, computer-aided animation involves the use of various software packages, such as a pencil test tool, an ink and paint program, a sequencer or editing tool, sound editing software and, in many cases, an extra compositing tool such as Adobe After Effects to create the final presentation.

Traditional animation, by definition, is any type of animation created nondigitally, such as classic cel animation where the images are penciled, inked, painted, and photographed entirely by human hands or, in the case of stop-motion animation, where puppets or figures are manipulated and captured on static film.

Cel animation can hardly be called traditional anymore. Most cel animation, whether full or limited, is done today with the aid of computers. Aside from the initial penciled sequences, most cel animation is now inked, painted, sequenced, and produced using state-of-the-art animation software in a process that makes Flash animation seem quite primitive.

Flash as a Pencil Test Tool

Professional animators looking for a cheap way to do a pencil test can import the series of images into Flash. Adjust the frame rate and publish a video file to see what the animation looks like and if it needs any further work. A pencil test is a video that plays back your hand-drawn animated sequence at a desired speed (frame rate), so you can test the animation for line consistency and other anomalies that tend to slip by us.

Using Flash as a Pencil Tester

Exploring all the various techniques and procedures of classical cel animation goes far beyond the scope of this book, but here's one technique that can be used by non-Flash animators as part of their everyday routine. This topic is covered here because this is the only place I reference pencil testing.

1. To perform a pencil test in Flash, first you need a hand-drawn animated sequence. Take your images and scan them in, using a scanner or a video imaging device.

2. Using a video capture device is, by far, the fastest and most efficient way to get your images from paper into your PC. Scanners are more trouble than they're worth and are better put to use for situations where the artwork itself must be of the highest possible quality, as in graphic design.

3. Make sure all your captured images are numbered in sequential order. Use double or triple digits for the numbering. This insures your computer determines the proper order for the images (for example, image01, image02, image03, and so on). If you plan to work with a hundred or more images, adjust your digits to something like image001–image255, and so forth.

4. Import these images into Flash using the Import Image command in the file menu, and then browse through the pop-up window to find the first image in your sequence.

5. Click Open and Flash automatically detects the image as part of a sequence and asks if you want to import the rest of the images as well. Select Yes and all your images are then imported as a sequence of frames.

6. Each image occupies its own frame in the timeline. Adjust the aspect ratio of the movie, so you can see the images played in sequence. You can do this by going to the Modify menu and selecting the Modify Movie option. Adjust the height and width to match the imported images. By default, Flash imports all images with their upper right-hand corner aligned with the upper right-hand corner of the stage. If this isn't the case, you must manually adjust the placement of the individual images. To align multiple images across several frames, the onion tool's Edit Multiple Object option works wonders. While you're at the Modify Movie panel, set the frame rate to the rate or what the final production should be. This depends on the production company you're doing the drawings for. Please check your guidelines and exposure sheets for the correct frames per second (fps) to use.

7. No way exists to ensure proper fps payback as a Flash file because so much of its functions are dependent on the computer's CPU power. Luckily, Flash also gives you the capability to export your final file in the form of either AVI or QuickTime video formats. So, to complete your pencil test, you need to export your file as video. If you like, you can also synchronize sound and voice tracks along with your tests. The file size of a pencil test file is irrelevant. This all depends on the quality of the image you want and the space available in the disk where you're saving the file. I usually set it to the highest possible quality. That way, I can also export to video cassettes and play them back on my television while I work on revisions or search for specific flaws in the line work or continuity.

8. A big plus Flash has as a pencil tester over other more expensive pencil-testing tools is the capability to add interactivity to your files. If published as QuickTime, you can also include buttons on your file that can help you jump from place to place within your sequence. You can publish multiple pencil tests as one file and use interactive buttons to jump from one test to the other to compare various versions of the tests.

CAUTION

Be aware that QuickTime is also an alternative to the Flash player and can read .swf files in their native form. QuickTime also has the capability to rename and convert an .swf into a *.mov file. This type of conversion doesn't transform your .swf file into a video file. This conversion makes it possible for the .swf to play with the QuickTime plug-in rather than the Flash plug-in.

Super-Duper Animatic Maker

An *animatic* is basically a production storyboard synchronized with the voice over and sound tracks to show the pacing of the film and give an idea of what's happening at certain times. To make an animatic, you first need to scan or capture the images in your storyboard. You also need at least the final version of the voice track for your film.

1. Take the entire voice track, in the form of a single file to ensure exact timing of audio events, and place it in its own layer within the Flash timeline.

2. To set the audio, select the first frame where the sound starts and open the Sound Panel under Window | Panels | Sound. Here, you can select the audio file that plays. From the same panel, chose Stream as your Sync method. To ensure proper audio playback, make sure you adjust your fps settings in the Modify | Movie menu to the production's desired fps.

3. You can see the waveform for that audio file in the timeline. Add as many frames as necessary to allow for the entire audio file to play, and then add a second layer in the timeline. You can add frames by selecting the layer on which you want to add them and going to Insert | Frame, or by simply selecting the area where you want your frame and pressing the F5 key. Be careful to add regular frames and not keyframes because keyframes cause a break in the continuity of that particular event.

4. Next, you need to import your images into Flash and place them along this new layer. Synchronize the images to the sound to indicate certain actions will be taking place at various points in the film.

5. Publish the movies as either a .swf file or a video file. You can also take advantage of Flash's advanced features to add interactivity to your file, as in the case where you might want to have a menu that jumps from scene to scene, or add special zoom or panning effects to the images in the animatic. In the case of a pencil test or animatic, I recommend exporting (publishing) to video because this is the best way to ensure proper fps playback.

6. Your animatic is a moving storyboard, which you'll find is a valuable tool to refer to as you work on your final production. In the case of a speculative work or submitting a proposal for funding, an animatic is an excellent tool to show your potential clients what their final product will look like without wasting valuable resources and time, other than making the initial storyboards and voice tracks.

A Powerful Graphics Program

With Flash, there's no need to rely on any third-party graphic design programs to create the images you'll be working with. Flash has all the tools you need right within the program itself. I created most of the images in this book in Flash, not only to demonstrate its robust graphic design application, but also because the only logical way to illustrate a book about drawing and animating in Flash is with images created with the program itself. The few images that weren't drawn in Flash are either drawn by hand or drawn by hand and later enhanced further with Flash's rendering options.

TIP

When drawing directly in Flash, you have the added benefit of drawing only those necessary lines and fills. When using third-party tools, you most often end up with extra unwanted debris. Drawing directly in Flash almost always guarantees smaller file sizes.

Graphics designed in Flash can also be exported in a wide variety of image formats, which can be used to publish to the Web, to print, or to be manipulated further within a different software package, like Photoshop or Fireworks.

For cartoonists, being able to draw naturally—without any of the technical jargon in many of today's most popular illustration packages—is a major plus. It's also nice to know that, for the techies who must have accurately drawn images, being able to manipulate lines and use Bézier points and curves is also an option that's been implemented in the form of a separate tool, which can be turned on or off. Being able to individually add, delete, and manipulate the actual points in a graphic is a great enhancement, especially if your ultimate goal is to keep file sizes as small as possible.

Flash Can Be Used as an Ink and Paint Tool

You can use Flash as a vector-based ink and paint program. Imported line work can easily be converted to vector images, using Flash's trace bitmap function. Vectorized line art can be edited and painted using the wide array of color mixing and texture effect tools readily available within Flash. Although vector graphics don't have the complexity of raster graphics, they still have a unique appeal. When used for this purpose, the quality of the images created in Flash is highly superior and can be exported for sequencing and further manipulation through higher-end animation software, such as Retas!Pro, CTP, or XARA, or my personal favorite new vector animation toy, Toon Boom Studio. As an ink and paint program, Flash can be a valuable timesaver because it enables you to render art much faster than many ink and paint software programs available today.

The possibilities are endless. You can create libraries of reusable characters, animation cycles, predefined sequences of characters, and backgrounds that are already inked and painted, and turn the animation process into a simple drag-and-drop operation.

An Animation Editor and Sequencer

As previously noted, you don't need third-party software with Flash. By importing or creating graphics and manipulating them using the various tools in Flash, you can effectively create and deliver high-quality animation. This animation can be exported in a multitude of media formats, which is discussed as we move ahead in the book. No law says a Flash movie must be made strictly for the Web. The same way you can sequence a pencil test, you can sequence finished raster images, which have been rendered using more robust graphic tools. As an .swf file, your production can be distributed complete with audio and interactivity, if applicable. It's no wonder Flash is quickly becoming the preferred tool for the creation of DVD and CD-ROM intros and interfaces, which traditionally was a job reserved for Director.

Web Development and Game Design Software

Because of the robust scripting and interactivity features, Flash is also an excellent tool for the creation of cutting-edge Web sites and Internet-based games. No other tool is so versatile and yet so affordable.

A Limited Sound Editing Tool

Flash has limited audio editing capabilities. You can use Flash to mix an entire audio track for your movies, work with sound events, modify the way sounds are played back, and work with various compression settings for export. This is a task better suited for a more robust third-party sound editing and sequencing tool, nevertheless. If, for any reason, you simply don't want to use an external tool, with a little bit of patience you can edit and sequence your own tracks all within the software.

What Flash Isn't

Although Flash can easily speed many tasks involved in cel animation, as in creating graphics and animation sequences quickly, inking and painting, or pencil testing, Flash is by no means a high-end cel animation software. Flash was never intended for that kind of use. Despite all the versatility and power Macromedia Flash has to offer, it's better suited for Web development purposes. As a production animation tool, Flash is terribly flawed. This isn't to say Flash can't do what other animation tools can do because it can. This simply means that as an animator, you must adapt to the software and accept it probably was never intended for the production of animated cartoons in the first place. Such software as XARA, Retas!Pro, Toon Boom Studio, USAnimation, and CTP is better equipped to handle this type of workload. Using Flash in conjunction with these programs or other video editing and compositing software, such as Adobe After Effects or Premiere, is often necessary to create high-quality full animation within the scope of cartoons, such as *Looney Tunes, The Tick,* or any other type of animation based on actual cel animation, as opposed to "motion graphics," such as spinning logos, moving text, and the ever-so-cheesy spinning 3-D box, which are far more simplistic in nature.

What Type of Animation Can Be Done in Flash?

Flash, as an animation and production tool, is best suited for limited style animation, such as what's seen in popular cartoon series like the *Powerpuff Girls, Dexter's Lab, Two Stupid Dogs, South Park, The Oblongs,* and *Angela Anaconda.* Flash is almost the perfect tool for the creation of simpler types of *Anime* cartoons like *Dragon Ball Z,* which isn't so much animation as it is a televised comic book with voices.

Limited animation takes the phrase "reduce, reuse, and recycle" and gives it a whole new meaning. The purpose of *limited animation* is to create a high-quality product extremely fast and within the constraints of a low budget. In most cases, emphasis is placed on the quality of the script and the method of telling the story, with a perfect blend of audio and animation. In short, a limited animation production is composed entirely of keyframes and rarely makes use of in-betweens or breakdown drawings. Camera technique and timing are key players in a limited animation cartoon. Extreme forms of visual effects, such as the ones shown on Figure 6-1 and 6-2 (*One Fine Ye Olde Day* copyright of Jerry Fuchs), aren't only visually appealing, but also allow animators to do less work and still produce great animation.

Figure 6-1   *A staple of limited animation is the capability to create the illusion of fluid motion through the use of special visual effects.*

While a fully animated *Looney Toon* walk cycle might be drawn with as many as sixty frames and, in some extreme cases, even more, in a limited animation presentation such as *Dexter's Laboratory* that walk cycle can be reduced to a good eight frames or less. In many cases, a walk cycle can effectively be created using a mere two frames!

Characters used in limited animation tend to be highly stylized and composed of parts that can easily be recycled over and over again. Aside from being limited forms of animation, there're also forms of other genres of animation that take this art form to an extreme.

Many animated style cartoons, such as *Dragon Ball Z,* which I mentioned earlier, are even simpler in nature than they appear. Study any episode of *Dragon Ball Z* and you'll realize that, aside from lip cycles composed of three or four mouth actions looping in sequence and the ever-so-often twitching vein on the forehead, hardly anything can be described as animation. Emphasis in this style of cartooning is placed on the quality of the artwork and completely overlooks the animation process itself, which is usually implied through camera-movement techniques and character posture.

Figure 6-2   *The entire sequence was created by using three distorted in-between drawings. This particular technique is known as the **smear**.*

Vector Graphics and Animation

At one point in time, the closest you could get to quality animation on the Web was through animated .gifs and extremely poor video files. Macromedia changed all that with its vector-based Shockwave Flash technology.

In simple terms, here's how this works: When you create your graphics in Flash, you aren't actually drawing the images in the traditional sense; instead, you're generating mathematical equations that instruct your PC on how to go about forming a line, its width, trajectory, length, angle, curve, and so on. These mathematical equations can also be programmed to include line color and shape-fill information. They can also be manipulated so they can change their state across a given number of frames (animation).

In traditional digital imaging, graphics are composed of actual pixels of varied color. When mapped in an ordered fashion, they compose an image.

Vector graphics aren't composed of a predefined cluster of pixels. They're merely a collection of mathematical instructions that tell the computer how to go about rendering an image once the user gives the order to display the contents of the file. Logically, when compared to a bitmapped image, the file size of the vector art is always smaller and easier to distribute over the Web, making it a perfect platform for delivering high-quality images through low-bandwidth restraints.

Another advantage vector graphics have over bitmapped images: Because vector graphics aren't a predefined cluster of pixels, they can be reproduced and rendered at any given size without any loss of quality. Large or small, the images always retain the same vibrant level of quality.

On the downside, because vector art must be decoded and rendered by the user's computer, the art is more dependent on processor power than already bitmapped images. The more complex your images are the more strain this puts on your CPU.

Flash files that play back poorly on your PC are often the result of vector graphics composed of overly complex information and your computer's inability to decode and render the images fast enough. Vector graphics are based on a point-plotting system that enables you to form lines from one point to another. The less points, lines, and complex curves you use to compose your images, the less likely you are to run into problems during download and/or playback.

 TIP

A great example of a CPU hog is transparency effects in Flash. Unfortunately, they are both cool and useful, and many times they add the needed effect.

The Flash Animation Studio: Equipment and Tools

Quite a bit more overhead is involved in jumpstarting a career in the field of animation. For one, if you plan to use Macromedia Flash as your tool of choice, you might want to consider purchasing a copy of the software. But you don't need me to tell you that. Once again, remember, the shoes or brand of clubs he uses doesn't make Tiger Woods an outstanding golfer. His talent and how he puts his tools to work for him make all the difference.

Having said this, Macromedia Flash is *not* the only tool out there used for Flash animation. The .swf is a vector animation format used by many of today's tools as an output option. Any other tool out there in the right hands can be used to create files in the Flash format.

Some of the tools currently available include *Kool Moves,* a software package that sells for about $30, which is perfect for students and people who want to explore Web animation without dishing out the full price of a more robust tool, such as Macromedia Flash, or Adobe Live Motion, which is an alternative to Flash.

People accustomed to Adobe products might find Live Motion a more intuitive product to develop on. Sometimes, it's simply a matter of what you're accustomed to. Macromedia Fireworks and Freehand both have the capability to publish to .swf now. A free plug-in is even available from Macromedia that gives users of Adobe Illustrator the capability to export directly to .swf.

For 3-D enthusiasts, a great product to keep your eyes on is *Amorphium Pro,* which is highly intuitive authoring software specially developed for 2-D animators who want to explore 3-D worlds. Amorphium Pro gives people with no knowledge of 3-D the capability to model and to animate objects and scenes, as well as to render them in .swf format in its many export options.

For the professional animator, you'll be happy to know a new sheriff is in town and it's called *Toon Boom Studio.* Made by the people who created USAnimation, which is one of the most respected animation products in the industry, Toon Boom Studio is actually a far more robust tool for Flash cartoon animation than Macromedia Flash itself. The new software doesn't aim to replace Flash because, although it's far superior to Macromedia Flash as an animation tool, its Web design and development application is quite limited.

Software

Countless plug-ins and alternatives to Flash are out there. The trick is to settle down, choose one, and get to work. For me, no better tool exists for working with

Flash files than Flash itself. I love this software so much, I married it and, if that wasn't enough, I consider every cartoon I make with Flash my child.

Toon Boom Studio is definitely a tool worth purchasing if you're already experienced in cel animation or you're interested in animating with a more advanced animation tool. The software was created specifically for the purpose of cartoon animation, so it's more adept at performing this task than Flash.

If your interests are in the creation of interactive content, Web design, or anything else that doesn't involve cartoon animation, Toon Boom Studio might not be a tool for you because you still must use it in conjunction with Flash when it comes to those purposes. Remember, Toon Boom's strength over Flash is in its application as an animation tool and not Web design. Flash, flawed as it may be, is still the more versatile tool overall.

Hardware

You need a decent piece of hardware. Your computer must be at least a 133 MHz system. Running Flash on anything below 133 MHz will probably crash your PC, and developing in computers higher than 550 MHz will probably cause you to create files that only play well on systems with higher possessing power. For optimal results, I recommend anything between 350 MHz to 550 MHz. If you want more power, you need to keep a close eye on the files you make and thoroughly test them on weaker systems.

Operating System

Flash works on all versions of Windows 95 or later. The Macintosh version runs under Mac OS 8.5 or later. The same pretty much goes for Toon Boom Studio.

Memory

You must have a minimum of 32MB of system RAM available, but you can never have too much RAM.

Available Disk Space

The program itself takes up about 40MB of disk space if installed in full, but you also need to have plenty of space in your hard drive to store and manage all your sound and source files. Ideally, I recommend setting aside an entire partition or a separate hard drive specifically for the use of Flash and the files you'll be working with.

Backup and Playback Devices

If you purchased the CD version of Flash, you obviously need a CD-ROM drive. I strongly suggest some kind of backup device, such as a CDR-RW drive or a ZIP drive, which enables you to back up, archive, and transport your files. Not too long ago, I lost many irreplaceable files because of a hard drive crash and, unfortunately, I learned the importance of backing up the hard way.

CAUTION

Don't lose your source files. Backing up your original project files (*.fla) is extremely important. The unfortunate experience of many newbies is to erase their source files accidentally, and then think they can recover their work from the published movie (*.swf). A project cannot be recovered from an output file, no matter how cool you think you are.

TIP

If your hard drive decides to "byte" the big one, it isn't only a matter of backing up your files that makes the difference. Back up your files regularly to an external device. Backup files that reside within your system should be considered a lost cause—if you lose your drive, you lose your files. Do me (and yourself) a favor and please back them up on an external device.

Display

A larger monitor! For cartoonists and animators working with Flash, the upgrade from Flash 4 to Flash 5 wasn't exactly a reason to break out the champagne and celebrate. Among the many, not-so-cool changes is the extra clutter formed by the new panel system.

A larger monitor enables you to have room to work at a comfortable resolution level, and the extra panels and windows in Flash's new look can be a nightmare to work with if you don't have that extra room to put them in. Obviously, you can accustom yourself to closing and opening them as you work but, for the type of work you do as content animators, you depend on many of these panels to remain open for quick and easy access. Closing the panels defeats the purpose, although you can also momentarily hide them by pressing TAB. Pressing TAB again brings your panels back.

If you can afford this, consider a dual monitor setup. Having an extra monitor in which to place all your most commonly used panels can dramatically increase your productivity, as well as enable you to draw and work on a larger work area. This type of setup is extremely useful for viewing all your layers at once because you can expand the timeline across the entire screen on one of your monitors and still have your work area available on the other. See the various setups in Figures 6-3 through 6-5.

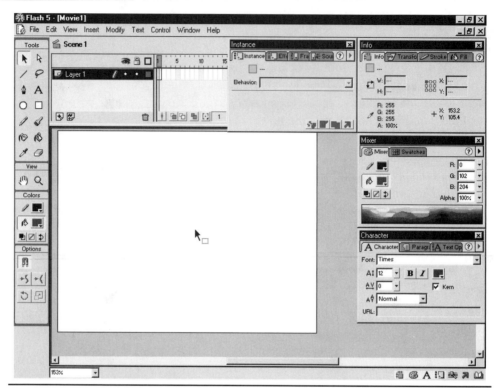

Figure 6-3   *This is Flash as it appears on a 17-inch monitor, at a resolution of 800 × 600 and with its default pane layout.*

Human Interface Devices

As for interface devices, all you need is a basic keyboard and a mouse. If you feel you need to spend the extra money on a graphic tablet, then by all means go ahead. The AIPTEK Hyperpen works wonders for me as far as speed and the capability to use Flash's pressure-sensitivity feature is concerned. The nice thing about the Hyperpen is it is similar to drawing with a regular pencil and paper. Best of all, the Hyperpen sells for around $50 after rebate, about a fourth of the price of the industry standard WACOM tablet, which isn't that different in usability. The drawbacks of using regular graphic tablets are you have little control of the actual drawing and the quality of the line work. When you draw on a graphic tablet, you're drawing by proxy. The images are rendered onscreen and not on the actual tablet, so getting used to it can be a challenge at first. Drawing on graphic tablets is almost like drawing on a piece of paper, and not looking at it directly, but through a mirror. Although you can still see the results of your drawing in the mirror, the process of drawing is impaired by the nondirect approach and often is quite disorienting. For this reason,

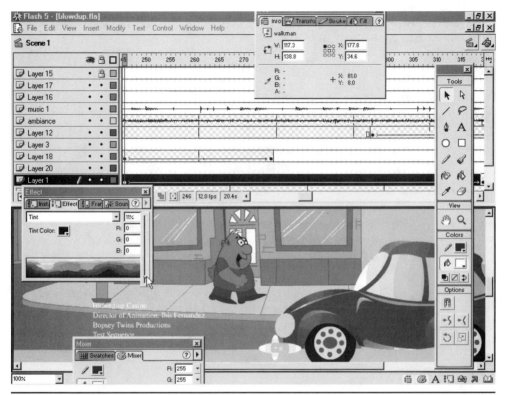

Figure 6-4   *This is what a typical Flash screen looks like as you work on a project. You rely on many of these tools to get you through the development stage.*

Figure 6-5   *A dual monitor setup can dramatically improve the efficiency of your work.*

many digital artists actually use the graphic tablets only for quick roughs and prefer a basic mouse to create their final renderings.

The Future of Animation: Promoting the Paperless Studio

For professionals working in any field within the animation industry, another promising product that has recently emerged on the scene is the LCD pen tablet. These graphic tablets are, by far, the most accurate and intuitive way to draw in a completely digital and paperless environment.

In a nutshell, *LCD pen tablets* are flat computer monitors, which are also graphic tablets. They enable you to draw directly on them with absolute control and accuracy. There's no doubt this type of product pays for itself in the hands of a professional; however, for an animation student or enthusiast, this type of investment isn't encouraged. The whole purpose of animating in Flash is to create high-quality animation with the least overhead possible. Before dishing out $3,000 for a graphic tablet like this, you should know they're an unnecessary commodity.

If you don't already own a computer system, however, I recommend you look into purchasing one that already comes with an LCD tablet, such as the Sony VAIO Slimtop PCV-LX90. The complete system costs about the same as the tablets shown in Figure 6-6.

Imaging Device

You need an imaging device for capturing hand-drawn images and importing them in your computer. Scanners are great for capturing images down to the smallest detail. The drawback is you have to scan in one image at a time and, depending on the speed of your

Figure 6-6   *The WACOM PL-300 and the PL-400 LCD tablets promise to revolutionize the way professionals animate in a completely paperless environment.*

scanner, it might take you several hours to scan and convert your entire animated sequence of images completely to a digital format suitable for import into Flash. Digital cameras, digital video cameras, and regular video cameras are the best and most efficient means of capturing animation sequences. The process is quite simple:

1. Hook up your camera to your computer according to the instructions provided by the manufacturer. If you're using a video camera, it needs to be hooked up to your video card using RCA jacks and a special adapter (basically the same way you hook up a VCR to a PC). Refer to the instructions supplied by the manufacturer of your video card, which should provide the necessary steps.

2. Set up your camera on a tripod with the lens approximately two feet above the surface where your images will rest. I normally set my camera above my animation disk, so I can use the pegs to help keep my captures within their registration parameters.

CAUTION

Be sure your camera is properly secured, especially if you're using it over a glass surface, such as on an animation disk or a light box. From personal experience, I can tell you that having a video camera crash through your animation disk isn't exactly a pleasant experience, not for me, not for the animation disk, and definitely not for the camera.

3. Support for a scanner or imaging device isn't available in Flash, although it should be. With the camera turned on, run any program that gives you the capability to capture images from your device.

4. Capture your images to a format such as .bmp or .jpeg. These formats can be imported into Flash for further manipulation. Be sure to name your images according to the order in which they should be played back if you're capturing an entire sequence. Capturing images this way is almost instantaneous and you can be finished in a matter of minutes.

5. Although good resolution is desirable, it shouldn't be too important, at least not important enough to justify buying a $3,500 Canon XL-1 Mini DV camera. Instead, you can go to a local pawnshop and buy a used VHS camcorder for about $50.

6. For those who live on the edge and don't mind taking risks, purchasing equipment online is another option. Places like **www.mysimmon.com** offer excellent comparison-shopping options allowing you to determine which places sell the product you are looking for cheaper. Online auctions also allow you to find new and used equipment and purchase it lower than its retail value. Be warned, however, that through online auctions you have a high risk of being ripped off or purchasing something that is defective.

Light Boxes and Animation Disks

The light box or animation disk is one of those tools that, for Flash animation artists, can be either a huge waste of money or one of the most useful tools you can have. It's all dictated by how you approach Flash animation on a personal level. A *light box* is basically what the name suggests: a box with a light bulb in it. You place your images on the semitranslucent base and the light coming from underneath enables you to trace and clean up images across several layers of paper.

For many animators working in Flash, relying on such devices is usually a waste of time. Many animators who still use a pencil draw on paper and clean up their drawings with tracing paper or vellum. They then scan their artwork to be further manipulated in Flash.

Other animators love to draw out their sequences or graphic elements by hand and rely on animation disks to see through the various images as they work their magic. An *animation disk* is basically the same thing as a light box, but with an added benefit: you can rotate your images around and attack the drawing from various angles much more easily while maintaining your drawings within registration parameters. Most people who draw tend to draw better and more comfortably with their paper slightly tilted in the direction of the hand they draw with. Many objects are often drawn better if you can approach them from various angles. A light box would have a harder time doing this for you.

What's Wrong with This Picture?

At press time, the going rate for a WACOM PL-500 LCD Pen Tablet is roughly a whopping $4,000. A comparable LCD tablet, manufactured by Sony, is bundled as part of its VAIO Slimtop series of high-powered computers. The funny thing is the entire Sony VAIO System sells for less than $3,000. Get a load of Figures 6-7 and 6-8 and compare for yourself.

The Expense of Creating Flash Content

Flash animation is all about doing the job with the least amount of out-of-pocket expenses. It's about making animation services available to small businesses at prices they can afford, and it's about creating content that rivals the quality of any multimillion-dollar entertainment company at an insanely small fraction of the costs. This is the formula that keeps independent animators and small animation houses thriving on the Web, while the multimillion-dollar production companies crumble before our eyes and become just another statistic in the so-called dot-bomb crisis.

Figure 6-7   *The WACOM PL-500 is a whopping $4K.*

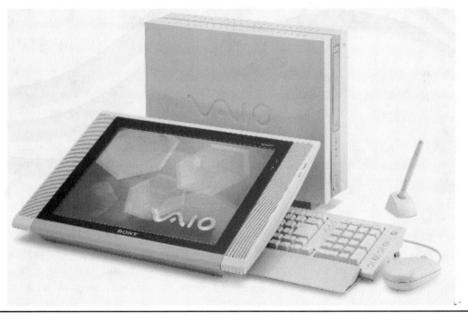

Figure 6-8   *The Sony VAIO Slimtop PCV-LX900 Pen Tablet computer is a high-performance PC (1,000 MHz Pentium 3 processor).*

Any time a product or service of the same or better quality can be created and sold for a fraction of the competition's cost will always hurt the competition. Especially if the competition spent thousands of dollars in overhead to produce its product, while you made yours during your lunch breaks at work or in your granny's basement over a holiday.

Production costs for Flash animation is cheap and should be made available—at an equally cheap price—to clients who want to hire you for your animation services or, perhaps, license your work. How you keep your overhead costs to a minimum and how you maintain balance between quality and affordability can determine how successful you are in this marketplace.

Summary

Macromedia Flash is a highly versatile tool, which can be used to perform a variety of jobs aside from simple Web design. Although the tool itself is designed with Web developers in mind, it proves adept at performing animation tasks such as ink and paint, pencil testing, sequencing, sound editing, and animatic making, and even lets you export in a variety of mediums. This can come in handy if your main animation software is something other than Flash.

Flash animation itself is no longer a proprietary form of animation. Many alternatives to Macromedia Flash are available that enable you to create vector-based Flash animation. Toon Boom Studio is perhaps the most powerful Flash animation product developed to date. Although Toon Boom Studio excels over Flash in every aspect of the animation process and workflow, its Web design application is rather limited.

LCD tablets and computers systems promise to convert the animation workflow into a complete paperless environment.

Flash animation simplifies the way we animate so much that anyone can do it. For professional and experienced animators, being able to animate in Flash not only creates the most cost-effective way to produce high-quality animation but, at the same time, makes animation services affordable to clients who traditionally couldn't have afforded them. Flash animation is faster and more efficient. A skilled animator can, in most cases, create a product of equal value to that created by a fully staffed studio by himself and, perhaps, even faster.

For the uninitiated, Flash animation is a great way to learn and gain experience as an animator. In the same way an average person can jumpstart a career in cartooning by simply picking up a pencil and paper, the average Joe or Jane can now turn himself or herself into a working animator. All you need is a PC and a copy of the software. You don't even need talent, as long as you're willing to learn the techniques and turn them into skills.

7

Introduction
to Animation

Now that you've tested the waters and are capable of creating your own drawings within Macromedia Flash, let's take it up a notch. In this chapter, we cover some of the most essential bits of information all animators should know before sitting down at their desks and picking up their pencils. This chapter discusses the origin of animation, the technical requirements behind various distribution technologies, and important technical information about vector art.

Origin of Animation as a Cartoon Genre

Animation toys, such as Zeotropes and Flip Books, have been around for centuries, so the art of animation itself has definitely been around for quite some time. In the early days of motion picture exploration, however, it was revealed that if a sequence of still images were presented at a rate of about 18 frames per seconds or faster, because of a phenomenon known as *persistence of vision,* the images would blend together, giving the impression of a continuous, uninterrupted image.

Someone also discovered that, if those images were varied slightly from one frame to the next to show changes over a period of time, the illusion of motion could be created when those pictures were played back in an uninterrupted sequence. These experiments led to the development of the motion picture and, consequently, established the art of animation as a mainstream genre of modern cartooning.

Persistence of Vision

Vision is a highly complex process, which works on a rather simple scale. Your eyes are basically a set of cameras that are constantly capturing images. Each individual image is processed and analyzed by the brain until whatever it is we're seeing registers. Once the image registers, the next picture is analyzed and the process continues, providing you with a seemingly uninterrupted stream of visual updates relating to the world around you.

To explain this concept better, let's look at a publicly accessible live video stream of New York's Times Square, which can be accessed from **http://www.earthcam.com/ usa/newyork/timessquare/**. By default, you'll see the streaming video running at approximately four frames per second. Each image will remain in view until it's replaced by the next most current image available.

The act of replacing an old image with an updated one is known as *refreshing*. The measure of how many times an image is refreshed over a period of time is known as its *refreshed rate*. The amount of time an individual image is displayed is called *exposure*. Exposure can either be measured in terms of time, in the case of an image being exposed for .25 seconds, or it can be measured in term of frames, such as in the case of a cel or image, which is exposed for a period of 30 frames.

Playback Film Speed

Two types of film speeds are involved in the production of a film. First is the *playback* frames per second (fps), which is the speed of the movie itself as it's presented to an audience. By conventional means, the playback of a film or video production must conform to standards available to your intended market. In North America, for example, the regional standard television playback rate is 29.97fps, while the theatrical presentation of films usually conforms to a universal 24fps standard.

Before you can see last summer's blockbuster hit on home video, which most likely was shot and displayed at the theaters at a rate of 24fps, the film itself has to undergo a process known as a *standards conversion*. In the case of a theatrical presentation, not only must the film be redubbed to play normally (in the United States) at a standard rate of 29.97fps, but it must also undergo several other image-formatting processes, so it can be presented within the constraints of the smaller TV field sizes.

> ### NOTE
>
> *Converting a film that originally played at 24fps to a video that plays at 24fps is easy. In North America, for example, because the video and television standard is 29.97fps, your video will be playing 6 frames more than its original rate of 24fps. This causes your video to appear to be playing fast and the characters to sound like chipmunks.*

Shooting Film Speed

The second of the film speed types is the *shooting fps,* which relates to the actual fps used to shoot or record the original production. There's no set standard for doing this. In fact, videographers and filmmakers might make use of several varied fps rates within the shooting of a single production.

Here's how it works. Suppose we're shooting a film where the police are chasing a gang of bank robbers. After a great chase scene, we come to a sequence where the characters have no choice but to jump off a high bridge if they want to escape. We want this jump to be dramatic and we want to see every little detail as it happens. What we do is take as many pictures of the action taking place as quickly as possible. If we know our film will play at 24fps, perhaps we could shoot the jump sequence at a rate of 48fps. Because for every one second of film, there are 48fps—rather than the actual 24fps—meaning when the film is played back at a rate of 24fps, the sequence will, in fact, be playing twice as slow as the rate at which we shot it. This is how slow-motion sequences are created.

For comic relief in our film, we're shooting a scene of a girl who's reminded she has a date only after the doorbell rings and the boy has come to pick her up. She realizes her house is a mess, her hair is a disaster, and she's wearing her comfy, but dirty, sweats and T-shirt. Maybe she even has a chunk of wax on her upper lip. What's she to do? The guy is right outside! She rushes to clean the house, takes a shower, brushes her teeth, does her hair, puts on her evening gown, feeds the dog, and does the dishes. What's funny is she does all of this before the guy can raise his hand to ring the doorbell a second time! This type of comedy sequence is usually shot at a slower fps: the lower the fps, the faster and more comical the action appears when it's played back at 24fps.

This is the same concept behind time-lapse photography. In time-lapse photography, the fps at which a scene is shot is slowed down to such a low fps, it's no longer accurate to refer to it as fps—maybe, instead, fpm (frames per minute) or fph (frames per hour). A flower blooming, the sun rising and setting again, the movement of clouds, a dying tree: we simply don't have the patience to sit there and look at the grass grow. Through time-lapse photography, though, the film can be shot at a rate of 60 frames per hour and, when we play it back on our TV set's monitor, we can see an entire hour pass by within the span of two seconds, making the growth of grass seem more exciting to watch.

Going back to the Times Square cam, we can see the video stream has a refresh rate of approximately four images per second (4fps), which means each image displayed remains in view (*exposed*) for a period of one-fourth of a second. Many changes take place within that quarter of a second time frame, and those changes are made quite apparent once that image is refreshed and replaced with a new one.

Choose a person (in the web cam image) and follow her as she crosses the street. Notice, as each image is refreshed, you can track her progress as she walks toward her destination. The background doesn't change much, her clothes don't change, the streets and buildings remain the same, and the color of the objects themselves doesn't change either. All the elements in the picture remain virtually the same. A blue car is still a blue car and a curly-haired woman is still a curly-haired woman when the image is refreshed. You can track that person crossing the street because even though her position and distance might be different from the previous image, her clothes, skin color, hair style, shoes, and so forth are still the same, giving you the assurance this is, in fact, the same person.

Many things change, however, once the image is refreshed. Things such as the person's position in relation to the last image, maybe her legs and arms are at a different pose. Perhaps she dropped something and is picking it up or maybe she's waving a cab to stop. If cars are in the picture, maybe they, too, have changed positions as they advance down the street.

When you see the world around you, you can track the movement of objects across a period of time because, for the most part, the physical appearance of objects doesn't change from one image to the next. When a change does occur, you notice it because not everything changes at once.

If a short, bald man wearing a yellow sweater is using a payphone in one image, but after the image is refreshed, you see a tall woman with long hair wearing a trench coat is at the payphone, your brain will have a hard time believing this is the same person. Your brain immediately analyzes the image and compares it to the memory of the last image you saw. The phone is still in the same location, the buildings haven't moved, the streets are still gray, and the sky is still blue. Everything is the same except your brain is trying to figure out where the short man is in the new image and where that tall lady was in the previous image.

The phenomenon responsible for your brain wanting constantly to analyze all visual elements such as shapes, colors, sizes, and distances, and to track their changes over a period of time is known as persistence of vision.

Persistence of vision is a function of the human brain, which animators have learned to exploit and manipulate by creating the illusion of living cartoons. We can animate a box moving from one side of the screen to the other side. If the box is drawn exactly the same way in every frame, with the only change being its position on the screen, the audience won't have any trouble believing it's the same box moving from one side to the other, rather than a series of totally different drawings.

If a character is drawn in a certain way using the same elements (formula) in every single drawing, no matter what pose you draw him in, your audience will perceive the hundreds of drawings as being a single entity. Persistence of vision allows animation not only to create the illusion of motion, but it can, in fact, enable you to create three-dimensional environments using a serious of two-dimensional drawings.

Frame Rates

Frame rate is a measure of film speed and has little bearing on the smoothness of an animation or the actual speed of the character's movements. Unlike 3-D animation software, where the environment is treated like an actual set and cameras can be adjusted to record the action at any given frame rate, Flash frame rates are handled in much the same way as conventional 2-D animation. From the beginning, it's made clear the film is to be displayed at a given frame rate and the actual shooting speeds are handled manually.

If you want a smoother or a slower sequence, you must create the action using more frames. If you want faster displays, then you must create the action using fewer frames.

Silent films generally used a frame rate of 18fps, which is perfectly fine for believable natural motion, but the technical requirements for sound playback in film made it necessary to increase that frame rate to 24fps. Unlike broadcast television, which has frame rates upward to 25–30fps depending on the country, to this day, film has maintained itself at a universal 24fps standard.

The National Television Systems Committee (NTSC) system used in the United States and many other countries reproduces pictures (frames) at a rate of 29.97 per second. While a motion picture camera records a sequence of static pictures on film, in a video camera, each complete picture is broken down into hundreds of brightness and color (digital) information. This information is then decoded on your television as a beam of electrons, in a left-to-right, top-to-bottom motion, electronically scans these horizontal lines onto the viewing area.

NTSC television consists of 525 scan lines in a 4×3 cubic unit aspect ratio (as shown in Figure 7-1). Remember this because, even thoughFlash animation is done primarily for web distribution, the majority of commercial animation is done for television. Today, Flash animation isn't exclusive to the Web. Even though its functionality is specific for web-based tasks, more and more animators and studios are adapting Flash for broadcast television production because of the low overhead involved in the creation of Flash-based animation.

Your Options

As a working cartoonist or animator, you should never put all your efforts into a single market. Sometimes a market doesn't exist until you invent it. Other times, we tend to overlook time-proven methods because we want to explore new technologies and venues.

Figure 7-1   *NTSC is created at an aspect ratio of 4×3 units. Whether this cartoon measures 288×216 or 400×300 pixels, it still falls under the 4×3 unit aspect ratio.*

Despite advances in technology and the Internet, film, video, and broadcast still continue as the most effective and profitable way to distribute content, ranging from commercials to educational programming, entertainment, and information.

Although broadcast-television bandwidth restrictions are now virtually nonexistent, over the Internet we're still at a stage where, as content developers, we're forced to conform. We not only conform to factors like bandwidth restrictions, but because it's such a new technology, we must also constantly fight to establish credibility for the work as a valid form of entertainment media.

The technology that empowers the Web itself may be far superior to anything we've ever seen but, as a platform for the delivery of media services, it's as primitive as television was 50 years ago.

For this reason, it's a good idea to consider the possibility of video distribution for your work even before you sit down to work on your Flash-based cartoons. After all, you never know when a company will want to license your work for a TV spot or commercial. Your work may be purchased and packaged in a short film anthology or you might decide to showcase your work at a film festival or two. Adapting something you made for TV to the Web is better and much easier than adapting a web-based feature to television. You aren't committed to a single format.

World Television Systems and TV Standards

Not all countries use the same television systems. And no set standard exists for authoring video, much less actual pixel dimensions, as many people will lead you to believe. In most cases, the country in which you live governs these methods and technical specs.

The presence of different broadcast TV standards means the exchange of information through video is made much more difficult. Videotapes made in the United States cannot be played back in Korea or England, at least not without having gone through an electronic standards conversion. In many cases, even among the countries using 625-line, 50-field systems, differences still sometimes exist that make them incompatible.

These inconsistencies in world television standards aren't entirely because of technical incompatibilities. Some political leaders at one point intentionally selected a television system for their country that was incompatible with one or more neighboring countries, in many cases, only a few miles away. This was done to regulate the type of programming their citizens were exposed to. In doing this, they attempted to isolate their citizens from "foreign" influences, viewpoints, and ideas. Of course, with the advent of the Internet, now virtually anyone in the world can have access to the same type of programming as everyone else.

Digital video has no restrictions. It can be designed at any aspect ratio or size and quality, and then distributed by any form of electronic means, such as CD-ROMs, DVD, or simply made available for download over the Web. Digital video can be played back by anyone with a computer independently from whatever distribution standards are in place.

The NTSC System

The U.S. National Television Systems Committee 525-line, 30fps system is shared by Canada, Greenland, Mexico, Cuba, Panama, Japan, the Philippines, Puerto Rico, and parts of South America. Because 30 frames consist of 60 fields, this is referred to as the 525-line, 60-field system. This was originally based on the 60 Hz electrical system, which was used in these countries. Because other countries in the world use a 50 Hz electrical system, however, it was logical for these countries to develop systems based on 50 fields per second.

PAL and SECAM Systems

Most countries in the world currently use one of two 625-line, 25-frame systems of television: Sequential Color and Memory (SECAM) or Phase Alternating Line (PAL). The extra 100 lines in these systems add a significant amount of detail and clarity to the video picture, but the 50 fields-per-second as opposed to the 60 fields-per-second used in NTSC means a slight flicker is often noticed.

HDTV a New International Standard

With the introduction of high-definition television (HDTV), the possibility of a single television isn't that farfetched. In many countries, productions are now being done in HDTV, which are later converted to film for theatrical release or to PAL, SECAM, and NTSC for video broadcast.

Because HDTV uses 1,125 scanning lines, the resolution and clarity of the standard broadcasting image is greatly increased. Instead of the raster (TV image) being four units wide and three units high (the 4×3 aspect ratio), the HDTV aspect ratio is 16×9 (Figure 7-2). Even though this new aspect ratio conforms itself more naturally to human vision, it does present some problems when making the conversion to the 4×3 NTSC ratio.

This conversion is handled in many ways. First, the sides of the picture can be cut off. If the production itself was created with the 4×3 cut-off area in mind, this won't be a problem. If the production wasn't shot to accommodate HDTV conversion,

Figure 7-2   *The HDTV aspect ratio is 16×9.*

however, and throughout the feature important visual information appears at the extreme sides, the entire production will need to be panned and scanned.

Pan and scan involves someone reviewing every scene in a computer and manually adjusting a 4×3 window over the HDTV area, which acts as a cookie cutter of sorts, favoring the area of the screen that contains the most important information at any one time, as shown in Figures 7-3, 7-4, and 7-5.

In some cases, the HDTV frame contains important bits of information, such as written material or titles on the extreme sides, which can't be cut off. You have two options. First, the entire picture can be inserted within the 4×3 area, resulting in a "letterbox" look, with the top and bottom sides displaying a computer-generated border. During the relatively short time it takes to display these titles, the video is displayed with a black border on the top and on the bottom (Figure 7-6). In many cases, the letterbox effect is applied only during the title sequences and the rest is pan and scanned.

The other less-visually appealing approach is to shrink the sides of the image to fit the window. This results in a skinny and tall people look, but it eliminates the need for the top and bottom borders (Figure 7-7). This is hardly ever used anymore, but it was quite popular in the '70s and early '80s.

Other conversion issues result in the difference of scanning lines used. Luckily, a wide range of scan converters is available to the public. These scan converters not

4x3 viewable area   Cut-off area

Figure 7-3   *A 4x3 viewing area is panned and scanned over the wide-screen formatted cartoon. This is normally done frame by frame.*

Cut-off area   4x3 viewable area   Cut-off area

Figure 7-4   *The area with the most important element will be viewable. The areas outside the 4x3 field of view will be cut off.*

Figure 7-5 *This film has been modified from its original version. It has been formatted to fit your screen (sound familiar?).*

Figure 7-6 *In this frame, both the titles and the small window are too important to cut off. So, a letterbox presentation is created during the short time the actual titles are displayed.*

Figure 7-7   *Here, the entire screen is shrunk to fit the 4x3 viewing area. This distorts the images and usually isn't an appealing look.*

only allow for conversion from your PC to video, they also aid in converting the formats to meet the standards required by the many television systems.

Note all these facts before you commit your animation to certain aspect ratios. Consider the steps you might have to go through to ensure a nice presentation across a variety of platforms, both online and offline.

Animation and the Web

Because of Macromedia Shockwave technology, we can now deliver rich media content to virtually anywhere in the world through the Internet, despite low-bandwidth restrictions. Macromedia Flash is an excellent tool for creating animated content for both online and offline purposes. The Flash format has rightfully established itself as the standard format for the creation of streaming animation over the Web.

Why the Web?

When it comes to the subject matter of entertainment over the Web, there are literally no rules. Your work might be fun for the entire family. The FCC or another government agency doesn't regulate your content. As the creator and distributor of your content, your work competes directly with the work of major production studios. This is an industry where anyone with a bit of talent, or at least some practice, can take part and compete. This type of freedom also allows for much experimentation in the field and, in many cases, has given us highly successful content. By conventional broadcasting standards, however, this content would be deemed completely unacceptable.

The Internet has given people the opportunity to expose a side of themselves (I don't know if that's a good thing), which, otherwise, would have been nearly impossible without years of academic training and a lot of out-of-pocket costs.

Just because you create the presentation in Flash, however, doesn't necessarily bind you to showcasing it as a Flash file. In many cases, converting it to video or another form of streaming media can increase the performance and enhance the presentation more than the native vector format.

Another thing to note is the Web can be accessed by virtually everyone in the world with a phone line, cable access, or a satellite dish, and those people don't necessarily need to have a computer to view your content. They can view your work through a multitude of wireless devices, computer systems, or even their web-enabled television sets. When it comes to web distribution, we aren't restricted to conform to any type of television standards. But, we are restricted to developing for an audience where a large majority is still limited to modem-based, low-bandwidth connections. With this in mind, we must find and develop ways to create great content that can be seamlessly streamed, while sacrificing as little graphic and audio quality as possible.

When creating content for the Web, you must also take into consideration other factors that will influence the proper delivery of the product (your cartoon). You must take into account that, although your cartoon plays perfectly well in your 1.5 GHz Athlon system, the majority of people who own computers are still within the 150–350 MHz range. Monitor sizes and movie dimensions are also a major issue. While sizes and aspect ratios can be accurately measured on a PC according to the number of pixels they take up, on television sizes they're relative and merely measured as cubic units of indefinite sizes. Whether you have a 12", 25", or 52" television screen, the resolution will always be the same as long as the content is formatted or edited to fit that screen (NTSC, PAL, HDTV, and so forth). On a PC, however, if your movie is 500 pixels wide × 400 pixels high, it retains its size, no matter how big or small the user's monitor is.

As explained before, the Flash player itself is extremely dependent on the user's processor, simply because of the way Macromedia's Shockwave technology works. As animators, it's often our duty to keep tabs on whether our content can stream from the server to the users' PCs efficiently and, as the data stream reaches the users, that their computer systems can decode the information fast and efficiently, with as few anomalies as possible. This is why developing content in Flash isn't only a matter of creating low-file sizes that stream well over the user's connection, but the content itself must allow their system's CPU to decode the information efficiently and as fast as possible.

Where File Size Comes From

The secret to creating small vector files is the way you draw the artwork. Optimization isn't only a step you do after a movie is completed. Instead, it's something that should begin at the character design phase, before your hand even touches the mouse. Most of the optimization should take place at the point where you initially sketch out and design your characters on paper. Try to minimize the number of lines and curves used in your drawings, so when it comes time to render them in Flash, your artwork is both animation friendly and lends itself to low–file size rendering much more easily.

TIP

In animation, the act of simplifying the artwork is more often done to make the characters easier to draw and to increase the speed at which an animation is created. It has nothing to do with file size. In Flash, however, because graphics for animation are supposed to be optimized, this conveniently goes hand-in-hand with keeping down the file sizes.

By definition, a *vector* is a one-dimensional mathematical array, which is formed between two given points. Saying that the amount of lines and curves in a drawing is what adds to the file size in a vector graphic is a generalization and not entirely true. Vectors are actually based on a series of points, which, until the release of Flash 5, people couldn't directly interact with. A vector can contain a variety of curves without necessarily increasing the overall file size of the project. Once you begin to add more points to your vectors, the file size begins to increase.

In Figure 7-8, you see a straight line created, using the Line tool. A straight line is composed of two points, which has no curves. These points are called *centerline points.* The line you see is created as the result of the computer being told to display the array formed between those two points.

Figure 7-8   *The line itself doesn't exist, only the actual points the computer uses to carry out the instructions.*

Figure 7-9 *On the left is the image as drawn. On the right, you can literally see hundreds of centerline points that make up the freehand drawing.*

When you draw freehand, you're actually plotting a series of centerline points along a flat one-dimensional plane. In Figure 7-9, I drew an image freehand and, as you can see on the right, all the actual points created number into the hundreds.

If, however, you plan ahead of time and decide how many lines your drawing is made up of, then perhaps you can bring that knowledge with you and apply it to a cleaner-looking drawing, such as the one in Figure 7-10.

Figure 7-10 *On the left is a more calculated drawing, using the least possible amount of points. The smaller amount of points not only makes this a cleaner drawing but, because it uses less points, this is also a much smaller file.*

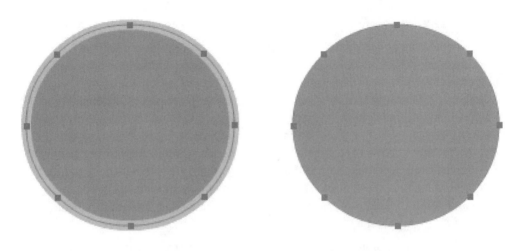

Figure 7-11   *The points that make up a fill are called contour points. Remove the outline and the same image is still made up of the same number of points.*

A shape, such as a circle, which also contains a fill color, is made up of points called *contour points* (Figure 7-11). This is because the fill is molded into the shape, not the outlines.

Drawings created using fills, such as brush strokes (Figure 7-12), are all created using contour points. Any shape drawn with fills generally requires at least twice the file size as graphics created with regular lines.

Figure 7-12   *This line has a few curves, yet it's still composed of two points. The brush stroke, which is a fill, requires at least twice the amount of points to mold the shape.*

Summary

In this chapter, we covered some of the most essential things every animator should know. We learned about the origins of the motion picture, and the science behind animation and vector drawing.

Here are some things to remember as you go through the rest of the chapters in this book and, ultimately, your own creations.

▶ The frame rate of a movie is merely the speed at which the film itself is played. It has little bearing on the speed and quality of the animation. The lower the frame rate, the more you must use visual tricks, like blurs and smears, to create the illusion of fluid movement. Faster frame rates mean you need to create more drawings and less visual trickery to achieve the same effects.

▶ Persistence of vision is dependent on using similar shapes, colors, sizes, and distances through your animation. If you're animating a character composed out of 18 individual lines, it's important to draw the changes of those same 18 lines in every frame that follows. Always adhere to your character's formula. If your drawings use a different amount of line shapes or colors from one frame to the next, your animation won't register well.

▶ Most animation is created for television, film, and video, which is where most of the money is. It's important to consider all possible venues before you commit to a specific format. By giving your work the ability to be distributed through as many markets as possible, your product can have a greater commercial value.

▶ Television standards vary from country to country. For a product to be viewed across the various standards, the product must undergo a conversion. Although 24fps is considered a true universal standard, HDTV is also rapidly becoming a new universal standard.

▶ To convert an HDTV or other wide-screen format to fit the 4×3 viewing area of general television standards, the film must also undergo an editing process known as pan and scan, in which each frame is edited to favor the best-looking 4×3 area. Try to keep this area in mind when you create your own animations. It will make the conversion process much easier, despite the actual dimensions you chose to animate the original work.

▶ Vector art is created through the plotting of a series of visible one-dimensional arrays across a number of points. The arrays themselves can curve and contour as they connect from one point to the next, without increasing the file size. Keeping the number of points to a minimum from the start can insure small file sizes and require less or no time at all to optimize the files after the work is completed.

▶ In a vector drawing, a fill always requires several more points to create than a regular line does.

TIP

A common occurrence when drawing in Flash is this: when you try to fill in an outlined shape with a color, the shape refuses to fill. This is because you have gaps in your shape. In case you're wondering, the width of a line (the size of the stroke) is merely a property of the array. The array itself is the width of a hairline, no matter what the actual size of the stroke is set to. It's often necessary to view your lines in Outline mode, which displays the arrays without their attributes and enables you to easily spot where the gaps are. This is also effective in determining where any unnecessary lines are located.

Drawing and
Painting in Flash

I n this chapter, you learn the basics of ink and paint in Flash. First, I discuss the various tools you need. Then, I explain the uses of each tool in combination with many of the other features and functions in Flash. All tools covered here are put to the test in a real-world task of importing and vectorizing an image file by hand.

The Tools Panel

At the heart of the Flash universe is the *Tools panel,* which contains the most essential tools for drawing, painting, scaling, resizing, and editing your artwork. The Tools panel is composed of four basic parts: the drawing and editing tools, the viewing tools, the color options, and the plain options. The tools appearing in the Options section change, depending on the tool selected. These options are also known as *modifiers.*

The Black Arrow (the Selection Tool)

The *Black Arrow* is the Selection tool, which works by enabling you to select a line or a fill for further modification. This tool is also in a way a Molding tool. You can use it to modify the length and curve of a line or a fill color.

The Black Arrow has several modifiers that affect the way the objects are manipulated, such as their rotation size, the curve of a line, or whether a selected object will lock itself against other objects. The following is a rundown of the Black Arrow modifiers.

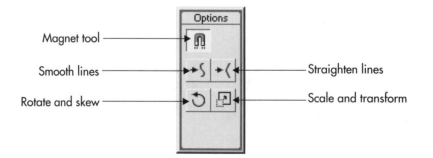

Black Arrow Modifiers	Description
Magnet tool	This option is also called the Snap tool because it affects whether selected objects will lock on to other objects when placed on, or drawn in proximity to, each other. In other words, when the Magnet tool is turned on, it causes objects you draw or placed close to each other to "snap" to each other. This is particularly helpful if you want to attach one line with another or snap a graphic symbol against a motion guide.
Smooth lines	This option affects selected lines or fills. It smoothes out the curves that make up the object.
Straighten lines	This option takes selected lines or fills and, instead of smoothening out the curves, attempts to straighten them.
Rotate and skew	This option forms a special highlight around a selected object with drag handles that enable you to rotate the object along its axis (pivot point), or to skew it horizontally or vertically.
Scale and transform	This option enables you to scale a selected object to a different size. This tool can also be used to manually flip a selected object vertically or horizontally.

TIP

You can keep a selected object's original proportions intact by holding the SHIFT key down, while modifying it under the influence of the Scale and Transform option of the Black Arrow tool.

The White Arrow (the Molding Tool)

The *White Arrow* tool is the *Subselect* tool (that's what it's called by Macromedia). This tool is known throughout most software packages as simply the Molding tool. The difference is, with the White Arrow, you have the benefit of viewing and working with a pivot point and handle system, which enables you to modify lines and curves. This is extremely useful if your graphics must be accurate or if you want to limit the number of curves because of the file size.

To modify a line properly using the White Arrow, you must first create a curve on the line using the Black Arrow selection tool. Once a curve exists, click the White Arrow and then on the line you wish to modify. All points that make up the line will be revealed, and you can alter the line by dragging the points to another place. A *pivot point*—or as it is more often referred to in animation, a *centerline point*—is a point in the line of extreme change, such as the beginning, the end, or the tip of an angle. The selected point changes color to let you know it's selected. If a curve exists on the line, you get a little handle or two protruding from that pivot point. Clicking-and-dragging those little handles enables you to adjust the curve of that line around the pivot point. A common name for this type of point is also a *Bézier* point.

The Line Tool

The *Line* tool draws straight lines from one point to another. Lines can be modified by using any of the two Arrow tools or the Pen tool.

The Lasso Tool

The Lasso tool is similar to a Marquee tool, which is quite common in graphic design programs like Photoshop and Fireworks.

The *Lasso* tool is used to select certain areas of a shape, literally by drawing around the area you want, and it will become the current selection.

Two modifiers are available for the Lasso tool. The first is the Magic Wand, which works by enabling you to select a certain color range within a shape. All similar colors are selected. This is helpful if your objective is to clean up certain unwanted areas or to remove a background. The Magic Wand works better when the areas you're trying to select are close in color consistency, such as removing a solid blue background from a bitmapped image.

The second modifier for the Lasso Tool is the Polygonal modifier. It allows you to make a selection around an object by anchoring a series of points around the object rather than having to select it all freehand on one try.

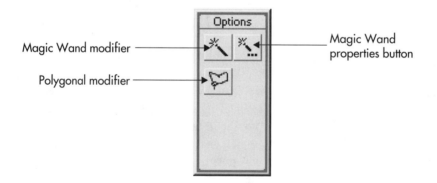

Magic Wand modifier

Polygonal modifier

Magic Wand properties button

The Pen Tool

The *Pen* tool is a drawing tool that enables you to modify your lines by giving you full control of your lines and shapes using Bézier curves and points. And, unlike the white arrow, the Pen tool isn't just a modifying tool; it also lets you draw and add points quickly and easily.

On the plus side, drawings created using the Pen tool tend to be smaller in size and more accurate. On the minus side, however, these drawings can look synthetic and lifeless, and lack the human quality that makes cartoons what they are. I personally recommend avoiding this tool for cartooning purposes. The Pen tool is better left for technical drawings, such as buildings and mechanical objects like cars and robots. It's also a great tool for whipping out web interfaces. A common name for the Pen tool is "the Bézier pen."

The Text Tool

The *Text* tool enables you to click your mouse on the work area and to place a block of text. The text can be further modified using any of the three text panels (Character, Paragraph, or Text Options), which can be pulled up by clicking the text icon (the one with the letter *A* on it), located on the lower right-hand side of your program window.

The Oval Tool

The *Oval* tool is used to draw circular objects. No special modifiers exist for this tool except, if you want to draw perfect circles, you can do it by holding down the SHIFT key while you draw the shape.

CAUTION

Another one of Macromedia's quirks in this new version of Flash is that, by default, these types of objects are filled with whatever color you select, which can be quite annoying when modeling out a character or wire-framing an object for rotoscoping. If drawing an oval with the color already filled in isn't what you're going for (it usually won't be if you're drawing cartoons), you can turn off the fill momentarily by clicking the No Color button directly below the Paint Bucket tool. The problem is, it won't stay off, so you must learn to keep clicking that button every time you need to draw an oval.

The Rectangle Tool

The *Rectangle* tool is used for drawing any form of rectangular shape. To draw a perfect square, you must draw the shape while holding the SHIFT key down. The Rectangle tool has one modifier in the Options area of the toolbar that enables you to define the roundness of the corners.

TIP

You can also define the roundness of the corners through a more natural approach. When you click to draw your rectangle — but before you let go of the mouse button — use your UP or DOWN ARROW keys to achieve the desired roundness without having to deal with specific numbers. Once you balance out your rectangle to the way you want it to look, let go of the mouse button and it'll be rendered with the round corners you defined.

The Pencil Tool

The *Pencil* tool in Flash is extremely easy to use and feels quite natural in the hands of a cartoonist. It works like the Pen tool, but without all the clutter and technicalities of Bézier points. In other words, the Pencil tool basically lets you draw freehand. Drawing with the Pencil tool is perfect for drawing anything quickly that pops into your mind, the same way you would draw on paper with a regular pencil.

Because drawing on a computer can sometimes be tricky, the Pencil tool has three modifiers to choose from in the Options area of the toolbar, which affect the way the lines are drawn. The following table provides a quick rundown of what each of these options does.

TIP

If speed is of importance, use the Pencil tool to sketch out your drawings quickly. On a separate layer, trace your initially penciled drawings using the Line tool. Modify the new lines with the Molding tool (white arrow) and, finally, delete the original sketchy line art, leaving behind the cleaner drawing created with the Pencil Line tool.

Pencil Modifier	Description
Straighten	This causes any lines to straighten out as you draw them. While under the influence of this modifier, Flash also employs its capability to recognize the oval and rectangular shapes. The effect is, if you draw anything Flash believes might look like a rectangle or a circle, Flash automatically renders it accordingly.
Smooth	This feature takes the lines you draw and minimizes the number of angles and curves, causing your lines to appear smoother and much cleaner in appearance.
Ink	Draw them as they come. Nothing is modified and your lines are rendered exactly as you draw them.

The Brush Tool

The *Brush* tool draws colored fills on to your work area. This tool has several modifiers that affect the way it works. The *Paint* modifier affects the way the brush paints shapes. It can be set to paint as normal, to paint only areas that contain other fills, to paint behind a shape, or to paint inside a selected fill.

CAUTION

In the Flash 5 environment, the Paint Selected modifier for the Brush tool is completely useless. You'll have better luck solving the mystery of your missing socks in the laundry than you will painting inside a selected object without changing the color of the entire fill area.

The Ink Bottle Tool

The *Ink Bottle* tool is also known as the Outline tool. To use it, simply apply it to any fill and it creates an outline around it. You can adjust the size of the outlines by modifying the attributes in the Stroke panel. You can also use this tool to change or modify already existing outlines.

The Paint Bucket Tool

This handy-dandy gadget is for filling an outlined shape with a color. Use the *Paint Bucket* tool to fill out large portions of an object quickly or to change the color of an existing fill. You can create various types of fills, including gradient fills, and use a bitmapped texture as a paint fill.

The *Gap* modifier is used to set how much of a gap can be in an outlined shape before it gets filled. If the gap is too large, no effect occurs. The *Lock* modifier lets you lock a color, so it cannot be replaced by another. The *Gradient* modifier enables you to adjust the positioning, direction, and size of a gradient fill within a shape.

The Eyedropper Tool

The *Eyedropper* tool literally sucks up attributes from one shape and lets you apply them to another shape. (*Shapes* are a line, a fill, or a bitmap, which has been broken apart into a fill.)

A common use for this tool is as a "color picker," which selects a previously used color from one shape and applies it to another one.

TIP

If you press and hold your left mouse color on to either of the two color selectors for the line or the fill, and then drag you mouse, your mouse pointer will transform itself into an eyedropper. This particular method is much more versatile because it also enables you to select colors anywhere on your screen. This is helpful when creating a palette that matches your web site.

The Eraser Tool

The *Eraser* tool lets you manually remove unwanted areas from an ungrouped shape. You can adjust the size of your eraser by way of its three modifiers.

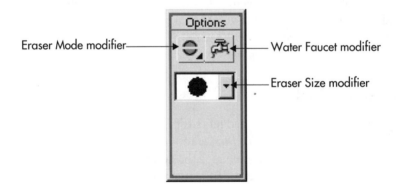

Eraser Modifier	Description
Eraser Mode	Works like the Pencil modifiers and enables you to adjust the eraser to selectively erase only fills, outlines, or selected fills, to erase inside an outlined shape, or to erase normally.
Water Faucet	Enables you to wash away larger areas of lines or fills.
Eraser Size	Lets you choose from various assortments of eraser sizes and shapes.

Vectorizing a Bitmapped Image Manually

My biggest ambition as an animator is to be the first person in the world to create a full-length motion picture entirely in Flash. I know many of the large, big-budget studios are already engaged in such an endeavor, so I'll settle on being among the first independent guys to achieve this.

I'd like you to meet Odesio Robles, who's the main character in my little feature film project, *Without You*. Having discussed the character design and personality types in previous chapters, you can pretty much make an educated guess as to how I went about designing him and the rest of the characters in the story.

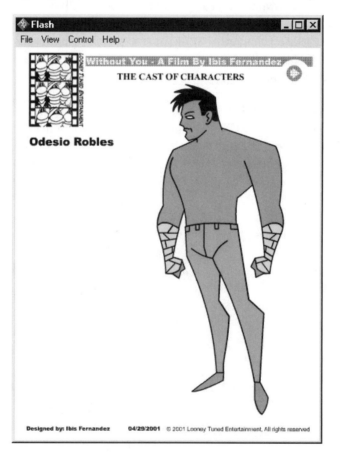

Many other factors that deal directly with Flash also have a strong bearing on the way the characters themselves were designed. The one factor that took more precedence over anything else is that Flash graphics are vector-based and the more simple the characters are drawn, the less file size the final output occupies.

I could design the characters and graphics as complicated and realistic as possible, but then I couldn't present the film over the Internet as easily, at least not without resorting to a streaming video format. I want to finish the film before the year is over and, as a one-man studio, time is always a big issue. Simplifying a character also isn't influenced by Flash in and of itself. Even in the most expensive productions, simplifying characters is the best way to increase production time and decrease anomalies caused when an animator decides to get creative and add unnecessary lines to a drawing.

Flash does make the work a lot easier and faster but, for Flash to work for you, you must work with it and come to a compromise somewhere in the middle.

Drawing ultrarealistic characters would defeat the purpose of using Flash as the production tool of choice. The average five-minute animated sequence created in *CTP,* a high-end raster-based animation software (and one of my personal favorites), uses up approximately 1.5GB of hard drive space! In Flash 5, I could easily create a ten-minute episode in under 5MG. Big difference!

The secret to creating low file-sized graphics in Flash lies in the simplicity of the graphics themselves. The less lines and curves you use, the less mathematical information the Flash player must decode to render the file when played back at the user's end. This also reduces the amount of strain placed in the user's CPU as the animation is delivered.

A major misconception is that because Flash is vector-based and limited to a certain extent, the products themselves will be limited. But the only limit is the user's imagination. If you're determined to create great-looking characters that can be fully animated in Flash, then you'll probably find a way to do it. If you've made up your mind that anything created in Flash is going to be stiff and lifeless, then there's little I can do to change your mind. In all cases, your own work reflects the way you feel about using the software.

Importing

Importing your images into Flash and tracing them by hand is by far the best method to obtain sharp-looking graphics and to keep down file sizes. Many are turned off by the thought of having to do anything by hand but, at the risk of sounding like an old fuddy-duddy, I want to remind you that in cel animation, animators draw anywhere from 24 to 60 drawings per second of film. Flash already makes your life simple enough, so learn to embrace it and make the most of it. A little grunt work never hurt anybody.

Flash enables you to choose from several image file formats and to import them into the work area, including a few sound formats and even QuickTime video. For this project, we only concern ourselves with an image file named Odesio.gif, which you can download from the Chapter 8 section of the book's web site (www.osborne.com).

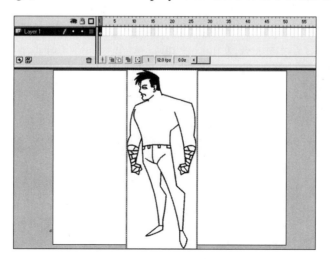

You can import this file in two ways into the Flash environment. The first and easiest way is to open the file in your default browser—Internet Explorer or Netscape—right-click the image and choose Copy. Next, you can simply right-click anywhere in the work area and choose the Paste option. The image is automatically pasted on to the stage.

The other, more common, approach is to go to your File menu and select the Import option. This brings up a file-browsing panel, which you can navigate until you find the image you want to import. Select the file and choose Open.

The image should now be imported in Flash. Be aware, this image, as any other raster-based image, is treated as a bitmap by Flash and not as a vector shape.

Basic Layer and Frame Functions

Now that the image is inside the program, notice a black dot is placed in frame one of the first layer. This indicates the frame is no longer empty. Click-and-drag the image to move it around and place it at a location of your choosing. When the image is selected, it's highlighted by a colored rectangle. You can set the color of the highlight to be the same as the layer that contains the object in the Preference panel. We've already discussed this, so we'll move right along.

The layer color is indicated by a colored square directly below the square icon. This colored square is also known as the *Outline View* button. Clicking it displays all objects residing in that layer as mere outlines.

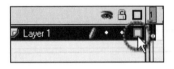

In the case of our bitmap, if you were to view it that way, you'd only see a rectangular outline.

To the left of the Outline View button on the layer is a dot and known as the Lock Layer button, which lies directly beneath an icon that looks like a padlock. Clicking this dot enables you to lock the objects residing in that layer, so they can't be edited or manipulated in any way. Click the dot and leave this layer locked. Notice how a little padlock icon replaces the dot when clicked.

To the left of the Lock Layer button is another dot. This dot resides directly under an icon that looks like an eye. Clicking this option hides all objects on that layer. Go ahead and click it, so you can see the results. A little *X* icon replaces that dot.

After you finish playing with this feature, make sure you turn on the visibility of that layer again, so you can see your bitmap.

The default name of the layer is usually something like Layer 1, depending on how many layers you create. Double-click the name and you can change it to whatever you want that layer to be called. For this project, name the layer "bitmap."

NOTE

Giving your layers custom names is extremely important. You often find yourself working on projects with lots of layers. If all you have is default names, you'll have a harder time determining what's where. A layer's name should be something relating to its content.

Directly below the name of the layer are three icons. The one that looks like a page with a plus (+) sign is the *Add Layer* button. Click that one now to add a new layer. The layer appears directly above the one previously selected and has a default name like layer 2. Double-click the name of the new layer and change it to **Character**. This is the layer we use to draw on.

If you created one too many layers, you can select the layer by clicking the name of that layer and, once highlighted, clicking the DELETE button, which looks like a garbage bin. This deletes the layer you don't want.

The button in the middle with a plus sign (+) and a little zigzag line is the *Add Guide Layer* button, which allows a Motion Guide layer for your Flash symbols to follow. You learn to use this feature in the animation portion of the book.

Tracing the Image

On your second layer, the one you named Character, select the first frame to make it active. This tells Flash this is the frame you'll draw on.

You want to draw using an outline color that contrasts the line work on the image. In doing so, you can see what you're doing much more easily. I like to use a bright color, such as red or orange.

1. Go to Window | Panels | Stroke and, in the Stroke panel, set the weight of your stroke to 2 points. This gives you a nice bold line to work with.

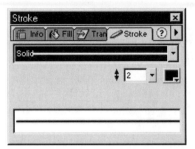

2. Find the points in the drawing where the lines start and end.

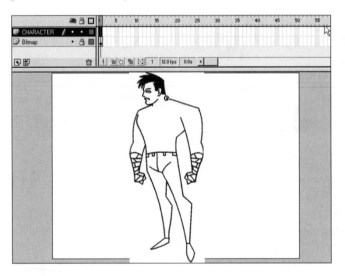

3. Using the Line tool, draw straight lines connecting them, beginning with the left arm (his left, your right).

4. Select your Black Arrow (select) tool and use it to mold the lines to conform to the curves of the arm in your bitmap. For better accuracy, after implementing the initial curve with the black arrow, use the white arrow (subselect) to further manipulate the fit of the curve against the original artwork.

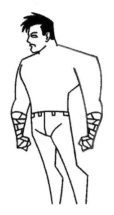

5. Next, select the outlines that make up the arm and drag them away from the main image. This enables you to trace the shape of the torso without messing up the arm you just traced.

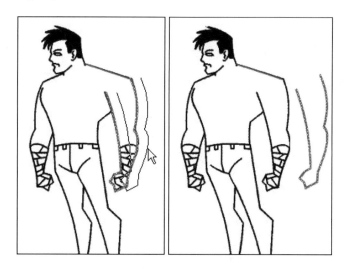

6. You already have the arm, so pretend it doesn't exist and make the torso area a single shape. Again, use the black and white arrows to mold the outlines accurately to fit the lines in the image.

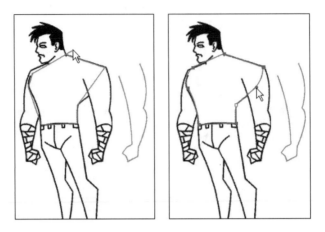

7. After this is done, select the torso and move it to the side.

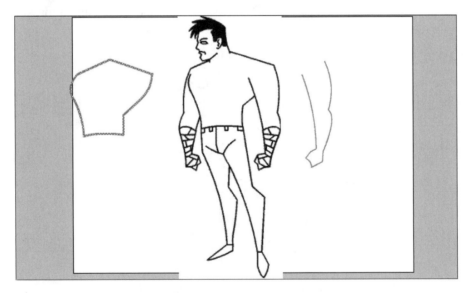

TIP

Double-clicking a line is a quick way to cause all connecting lines to become selected. Use SHIFT-CLICK to deselect or select individual lines.

8. Next up are the pants and the feet. Use the same technique to mold your lines, contouring and adjusting their curves as necessary.

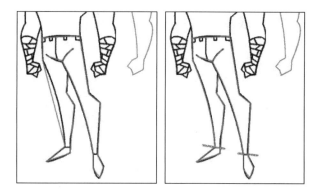

9. Do the same thing for the head. The head is quite small, so you need to zoom in on it. You can do this by holding down CTRL and the + key at the same time.

10. Let's go back to the original arm and, this time, trace the straps he wears wrapped around his fist and forearm.

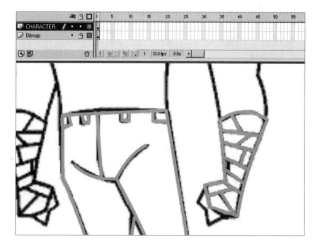

11. Go back to the arm you traced earlier and, using a different colored line, connect the two points on the top of the arm where the outline was left open. This defines the shoulder area of the arm and lets you blend this shape back into the final drawing later.

Flash recognizes intercepting lines, which is a great benefit because it easily enables you to delete unwanted debris created by the excess lines.

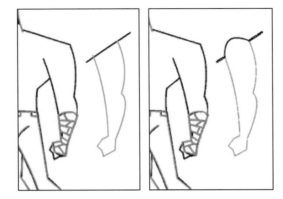

12. You should now have complete outlines with no openings. Use the Black Arrow tool to round off the top area of the shape. Use your Outline tool (the Ink Bottle tool) to change the color of the lines to black.

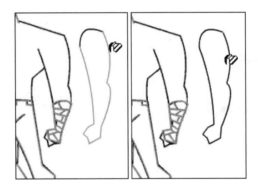

TIP

A quick technique you can use to change the color of the outlines is first to select all the lines whose color you want to change. Then, while those outlines are selected, change the color of the pencil to whatever color you want and the changes occur instantaneously. The longer, more calculated, method is to open the Stroke panel (Windows | Panels | Stroke) and modify your selected lines using the given options.

13. Click the Hide Layer button on the Bitmap layer to hide the image. This way, you focus your attention exclusively on the new vector shapes. Using the Bucket tool, fill in the shape of the arm with a flesh color.

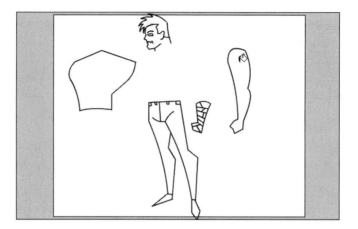

14. Next, fill in the torso shape. To fill in the head, you need to enclose the shape by drawing another line, connecting the two points below the neck in the same way you enclosed the area of the arm. You also need to round off that line, so it isn't jagged. Fill in the face with a flesh color, and then fill in the hair with black.

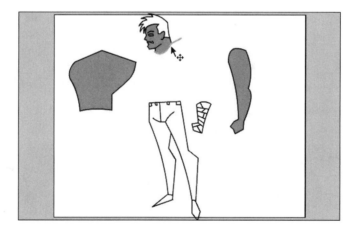

Building a Library of Reusable Symbols

Flash gives a whole new meaning to the phrase "Reduce, Reuse, and Recycle." By letting you create reusable graphic elements, known as *symbols,* you can dramatically reduce the file size of your work. Each symbol is like a general image file on a web site. Once that symbol is downloaded and cached, it needn't be downloaded again every time it appears. That is, until you clear your cache, of course.

Basically what this means is, if a symbol is 1K in size, you can actually use 100 instances of the same symbol and your file size will still be in the vicinity of 1K. Any extra amount of size generated from the use of this symbol is because of the way you use them across a number of frames or as you have them perform various effects, such as tweening and alpha fades.

1. Using the Black Arrow tool, select a rectangular area around the shape of the arm. This causes the entire shape of the arm to be selected. You can also use the Lasso tool to select the shape.

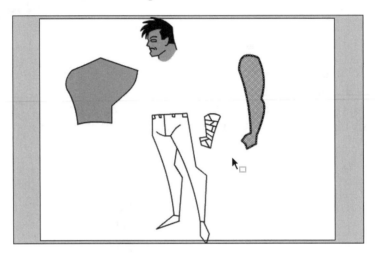

2. Press the F8 key to bring up the Convert To Symbol panel. This panel can also be activated by choosing the Covert To Symbol option in the Insert menu. Here, you specify a name for your new symbol (name it "Arm").

Three types of symbol behaviors exist: *Movie Clip,* which, if animated, plays independently from the main timeline; *Button,* which is used to create symbols the user clicks to perform various tasks of interactivity; and *Graphic* symbols, which are static graphics or sequences that attach themselves to the timeline.

3. Choose Graphic and click OK. You've now created your first symbol.

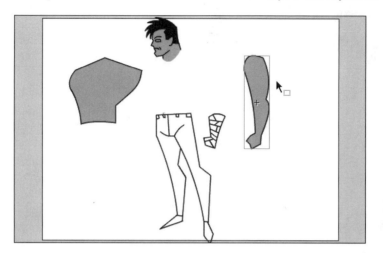

4. Select the torso shape and covert that to a graphic symbol. Name it "Torso." Do the same thing with the head and name it "Head." If you haven't done so already, color in his blue jeans and feet. Convert the entire shape into yet another graphic symbol named "Pants" and don't forget the arm straps. Make the arm straps into a graphic symbol named "Straps."

5. On the lower right-hand side of your project window, notice a little icon that looks like a book. Clicking that icon enables the display of the Projects library. The library contains all the symbols you created in alphabetical order. Clicking a Symbols icon in the library displays the contents within the preview area of the library. Your symbols can now be dragged-and-dropped on to the work area any time you want to use them. The library can also be activated by choosing the Library option in the Window menu.

Duplicating Objects

Using the same images in the previous section, you can duplicate objects:

1. Use the Black Arrow tool and select the Arm symbol in your work area. This activates the symbols you want to affect. You can select multiple objects by holding down the SHIFT key as you click the various objects you want to target. Try this now. While the Arm symbol is activated, press and hold your SHIFT key. Now, click the Straps symbol. You'll notice both objects are now selected. Let go of the SHIFT key and perform a duplicate symbol command by pressing

CTRL and the letter *D* at the same time. Voilà! You've now created duplicate instances of the two symbols.

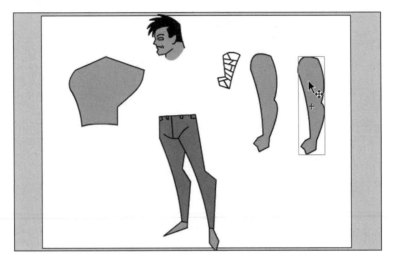

TIP

Another way to perform the duplicate symbol function is to select the Duplicate option in your Edit menu. You can also copy-and-paste the symbols using your right-click menu.

Great! Enough playing around and back to the task at hand (no pun intended).

2. Take both instances of the Straps symbols and align them in their rightful place on top of the Arm symbols. Notice, because you never filled in a color for the straps, the arms show through the open gaps between the outlines of the straps. I did this on purpose to demonstrate this next trick.

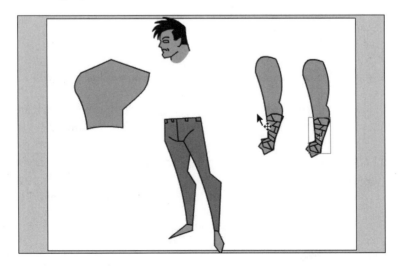

Editing a Symbol

Now, you're going to modify the Straps symbol. You can do this in several ways:

▶ In Flash, you can go directly inside the library and modify a symbol away from the main work area in its own environment: simply double-click the name of the symbol as it appears in the Library panel. You can also do this by right-clicking the symbol you want to modify, and then choosing Edit from your list of options.

▶ You can edit your symbols in two other ways. *Edited In Place* takes your symbol and opens it in a virtual layer above all others and automatically locks the other elements on the stage, so they won't be affected, as shown here:

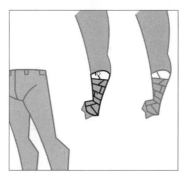

This method enables you to modify your symbol in relation to the surrounding objects. The other method is to edit in a new project window altogether. Choosing this option opens the symbol and enables you to modify it as if the symbol were a totally separate project. This is extremely helpful if your symbol is complex. All changes made in the new project window are reflected on the original project. To end your session, simply close the window.

TIP

If you need to modify several symbols simultaneously, editing in a new project window enables you to do this. This also adds the functionality of being able to keep a set of symbols you can maximize and minimize, rather than opening the library itself and taking up your desktop real estate.

1. For this next step, use the Edit In Place option. You can also activate this option by double-clicking the desired symbol—in this case, the Straps symbol.

   Notice the other objects residing in the work area become slightly out of focus. This is to indicate you aren't able to edit anything other than the one symbol you chose to modify.

2. Select the Paint Bucket tool and the color white. Fill in the gaps within the outline of the straps. As you do this, notice that, in the background, the other instance of the Straps symbol is also changing as you paint. These may be two different instances, but it's the same symbol nonetheless.

3. Once you finish painting, double-click any empty area in the stage and you're taken back into the regular mode.

Grouping Objects

Grouping certain objects together allows you to manage them easier. To group objects, you must first select all of the elements you want to group and press CTRL-G. Alternately you can also do this by selecting the Group option in your Modify menu. Let's do this now.

1. Select one instance of your Arm and Straps symbols, and group them by selecting them and pressing CTRL-G.

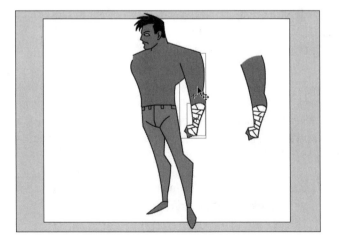

2. Do the same with the other Arm and Straps symbols. Arrange the different objects to form the character. Feel free to turn on the visibility of the Bitmap layer to help you with the placement.

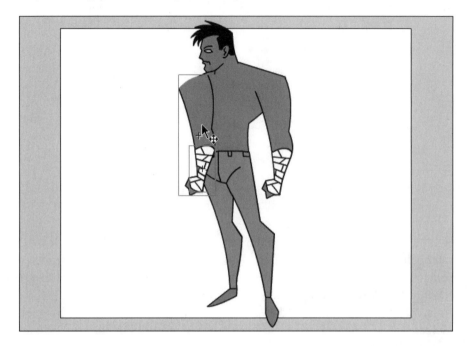

3. In this case, we only created one left arm symbol for Odesio, so we'll remedy this by using the second instance of the arm to give him a right arm. To do this, select the extra Arm and Straps group, and choose Transform | Flip Horizontal from your Modify menu.

4. Now that the arm is flipped, you can place it on the other side to use as his right arm.

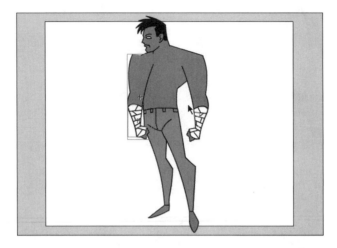

5. Unlike the left arm, whose shoulder faces us, the right arm needs to be away and behind the torso area. Graphical objects are always arranged in various planes even if they reside within the same layer. We need to bring this arm down to the lowest level so that it can lie underneath the torso symbol. To do this, select the arm and hold down CTRL. Use the DOWN ARROW to move the selected object further down, so it rests below everything else. To give an illusion of perspective, use the Transform tool to make his right arm slightly smaller than his left arm. Feel free to experiment with the Rotation tool, to achieve the desired pose.

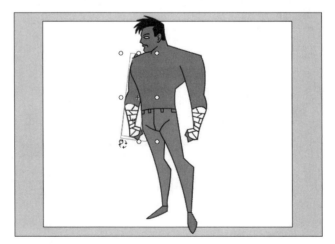

6. That's it. At this point if you like, you can ungroup any grouped objects by selecting them and applying the Break Apart command which can be accessed through Modify | Ungroup or Modify | Break Apart. You may also use the keyboard shortcuts CTRL-B or CTRL-SHIFT-G.

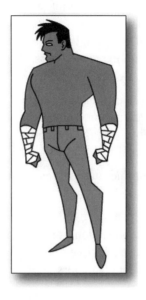

NOTE

The only difference between the Break Apart and the Ungroup commands is that the Ungroup feature will not destroy a symbol's basic integrity. The Break Apart function, if applied enough times, has the ability to break apart both groups and symbols, leaving behind nothing but lines and shape fills. Ungroup will not go that far.

To finish off, select the entire character, convert it to a graphic symbol, and name it whatever you want. You can now delete the Bitmap layer by selecting it and clicking the DELETE button (the little trash can icon). You can delete the bitmap itself by selecting it from the library and doing the same thing there.

Congratulations! You've now taken a simple line drawing, which as a .gif file weighed in at a little over 3K, and created a colorful vector drawing whose aspect ratio can be increased or decreased without loss of quality and which will always weigh in at approximately 1K in file size!

Summary

In this chapter, you not only learned the tools in the toolbar, you also learned how to use them through practical application. And, you learned an everyday approach to using keyboard commands. Here a few more things this chapter examined.

▶ Defining the roundness of a rectangle is a task that can be performed visually without having to deal with exact numbers. Simple keyboard commands do the trick, which is often easier and faster.

▶ To modify the curve of a line using the White Arrow tool, better known as the Molding tool within the animation community, it's best first to create the curve using the Black Arrow tool. Using these tools in combination enables you to create more precise lines and curves.

▶ Keep it simple. The fewer lines and curves you use, the smaller your file sizes will be, which allows the files to render faster on the user's PC.

▶ To keep file sizes down even more, take advantage of Flash's capability to create reusable library symbols. Don't create unnecessary graphics if you can avoid it. You can simply use multiple instances of one symbol to create various parts of the same or different characters.

▶ If you want to manage several objects as one, but you don't want to make them part of the library, you can simply group these objects together. They won't have the properties of a symbol, but they'll be more manageable and you can move them around and manipulate them much easier.

▶ You can edit a symbol in several ways. Any changes made to a symbol are reflected on all other instances of that same symbol.

CHAPTER

9

Using Flash to Animate

Because the use of Macromedia Flash is geared for purposes of web design, much of what is known and practiced in the field of Flash animation is usually built on concepts that only apply to web design, not to real-world animation.

To get the full benefit from this book, especially this chapter, put aside all you ever learned about Flash animation from web design books and approach the material from the standpoint of someone who wants to animate content and not simply move text around, build interfaces, or create cheesy, spinning logos.

In this chapter, we establish a naming convention for individual cels in Flash. You learn how real-world animation techniques and principles are applied to Flash animation, and we create an animated movie of a ticked-off wrestler on his way to kick some major booty.

Walk the Walk

Let's begin by setting up the work area. First, you want this sequence to be NTSC-compliant, so the first thing you need to do is to plan for your field of view to comply with the 4 × 3 aspect ratio. We could take the easy way out and simply set your stage to be 400 pixels wide × 300 pixels high, but we aren't going to do this. We also want our cartoon to be as Web and CPU friendly as possible, so instead we'll set our movie dimensions as 288 pixels wide × 216 high, as shown in the following illustration. Twelve frames per second is a good-enough frame rate for this type of animation, so let's leave the default frame rate as is. Save the project file under a unique name, such as walkthewalk.fla.

"Why the smaller aspect ratio?" you ask. Flash believes the smaller the aspect ratio, the smaller the actual file size of the movie will be. Remember, vector art will always retain its same level of quality, no matter how much you resize your graphics. Flash, however, doesn't seem to realize that once you export your movie, you can resize it to any proportions you want, and so, believe it or not, it will render your files at much smaller file sizes! This little quirk enables your movie to stream (download as it plays) and play more efficiently on any given CPU and at larger screen resolutions.

Animation Levels and Flash Layering

Levels and layers are the same thing. Macromedia uses the term *level* to describe the placement of a separate .swf file when it's loaded on top of another. Technically, this isn't inaccurate because it does describe one object on top of another but, like other quirks in Flash, it's created a bit of a communication barrier between animators and web developers.

Animators use the word "level" to describe the placement of individual drawings in a stack of cels. In the Flash *timeline,* which is basically a spreadsheet or a table, a *level* is represented as a row and is referred to as a layer rather than a level. When you insert a new layer in Flash, you're inserting a new level of animation. The two terms are the same thing.

Given the nature of this book, when I refer to an object's level, I'll most likely be referring to the layer where it may be placed and not to a separate .swf file.

Traditionally, most animation is designed to take place within five levels (layers) of cels stacked on top of each other. The number of levels an animation uses is largely dependent on the type of setup to be used to capture it on film. While many studios are able to produce animation using five or more levels, for the most part, my experience is they only rely on three or four of those levels. Not only are four levels easier to manage, but the more cels you stack on top of each other, the harder it is for the camera to pick up the lower levels. In Flash, you don't have that problem. The software enables you to create an unlimited number of layers in your animation but, in appearance, the depth of each layer is always flat and never changes. This, of course, can be viewed in two ways: good, because you can create unlimited numbers of layers without any visual distortion; not good, because the fact that there is no visual distortion between the layer means that there is no depth of field created between the layers.

The walking wrestler sequence we make in this chapter only requires three layers to be created. Create these layers in your timeline and name them from top to bottom as Announcer, Wrestler, and Background. When you finish, take your project file and minimize it. We'll come back to it later.

Applying Conventional Terminology to an Unconventional Animation Tool

Because Flash was not originally intended to be used for production-style animation, there was very little attention paid to conventional animation standards and terminology. Although most of the function and features available to the animator are the same as those available in standard animations tools, Flash uses nonconventional and sometimes even contradictory terms when naming its tools and features. It makes the adjustment of an animator to the software a lot more difficult than it should be.

This may come as a shock to you, but in Flash there's no such thing as inserting or deleting a frame. In fact, if you're an experienced Flasher, you may find it even more shocking or, perhaps, even confusing that what you've been accustomed to calling frames or key-frames aren't even frames at all. In animation, they're called a "cel."

All the frames that can possibly be created in Flash are already there, just waiting for you to place cels on them. *Frames* are the columns you see on the timeline and are numbered in increments of five from left to right. Another thing to notice is the column on every fifth frame is slightly shaded. This is merely a cosmetic effect to help you keep track of frames but, as an animator, you can also use these shaded columns to keep track of beats in your animation. When a movie is exported, only the range of frames containing cels are the ones published.

Hold on There, Mulder, What Exactly Is a Cel?

A *cel* is an individual drawing (shown right). Traditionally, cels were drawn on clear sheets of acetate called cels. Because the acetate is transparent, as seen in the next illustration, it enables us to layer or *stack* several cels on top of each other to form a single frame of film. As mentioned before, most animation is usually done using five levels. In short, this means five sheets of acetate are stacked on top of each other when a single frame of film is finally captured. Also important to note is, in film, even when an animation doesn't require all four or five layers of animation, empty cels are used to preserve the sense of depth created by the use of those four or five levels. *Empty cels* are sheets of acetate that don't have anything drawn on them.

Layer 4 (Mouth)
Layer 3 (Arm)
Layer 2 (Body)

Layer 1 (The background is usually a hand-painted image.)

The actual frame is an image composed of several cels stacked on top of each other.

Because Flash enables you to draw directly on what Macromedia refers to as a "frame," the real distinction between a frame and a cel has never been brought up in any Flash-related resource. For the most part, because web developers haven't been exposed to production-type animation, these terms don't bother them, but animators and filmmakers have to contend with this difference daily.

Difference Between Frames and Cels

Suppose your Flash movie is made up of ten layers and each of those layers contains ten of what Macromedia calls a "frame" on it. Let's see . . . there are ten layers and each layer has ten frames—does this mean your movie is made up of 100 frames? Absolutely not.

That movie would only be made up of ten frames. Each frame in that movie is made up of ten individual cels, which are stacked on top of each other in layers. Although the sequence in question is created using a total of 100 cels, this doesn't change the fact that the movie itself is a mere ten frames in duration. Are you confused yet? Perhaps looking at an image can help.

As shown in the following illustration, I used up a single frame of film in the timeline. This frame is composed of ten layers. Each layer contains one of what Macromedia refers to as a "blank key-frame," but these key-frames are *not* frames at all. What you're really seeing is one frame made up of ten empty cels.

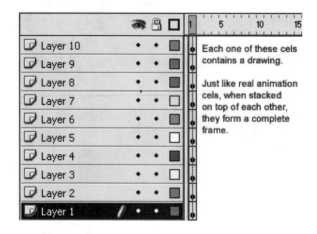

Each one of these cels contains a drawing.

Just like real animation cels, when stacked on top of each other, they form a complete frame.

TIP

Think of cels as actual sheets of acetate. Just as in regular animation, they contain a single drawing. If five cels are stacked on top of each other, the lowest cel is at level 1, while the uppermost cel is at level 5.

To make sure we're on the same page here, the real frames in the timeline are the columns, which are numbered in increasing order from left to right. Layers or levels are the rows, which, by default, are numbered in increasing order from bottom to top. An unlimited number of layers can be in the timeline; therefore, a single frame of film can be created using an unlimited number of cels.

The Flash timeline is basically a spreadsheet with rows and columns, which form cells as they intercept. Ironically, animation cels are placed onto the cells in the timeline.

TIP

A published Flash movie has a maximum frame capacity of 16,000 frames. Be aware of this when you're deciding the frame rates. A movie set to play at 12 frames per second enables you to create a file a little over 22 minutes long. At 24 frames per second, 16,000 frames give you a mere 11 minutes of actual film time to work with.

New Terminology

If animators and Flashers are ever to come together effectively as Flash filmmakers, it's important not only to establish a naming convention for the cels in Flash, but also to incorporate more conventional animation terminology rather than traditional web-design jargon.

The following list includes some of the terms Macromedia uses and what they are according to animation standards.

Macromedia Calls It	Animators Call It
Frame	A regular "frame" in Flash is nothing at all. It isn't even a cel. Whenever you perform an "Insert Frame" in Flash, you're actually telling Flash you *don't* want to insert a new cel, but instead you want to extend the exposure of the previous cel in that layer.
	Applied by selecting Insert | Frame (F5)
Key Frame	The term "key-frame" applies to a new independent cel whether or not it contains graphical elements. Again, be aware that Flash key-frames aren't frames at all. The entire column is the frame.
	Applied by selecting Insert | Key Frame (F6)
Blank Key Frame	In Flash, a blank key-frame refers to a new independent cel that absolutely doesn't contain graphical elements or any other elements, for that matter. Whether a cel is empty or not, it's still just a cel.
	Applied by selecting the cell on the timeline and selecting Insert | Blank Key Frame (F7)
Insert Key Frame	When you apply this command in Flash, what you're really doing is duplicating the previous cel on that level. If there's no cel to duplicate or if the previous cel is an empty one, then it creates an empty cel.
	Applied by selecting Insert | Key Frame (F6)
Insert Frame	This is really an extended exposure command. It merely tells Flash to hold the exposure of a given cel for one or more frames. This could also be referred to as a "hold cel."
	Applied by selecting Insert | Frame (F5)

A Bit More about Empty Cels

As previously mentioned, a cel is traditionally a sheet of acetate that contains a drawing. In animation, an empty cel is used to maintain a consistent depth between the various levels. If a film is created using four levels and a particular sequence requires only two of those layers, say Layer 1 and Layer 2, to have actual drawings on them, that particular frame is still shot using four cels. The top two cels will be empty. This ensures that the same depth perception is maintained throughout the entire film.

In Flash, we don't worry about maintaining a sense of depth between levels because there isn't any. You can create an image using 100 layers and your image will still look as if it's on a one-dimensional plane. Empty cels do have their place in Flash animation, but they are used more or less for organizational purposes and to break the exposure of a held cel. Flash uses what's referred to as "blank key-frames" when it's referring to an empty cel.

A Bit More on Held Cels

Characters and objects are only animated when the animation itself is of extreme importance, so animation is rarely a 100 percent, frame-by-frame process. Just because an animated film, such as a *Bugs Bunny* reel or a *Teenage Mutant Ninja Turtles* cartoon, is shot and played at 24 frames per second, this shouldn't imply that 24 complete drawing were actually drawn for every second of film. Instead of drawing every single action one frame at a time, certain cels across many layers are often held for longer periods of time than others.

To hold a cel means you'll continue to display that same cel until the object in that particular layer is required to move again. At that time, you'll replace it with a new cel and it will no longer be held.

On many occasions, only a character's arm, mouth, or head is required to move while performing an action, so those parts of the character will be animated on separate levels (layers). The parts of the characters that aren't required to move are drawn in a cel, which is held for as many frames as necessary.

NOTE

Look at any cartoon on TV and notice how sometimes a character is talking to someone, but only his lips are moving while the rest of his body remains frozen. The body of the character is a single drawing, which is being held, while the mouth is animated on a separate layer. Sometimes, a cel is held for a long time and becomes easily noticeable but, at other times, held cels are hard to catch. Nevertheless, this technique is relied on heavily in animation because it keeps us from having heart attacks while trying to draw hundreds of unnecessary drawings.

Basic Key-Framing

For a classical animated sequence to be properly executed, it must be timed to perfection. Once a certain rhythm or timing is established that's consistent with the sound track and overall timing of the film, the job of the animation director(s) and principal animators is to draw the sequences using key-frames. Key-frames feature the animated characters performing their actions using only the most important drawings in the sequence. These drawings are timed to perfection and, in most cases, are indicative of the final version of the product.

Key-frames are often drawn rough and unpolished. Assistant animators are hired to clean up the drawings and polish up the line work.

I've drawn and assembled a little something for you that I like to call a Bopsey Model. This is a set of Flash symbols which, when assembled in a particular order, create a character that's animatable in Flash.

Head on over to this book's web site at www.osborne.com and take a look inside the Chapter 9 directory. There you will find all the project files you will need to complete this assignment. Start by opening up the file named charhogan.fla, and maximize it so that it takes up the entire program window.

Because the creation of the wrestler's walk cycle takes place within a single layer, don't worry about the actual names of the cels yet. We'll call the cels what Flash calls them (frames) for now. Notice the model is already assembled on frame 1 of the timeline and is ready for you to mess with it. At this point, we also want to create our initial key-frames. But unlike regular animation, we won't draw them. Instead, we'll simply duplicate the cel and manipulate the various symbols individually to achieve our desired actions.

1. In frame 1, take the symbols and manipulate them, so they form a nice action pose, such as the one in the following illustration:

2. The next step is to duplicate the cel (Insert | Key Frame). Do this by selecting the cel in the timeline and pressing F6. A new key-frame is added directly after the original one (it's not really a key-frame, but a duplicate cel). This new key-frame also contains the same graphic elements (symbols) that were on frame 1 of your movie. This frame marks the middle of the first step, so assemble your character as the following illustration shows:

3. So far, so good. Create a third key-frame. Here, you'll pose the character as he would look when he has completed the first step, as you can see in the following illustration:

4. Characters walk using both feet, so now let's repeat the same three actions featuring our character taking a step using his other foot. (Feel free to refer to the chapter on animation cycles as you work on this project.) Because, in the last frame, your character was ready to switch legs, in this next frame, he should be performing his action in the middle of the second step.

For the last and final frame, we want our character to end up the same way he started, so the animation will play in a nice little loop. If we create another frame that's the same as frame 1, though, we'll have two frames that are the same playing against each other. This would make the loop seem like that particular cel is being held for a period of two frames and we don't want that.

Because the movie will go back to frame 1 and play again anyway, we won't create a final frame, so the cel that immediately follows the last one will be frame 1.

We created our initial sequence using four key-frames. It still looks a bit odd, though, as if it's missing something and it's actually missing plenty. Go to the cel on frame 4 and select it. Insert a regular frame by pressing the F5 key. Now, notice that the new frame hasn't duplicated the cel on frame 4 yet. The same graphics that rest on frame 4 are also displayed in frame 5. This is because when you add a regular frame after an existing key-frame, you are neither adding a new cel nor adding a new frame. In fact, you're simply telling Flash to hold the previous cel for an extra frame.

5. Let's select the newly created cel in frame 5 and convert it into a Flash key-frame. Select the cel and press the F6 key on your keyboard (Insert | Key Frame). Here you can create and assemble your character into a drawing, shown next. Feel free to play around with the symbols using the transform tools.

6. The entire sequence should now look a little something like the following illustration. Press ENTER to do a quick animation check. The timing still isn't right. The cycle is composed of a mere five frames and, for a normal walk cycle, this is way too fast.

7. We'll slow down the cycle and make it a bit smoother by adding extra frames. This wrestler is walking in a very determined manner, so the actions themselves will be a bit more violent than the normal speed of a generic walk cycle. Add one "frame" in between each of the existing "key-frames." This should do the timing of our character's walk cycle a bit more justice, shown here:

Fill in the Blanks (Basic Inbetweening)

In regular animation, once an entire movie has been key-framed, the various sequences are turned over to several people whose job is to draw the frames that will go in between those key-frames. These people are known as *inbetweeners*. Sometimes inbetweeners work at the studios but, in most cases nowadays, they are contractors who do the work from the comfort of their own homes. By outsourcing the work in this manner, studios can save a lot of money in production costs.

Going back to our walk cycle, you can see that although the animation itself has a rather comfortable timing, the performance of the walk cycle is still rather choppy. The held cels work okay for the purpose of establishing the timing, but the playback of the sequence still isn't as polished as it can be. To smooth out the animation, we need to create new cels to serve as a transition between the action being performed in one key-frame to the action being performed in the next. In animation, these drawings (cels) are called *in-betweens*. In Flash, you create in-betweens by simply duplicating the previous cel and modifying the graphics accordingly so that they smoothen out the transition from the previous frame to the next.

We already set up the cels in our key-frames to be *held* at frames 2, 4, 6, and 8 to adjust our timing, as shown in the previous illustration. In a previous step, we also learned how to convert a held cel into a key-frame. Because only one held cel is between each of the existing key-frames, our particular setup allows for only one inbetween to be created within the gaps of the key-frames. This is, of course, provided you want to stay within the established timing of the sequence. Go ahead and convert those held frames into regular Flash key-frames. The new key-frames are basically just duplicate cels, which need to be modified. Manipulate the graphics in those new cels, so they reflect a transition between each of the original key-frames to the next, as the following illustration shows. The newly added in-betweens will make our walk cycle an eight-frame sequence. When this sequence reaches the last frame it will simply be made to loop back to frame 1 and create a never-ending cycle.

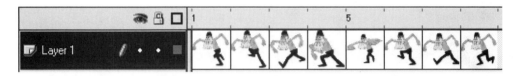

The Onion Skin Controls

A nice little feature in Flash that allows you to create better in-betweens is the Onion Skin controls. These *Onion Skin controls* enable you to view several adjacent frames behind or ahead of your animation as if you were working on a light table or an animation disk.

The Onion Skin controls are located to the right of the garbage bin icon next to the Center Frames button in the timeline.

Normal Onion Skin   Edit Multiple Frames

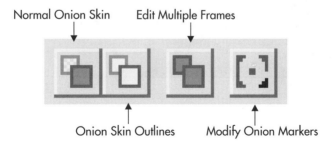

Onion Skin Outlines   Modify Onion Markers

▶   From left to right, the first button is the Normal Onion Skin control button. With this feature on, you can see the additional frames in color. The farther away a particular frame's order is, the lighter it appears. This is the only time you can see some kind of native form of depth perception in Flash.

▶ The second button is the Onion Skin Outlines button, which works the same way as the original control, except you don't see the full shapes of the objects; you only see the outlines.

▶ The third button, Edit Multiple Frames, enables you to modify multiple frames at a time, which you learn about later in the book.

▶ Finally, the Modify Onion Markers button enables you to choose from several modification options in your Onion Skin controls.

Our entire sequence was created on one layer and across eight frames. Let's review each of the frames and see what we've done so far:

▶ On frame 1 of the animation, the wrestler begins his walk cycle.

▶ Frame 2 is an in-between, which displays the transition between frame 1 and frame 3.

▶ Frame 3 is another one of our original key-frames.

▶ Frame 4 is an in-between, which shows how our character gets from frame 3 to frame 5.

▶ Frame 5 was the high point of this particular cycle. This is where the major change occurs.

▶ Frame 6 is yet another in-between, which displays the change from frame 5 into frame 7.

▶ Frame 7 is technically our final key-frame. This is where the last major action in the sequence takes place.

▶ Frame 8 is an in-between. It should show a transition between frame 7 and frame 1.

▶ After frame 8, the animation once again reverts to frame 1 and plays all over again. This creates a never-ending cycle.

Frame 7   Frame 8   Frame 9

Convert Your Sequence into a Reusable Symbol

In a previous chapter, we learned how to convert simple graphical elements in Flash into symbols. In this particular walk cycle, the character is composed of many of these graphic symbols, which you manipulated to achieve the desired poses. Now, let's convert the entire walk cycle into a symbol we can use on a movie.

1. To do this, hold down the CTRL key and scrub across all the cels that make up the entire walk cycle. To *scrub,* you run your mouse across all desired frames or cels. This enables you to select all the frames you want in the timeline. The selected cels are now highlighted.

2. Take your mouse and right-click anywhere on the selected frames and, from the menu that pops up, select Copy Frames. A copy of the entire sequence now resides in your clipboard.

3. Go to the Insert menu and select New Symbol, or simply press CTRL-F8. A panel prompts you to enter the details for the new symbol. Name it "Walking" and select the graphic option from the list of behaviors. Click OK when you finish. Now, you're immediately transported to Symbol Editing mode for that particular symbol.

CAUTION

The only time you should select Movie Clip as your symbols behavior is when you plan to target it using action script or when you want it to play independently of the main timeline. Otherwise, you're simply using up unnecessary system resources. Graphic symbols should always be your symbols behavior of choice when it comes to animated characters because they bond with the main timeline. Graphic symbols enable you to test the animation while on Normal Timeline mode and also translate better if you decide to publish directly to video. Setting your symbols behavior to Movie Clip is just unpractical in a standard cartoon.

4. Notice a whole new timeline is created for this symbol. This timeline is completely separate from the main timeline and the events that occur here will occur only within that particular symbol. Go to layer 1, frame 1 of your movie. An empty key-frame should be there. Right-click it and select Paste Frames from the right-click menu. The entire sequence of cels has now been duplicated in this timeline.

5. To switch back to the regular timeline, go to the upper-right corner of the project window. Two buttons are there. The one that looks like a production slate is the Edit Scene button. Clicking this button displays a list of all the scenes in your production. You only have one scene so far, so you'll only see Scene 1 on the list. Select Scene 1 and you'll now be transported back to the main timeline.

6. The other button is the Edit Symbols button. This button works the same way as the Edit Scene button, except it's used to go into Symbol Editing mode for any of the symbols that appear on the list.

7. Now that you've created your symbol, save the file to your computer's desktop and close the project window. Be sure to give the file a memorable name because you'll be asked to access it a little later.

Establishing a Naming Convention for Individual Cels in Flash

Let's maximize our previously created project file, walkthewalk.fla. Our movie consists of three levels (layers): layer 1 is named "Background," layer 2 is named "Wrestler," and layer 3 is named "Announcer." Notice Flash has, by default, placed one empty cel on each layer. These cels are all located on the first frame of our movie.

For a better understanding of how we're going to lay out the elements in this movie, I want to make you aware of conventional animation terminology and how it applies to Flash animation. From here on, we'll call "frames" cels, which is what they really are, and we will only refer to the term "frame" when we are referring to an actual column on the timeline, which may hold any number of cels at any given time. Each individual cel in Flash may also be referred to by its own unique name, which can be determined by a set of coordinates that tell of their location in the timeline. In other words, a cel's name in Flash is also the actual coordinates of the cell where it's placed.

A typical name for a cel looks something like c(17,22). First, the letter c immediately tells you this is a generic animation cel. The second part is a set of coordinates, which are enclosed in parentheses and divided by a comma. The first number tells you the level number where the cell is located and the second number gives you the number of the frame. Remember, frames are the columns and levels (aka layers) are the rows, so c(17,22) is a cell in a table that's located at the intersection of layer 17 and frame 22. The quirky thing here is an animation cel in Flash is generically named after the cell in the table it occupies.

In traditional animation, a cel often tends to have a more descriptive name based on the drawing it contains. For example, suppose layer 2 of my animation held drawings of the left arm of a character named Ronald and I wanted to point this out for c(2,17). In conventional animation, this cel would be referred to as something like (Ronald's Arm 2,17) or some shorter form of the same name. This is something that could also be done in Flash, but usually we use the generic format, such as c(2,17), because it's easier to read, write, and locate.

NOTE

In Flash, the only way to go in and give a cel a unique name, which would be totally independent from the cel name, is to ad a frame label to it. While a cel may be moved from c(1,100) to c(20,150) the label never changes. The primary use of frame labels in Flash is so that you can refer back to them either by normal browsing or by targeting them using action script.

TIP

As a rule, a cel's level is always written first and the frame number is always written second when referring to its coordinates. In the Flash timeline, levels are numbered incrementing in value (that is, 1,2,3,4,5) from the bottom layer to the uppermost layer, and frames are numbered from left to right. In a true exposure sheet (x-sheet), levels are written from left to right in decreasing order (that is, 5,4,3,2,1) leading to the BG (background) level, which is reserved for the background. In an x-sheet, frames are numbered from top to bottom.

Pop Quiz: Locate the Cels

Now, let's see if you were paying attention. Look at the next illustration and see if you can locate the following cels. Also see if you can determine whether these are empty cels, new cels, held cels, or simply cells on a table waiting for a cel to be placed on it?

▶   c(3,175)

▶   c(4,180)

- ► c(1,213)
- ► c(7,215)
- ► c(5,223)

See if you can pinpoint the cels by using the following illustration.

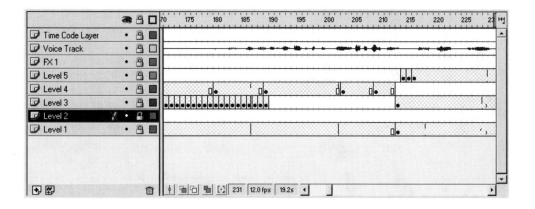

How well did you do? Refer to the next illustration and table for the answers. Make sure you understand this concept before continuing with the rest of the project. From this point, each individual cel is called out by its rightful coordinate name.

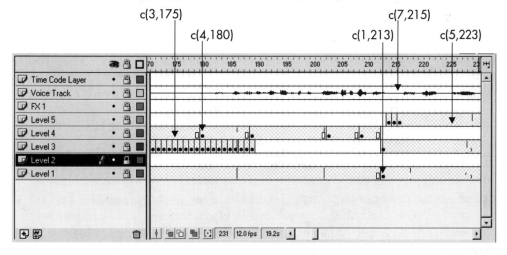

Cel Name	Location
c(3,175)	This is a regular cel. The dot indicates some kind of graphic element is on that cel.
c(4,180)	This is also a regular cel, which contains a graphic element. This particular cel is being held for a total of nine frames.
c(1,213)	This particular cel is being held for an even longer period of time.
c(7,215)	The entire Voice Track layer is based on a single cel, which has its audio content set to stream. This cel is being held for the duration of the entire movie. In this particular case, c(7,215) isn't a cel but is, instead, a cel exposure. The original cel that's being held is located all the way at c(7,1) and contains an audio file, rather than a graphic. Cels containing audio elements display a waveform along the timeline.
c(5,223)	This, too, is a cel exposure and not a true cel. This cel exposure is extending the display time of the cel located on c(5,216).

Tweening the Action

At this point, many of you might be thinking, "Why do we have to animate the character by hand? Doesn't animating the entire sequence by hand defeat the purpose of using Flash? And, what about tweening? Why can't I let Flash tween my character's parts, so I don't have to inbetween it by hand?"

While Flash does have the capability to let you tween each piece individually—essentially doing the work for you—there's no substitute for good old-fashioned, hardcore animation. Remember, we aren't animating logos or text, but instead we're animating characters that must give the illusion of being alive. Not only does the synthetic tweening feature in Flash make your movies more CPU- dependent, it also makes your characters look robotic, lifeless, and boring. The rule of thumb here is this: in animation (character and performance-based animation), unless your character is a robot or an inanimate object, you should avoid tweening like the plague.

Inbetweening and tweening aren't the same thing. *Inbetweening* implies you have done the work manually. *Tweening,* on the other hand, is a software-based feature that allows the computer to generate the drawings you need automatically between two key cels (Flash calls them key-frames). In Flash, tweening can be created only between cels that contain single objects. Multiple objects in tweened cels generate unpredictable results, and this isn't recommended.

We already have our symbol of the walking wrestler, which we animated by hand. Because we animated the wrestler by hand, it makes him look more lifelike and gives him more personality. This wrestler will walk from one place to another, something that doesn't require much personality, unless your objective was to maintain proper beats with a sound track or music file. In our case, all the important animation has already been done. Now, to get our character to move from one place to another, we can afford to take a break and let the software work for us.

1. For our next step, we need to import the background into our movie so be sure you have downloaded the file bgarena.fla from the book's web site at www.osborne.com. Once you have done this, select Open As Library from the File menu and locate the file bgarena.fla. Rather than opening a project file as a project, Flash simply opens it as a standard library as shown in Figure 9-1. Objects in this library cannot be modified unless you import them into an already open project.

2. Select c(1,1) to make this the active cel. Take the Background symbol in the library (Figure 9-2) and drag it onto the stage. Close the library; you no longer have any use for it.

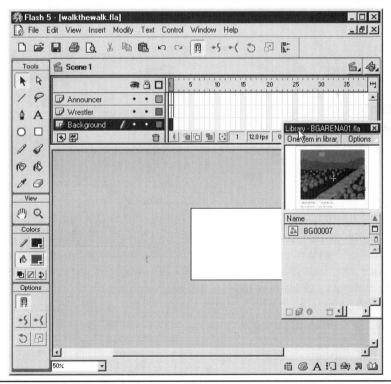

Figure 9-1 *The file has been opened as a library.*

Figure 9-2 *Drag the background onto the stage.*

3. The background is much larger than the stage. Activate the outline feature in layer 1 (named Background), so you can see the work area better. Use the Transform tool to resize the background so that the image area of the background will fit within the stage area (field of view), while the border and illustration data remain away from the public's eye on the gray work area, as the following illustration shows. In short, we only want the actual image area and not the data or borders to be displayed.

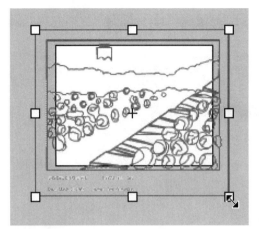

4. Lock the Background layer to prevent further modification to it and click c(2,1) to make it the active cel. Open the file you created earlier as a library and drag the symbol of the walking wrestler onto the stage. Resize the wrestler, so he appears in proportion with the background and move him to the upper right-hand side of the stage, as the following illustration shows. We're going to animate this wrestler walking down the walkway in the background.

5. Open the file charannouncer.fla as a library. You can download this file from the Chapter 9 area of this book's web site. Lock the Wrestler layer and select c(3,1) to make it the active cel. Import the graphic symbol named "Announcer" into the stage and place him on the right side of the stage, as shown in Figure 9-3.

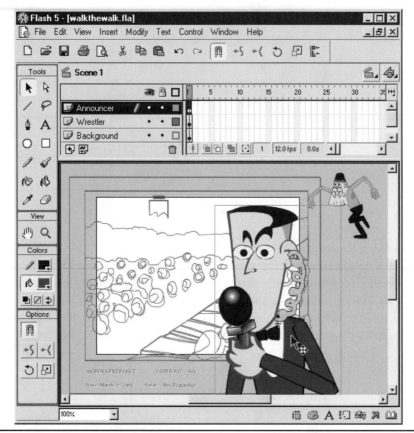

Figure 9-3   *Place the announcer on c(3,1), and then resize the symbols as needed.*

We don't want our wrestler simply to waltz onto the stage, so what we want to do is set up the action a little bit. Let's wait until frame 20 of the movie for our wrestler to make his grand entrance.

6. To relocate a cel to another place in the timeline, hover your mouse over the desired cel (see Figure 9-4). The mouse pointer changes into a little hand, which means you can literally grab it and drag it to a different place in the timeline. Cels can be relocated to any level or frame. Use this procedure to relocate c(2,1) from its original location and place it on c(2,20), as shown in Figure 9-5.

When you relocated the cel to c(2,20), you left behind an empty cel on c(2,1). By default, Flash holds that empty cel until the timeline reaches frame 20, at which time the relocated cel is displayed.

Figure 9-4   *Hover your mouse over the cel. Click it, and then drag the cel to its new location.*

7. Apply an Insert Key Frame command at c(2,50). This creates a new instance of the cel (a copy). If you click anywhere between c(2,20) and c(2,49), you'll notice the entire area becomes highlighted and you could, if you want to, drag the entire area to a different location. The area between c(2,20) and c(2,49) is actually the same cel that's merely being held for a total period of 29 frames. Because the entire exposure is the result of a single cel being held, it can be referred to as c(2,20-49). The cel is held all the way until frame 49, as shown here:

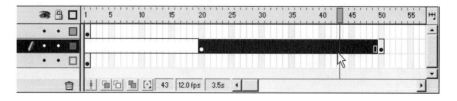

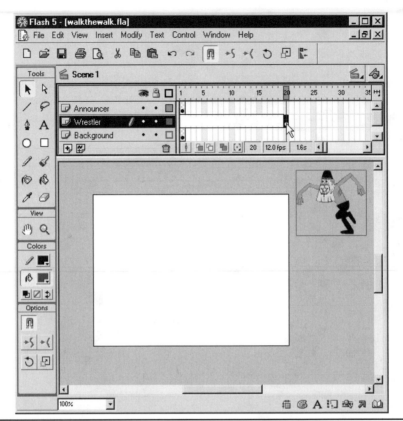

Figure 9-5 *c(2,1) has been relocated to c(2,20).*

NOTE

Remember, tweening is a way of getting the software to generate fake in-betweens from one cel to the next.

8. The first cel containing our wrestler is located first at c(2,20) and the second cel is at c(2,50). We want to make it so the wrestler walks down the path and exits toward the bottom corner of the background. Locate c(2,50) and activate it. Take the symbol of the wrestler and place him slightly outside the lower-left corner of the stage, as shown on Figure 9-6.

Figure 9-6   *The wrestler is placed slightly outside the lower-left corner of the stage.*

9. We have now officially created two points of extreme change in the main
    timeline (key-frames). Right-click on any coordinates between c(2,20) through
    c(2,50) and from the right-click menu select Create Motion Tween. The tween
    is generated only within those two cels and not the entire frame. Tweening can
    be effectively performed on many layers at the same time provided that the two
    cels being tweened are located in the same layer and that they contain the same
    symbol and nothing else. The color of the two cels being tweened turns to blue
    and an arrow is placed across all the fake cels that Flash has generated for you.
    See Figures 9-7 and 9-8.

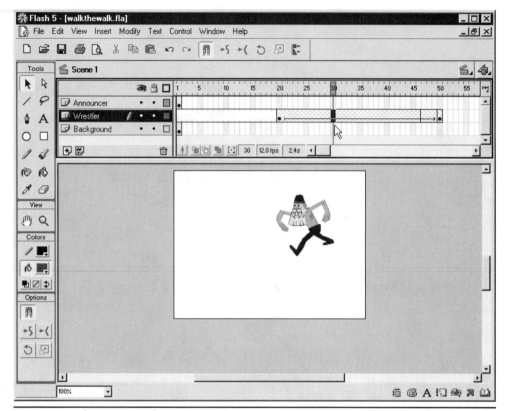

Figure 9-7   *The generated tween*

The two cels are now joined by a common cause; they're tweened. As a result, clicking anywhere between c(2,20) and c(2,50) now enables you to select the entire cluster of cels and relocate it to any other place in the timeline as a single unit. Because this particular type of cel cluster is a Motion Tween generated between two independent cels, I like to refer to it as c(2,20–50). Let's now turn our focus to our background, which won't change at all for the duration of the movie, and will only be displayed for 50 frames. Take your mouse and click c(1,50) to activate it. Press the F5 key to give Flash an Insert Frame command. Again, you haven't created 50 new frames or 50 new cels; instead you've extended the exposure of the first cel all the way to frame 50. This command should be called Hold Cel or Extent Exposure; either one is better than Insert Frame.

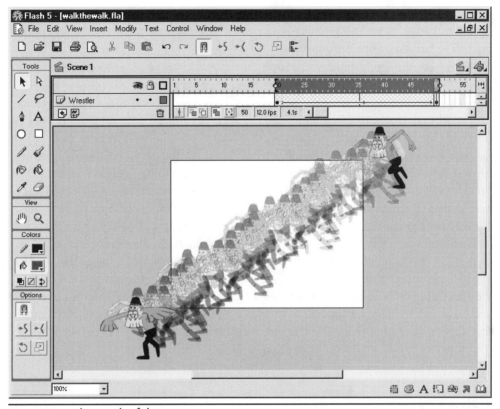

Figure 9-8   *The result of the tween*

The announcer will also be part of the picture for the duration of the 50 frames. So, let's turn a simple c(3,1) into a c(3,1-50). In other words, extend the exposure of c(3,1) all the way to frame 50.

One thing about animation—and not just Flash—is you can't modify an exposure. An exposure is nothing; therefore, there's nothing to modify. Look at the Announcer layer (layer 3) and notice how the entire thing is the result of a single cel being held for a period of 50 frames. The real cel is the one with the dot on it, c(3,1). Try to click c(3,25) and notice the entire 50-frame exposure gets activated and you can't grab that particular exposure and relocate it without taking the entire thing with you. The *frame indicator* is a little pink bar that tells you which frame of the film you're looking at currently. When you clicked c(3,25), the frame indicator naturally moved to frame 25.

Because you're on frame 25, take the Announcer symbol and move it to the right side of the stage. Now, click anywhere on any frame column from 1 to 50 and notice the image has changed location across all 50 frames.

When you moved the announcer from the right side of the stage to the left side on frame 25, you never actually modified c(3,25) because nothing was there to modify. The only real cel that can possibly be modified is the one located at c(3,1). Everything else is only an exposure of the same cel. Go ahead and place your announcer back on the right side of the stage.

Let's suppose we wanted to modify c(3,25) to show the announcer looking down toward the walkway without having to modify the entire thing. This is simple. All you have to do is right-click c(3,25) and, from the right-click menu, select Insert Key Frame. The duplicate cel, which is created at that location, can now be modified. Notice how the duplicate cel is now being held from frames 25–50.

Go ahead and apply a Break Apart (CTRL-B) command to the Announcer symbol on c(3,25), so you can manipulate the various little symbols individually. Be sure to apply the command one time; otherwise, you might destroy the symbols. Take the various little symbols on the announcer's face and use the Transform tool to resize and skew them so that he appears to be looking down toward the crowd. Now, every time the movie reaches frame 25, it'll appear as though the announcer is turning toward the crowd to see what all the commotion is about.

Scrubbing

When an animator is animating the old-fashioned way, he will test the progress of his animation by holding the pages in such a way that enables him to flip them back and forth, so he can check the consistency of the line work and the motion of the character. A similar technique is available to Flash animators, which is called *scrubbing*. When you scrub the timeline, you're flipping the frames of the film back and forth, and testing your animation. To scrub the timeline without messing up your carefully laid-out cels or accidentally relocating the contents of a frame to another location, make sure you're pressing and holding down the CTRL key. While the CTRL key is pressed, use the mouse to click-and-drag your pointer across the timeline. As long as you're pressing the CTRL key, you won't be able to modify the cel in your timeline.

Let's try this technique to test the accuracy of our sequence (see Figure 9-9). Notice, when you scrub to the right over frames 20–50, our wrestler walks across the stage. If you scrub to the left, you will see the action performed backwards. Continue to scrub back and forth, and notice the placement of the character in relation to the background. Look for any mistakes and try to fix them by modifying the graphics in the key-frames. Is the wrestler too large for the background? Is he too small? Does he walk along the pathway correctly or does he seem to walk on people's heads? Because we elected to use a graphic symbol, we can see him walking as we scrub across the timeline. If we were to have chosen Movie Clip symbol as its property, then this character's animation would have been impossible to assess properly within the general editing environment. Modify the key-frames (or rather key cels) as necessary and scrub again, until you fix all those little glitches. Continue to scrub and notice the announcer's action. Does it look all right? Perhaps it would look better if he turned toward the crowd at frame 35, so he appears as if he's looking toward the wrestler. Go ahead and relocate c(3,25) over to c(3,35). Scrub again. This should look much better now.

Figure 9-9   *The scrubbing technique is the most effective way of troubleshooting the quality of the animation.*

Testing and Publishing Your Movie

Flash also has an embedded Flash player, which is a more advanced way to test and troubleshoot all areas of your movie from the playback at various bandwidths to the file size of each individual frame. To activate this feature, press CTRL-ENTER and a window appears playing back your movie.

If you have HTML set up in your publish settings, you can launch the movie in an .html file and see through your default browser. To do this, simply press the F12 key. Any resulting file, which is published, is created on the same directory as the FLA file. So, if walkthewalk.fla is located on your desktop, any .swf, .html, size report, and so forth is created on that spot as well. You can adjust how your software publishes through the File | Publish Settings feature.

The .swf file we create is 288 × 216 in dimension and should be approximately 35K in size. When you embed the .swf file onto an HTML page, you can change the aspect ratio to anything you want. I usually present my NTSC-formatted movies at 400 × 300. Creating the file at a much smaller aspect ratio allows it to perform better when played at larger dimensions and it's less likely to drop frames.

a.

b.

c.

d.

Summary

In this chapter, we created a little Flash movie featuring a hotheaded wrestler on his way to kick some major booty. The most important thing we discussed in this chapter was how much of what is practiced in Flash animation centers on a naming convention established by Macromedia as it developed its product. Although Flash was created as a web development tool, it does have its place within the animation industry.

Here's the quick rundown of all the other important stuff you learned in this chapter.

▶ A movie created at 288 × 216 will be smaller in file size than if it was created at 400 × 300. The smaller-dimension movie will also tend to play more accurately and be less likely to drop frames than the larger one, even if it's enlarged to the same aspect ratio as the larger movie.

▶ The Flash timeline is basically a spreadsheet or a table that interacts with your animation project, allowing you to navigate through the frames and the cells that make up those frames. The columns of this table represent the actual frames of the movie, while the rows are the layers or levels. Just like any table, the Flash timeline contains cells. Ironically, in animation an individual drawing is called a cel, so when it comes to Flash animation you are placing animation cels onto a table's cells.

▶ A cel can be located on the timeline according to its name in relation to level and frame value. A generic cel's designation in Flash would look like $c(3,87)$. The numbers inside the parentheses are the coordinates. The letter c is generic and can be replaced with the name of the drawing contained in the cel.

▶ In animation, a level is the placement value of an individual cel in a stack. In Flash, a level is referred to as a layer. This is perfectly fine because a level and a layer are the same thing.

▶ In animation, a cel is an individual drawing placed as part of a stack, which forms a single frame. In Flash, a cel is called a frame or a key-frame.

▶ In animation, an empty cel is a cel that doesn't contain any graphic elements. The Flash equivalent of this is referred to as a blank key-frame.

▶ A held cel is a cel whose exposure has been prolonged over a period of several frames. In Flash, this is called a frame.

▶ A held cel that begins at $c(10,25)$ and is exposed all the way to frame 100 would normally be referred to as $c(10,25–100)$.

▶ Inbetweening is the act of manually creating the drawing within two key-frames. Tweening is a software-based solution that essentially does the same thing.

▶ Animation is rarely a 100 percent frame-by-frame process. A combination of held cels across multiple layers and frames, as well as frame-by-frame actions, makes our job easier and more productive.

▶ The Onion Skin controls are like a virtual light box at your disposal.

▶ Just as you can convert a single graphical element into a library symbol, you can also convert an entire cluster of cels. Use the Copy Frames or Paste Frames commands.

▶ Scrubbing the timeline is the equivalent of page flipping, which is a technique used for testing the quality of the animation across multiple frames.

▶ Control | Test Movie enables you to test the playback of the entire movie using a special Flash player, which provides you with various types of data.

▶ Any file published from a project file will be created on the same directory as the original project file, unless the file was made not to do this.

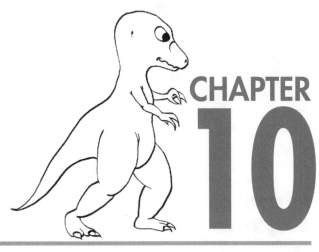

CHAPTER 10

Advanced Techniques

In this chapter, you learn alternate import methods and advanced techniques, such as the use of a live video feed as a way to increase productivity. This chapter also shows you how to project a live video stream onto the Flash work area to increase productivity further and to do other cool stuff, like painting with video and compositing Flash animation with video footage. You learn to animate gradient fills, rotoscoping techniques, and how to create those wonderful starburst and speed line effects to enhance a character's dramatic actions. This chapter also provides you with valuable information on the use of color, using bitmaps, and creating entire color pallets based on a single bitmap.

Alternate Import Methods

Hand-drawn images add a certain quality to the overall look of any type of animation, whether it's a vector- or raster-based image. As a personal preference, many animators choose to draw their animated sequences by hand first, and then later incorporate the digitized images into the vector format.

TIP

When drawing images for this type of conversion, the recommendation is that you draw your final sketches using a blue nonphotocopy pencil. This reduces the chance of the software picking up any unwanted pencil lines. Another recommendation is that you properly ink your drawing, so the software can better capture and render the lines and fills you want captured.

Adobe Streamline

Adobe Streamline is software that enables you to vectorize any bitmapped image so it can be worked with in Adobe Illustrator. The good thing about the Adobe Illustrator (.ai and .eps) format is it's 100 percent compatible with Flash and the images you create can be effortlessly imported into Flash. These are the steps to follow to perform the conversion.

1. Begin with a cleanly drawn and inked image. Streamline enables you to scan the images directly into the software.

2. Use the Eraser tool to remove any unwanted debris from the image.

3. Use the conversion settings to adjust the degree of line recognition of the software. This option can be found in the Options menu of the software.

4. In most cases, the predefined Inked Drawings option will be sufficient.

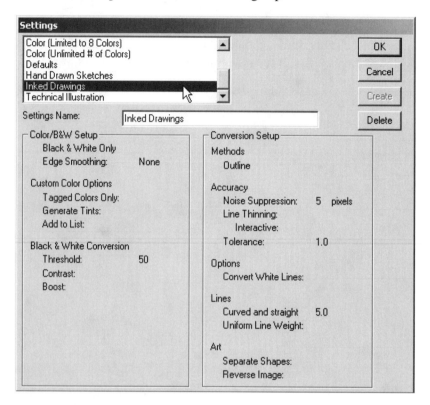

5. Also, be sure to adjust the color levels of the image. This option can be accessed from the Edit menu. Adjust the levels so your line work appears clean and crisp against a solid white background. This reduces the chance that the software will render any unwanted debris on the paper and it helps to insure that the line work itself will be picked up as cleanly as possible.

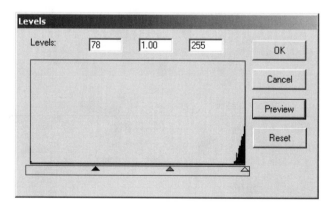

6. Using the Convert command in the File menu, the software will render a vector-based representation of your image. If you don't get the desired results right away, you can always go back and play around with the settings and color levels, and then try again. A lot depends on the way you ink the drawing and how clean the paper is.

7. The resulting image won't be displayed in anti-alias form (smoothed edges), so you won't get a true appreciation of what the new vector image looks like until you import it into Flash. In some cases, lines that appear to have been broken up in Streamline look fine once the image has transferred over to Flash.

8. Next, choose the Save As option from the File menu and save your image using a distinctive name. The file will then be saved in .eps format by default, which is native to Adobe Illustrator as well as Macromedia Freehand. Flash, however, is capable of importing all image files that result from Streamline.

9. In Macromedia Flash, choose the Import option from the File menu and find the recently saved .eps file.

10. The image is imported as a grouped object, which you must break apart before completing the conversion. Because the image groups are automatically selected when you import them, all you need to do is press CTRL-B to break it apart into a solid shape. Once the image is broken apart, it can be manipulated any way you want.

You can color it, delete any unwanted areas, and create symbols from the image to use and reuse as you please.

Converting your image files by way of Adobe Streamline is one of the most preferred methods among animators. Not only are you able to convert single image files one at a time, but you can also batch-select an entire sequence of images to which you can apply your predefined conversion settings.

One of the most common uses for the Batch Select feature in Streamline is the conversion of video sequences into vector graphics. The artist will first convert the video sequence into a sequence of independent images. The batch conversion is applied to the entire lot and the newly created vector images are imported into Flash as an image series.

The converted video sequence can then be resynched with its original audio and used in a variety of ways, as seen in these images from the "Rastaman," a music video by La Fabrica del Immaginario.

Macromedia Freehand 10

Users of Freehand 10 are also able to create vector rendition images through the Trace Image option, which works best if it's used for line work. Follow this procedure to create vector rendition images.

1. Import your image into Freehand via the Import option in the File menu. Select the Trace tool in your Tools panel.

2. Take the Trace tool and select the entire area of the image you want converted into vector shapes by placing the tool on one corner of the image and dragging a rectangle to the other side of the image.

3. The image is now traced over the original file. To import the new vector image into Flash, make sure the image is selected and drag it from the Freehand window to your Flash project window. You can also use copy-and-paste.

CAUTION

Freehand isn't as clean as Adobe Streamline when it comes to the conversion, though, and it might create some unnecessary shapes and colors. You might need to tweak these further once the graphic is imported into Flash.

4. To clean up your newly formed vector graphic, begin by removing any unwanted and unnecessarily generated colors and shapes.

5. Select the entire image and break it apart (CTRL-B).

6. Change the color of the entire shape to black by selecting it, and then selecting the color black from the color fill selector.

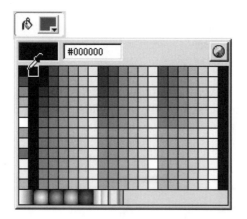

7. While the shape is still selected, apply the Smooth modifier to the shape. This will dramatically reduce the amount of unwanted points in the image, but it isn't a perfect process. You'll have to go in manually and use the Subselect tool (aka the White Arrow tool or the Molding tool).

8. With the white arrow, select all unwanted points and press the DELETE key to remove them.

9. Use the little handles to modify your curves.

10. As a final step, check any areas in your image that were incorrectly converted and modify them using the standard tools. In this sample, you can see the bully's teeth were traced badly, as was his right eyebrow. I corrected them using the Eraser and Arrow tools.

Macromedia Flash—Trace Bitmap

You don't need third-party software for converting an image into vector format. Flash itself has an extremely powerful and often underrated tool for performing this task. This feature in Flash has a not-so-great reputation for vectorizing images, but the truth is the misuse of this feature often leads web designers and animators to believe it isn't as good as it could be. If it's used for converting properly inked line work, the result can be quite gratifying and, in most cases, better than those provided by any third-party tool out there. The steps to use for this procedure follow.

1. Begin by importing your image into Flash. Select it to make it active, and then choose Trace Bitmap from the Modify menu. An Options panel will pop up and provide you with various tracing options.

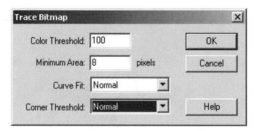

2. Feel free to mess around with these settings, but if your line work is nicely inked and the white areas are clean, the default settings should work fine. Press the OK button to perform the trace.

NOTE

Flash will always try to trace color information, including all the white areas of the image, so the important thing to realize is your image should be limited to as little color information as possible.

3. Use the Selection tools to remove all unwanted areas completely, especially the white color fills, leaving behind only the dark line work. I like to change the color of the stage to something other than black or white, preferably a shade of gray, so I can tell where all the white areas are more easily and delete them.

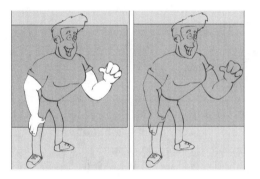

4. Flash will most likely have traced your line work using multiple shades of gray. So, now that all the unnecessary fills and debris have been cleaned up, select the entire image and change the color of the entire shape to solid black.

5. You should now have a great-looking vector image, which you can further optimize, if you choose. You can color it, convert it to a symbol, and use it any way you want in your animation. Look at this side-by-side comparison of the same illustration, traced using the three methods described so far in this chapter.

Adobe Streamline   Macromedia Freehand 10   Macromedia Flash

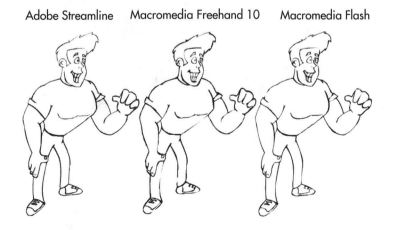

The reason most web developers misuse this feature is because vector graphics are always smaller in file size than bitmapped images. This isn't always the case, though. In fact, in many instances, especially when the object being considered is a photograph or another type of complex image, the use of unmodified bitmapped images is often a better idea than converting it to vector shapes. You learn more about when to use bitmaps later in this chapter.

Work with a Live Video Feed

You might want to work with a live video feed as an aid for importing images into Flash for two reasons. The first and most important reason is speed: a video camera connected to your video card can capture images a hundred times faster than any scanner. Most graphic design software enables you to select a camera connected to your video card as an input device, and then use it to capture the images into digital files. You can then convert them using any of the previously described methods. However, there's another way to use a video feed in conjunction with Flash, which most people aren't aware of: by literally projecting the video feed directly onto the program window and using the projection as a virtual light box to trace over the image being displayed. This procedure requires the use of a video card with TV tuner capability, such as TV tuner software that uses a special color to display the picture onto the TV software's window. I've found the most reliable cards for this procedure are the ATI ALL-IN-WONDER series, which are also bundled with the ATI Multimedia Center for use as the TV display software.

NOTE

As far as using this method for rendering vector graphics, you still must trace the images by hand, as demonstrated in Chapter 8. Your production time will be dramatically decreased because there's no messing around with scanners or digital files of any kind. The following paragraphs explain how this works.

The television tuner in the ATI video cards, such as the ALL-IN-WONDER Pro and the TV WONDER, enable you to see television on your PC while you work. The television picture is projected onto the program window through a process similar to that of Blue Screen imaging or Chroma-Key compositing, which is quite common in today's motion picture industry.

Blue Screen Imaging is a technique that involves shooting a subject against an evenly lit background, which is often painted with a special shade of blue or green.

The background is then electronically replaced with a separate video feed or a still image and the result is a merging of the two images (Blue Screen composite). The ATI software used to display the television picture onto your desktop also uses a special color to composite the video feed onto your desktop, which varies depending on the version you use. While older versions of the software used a bright purple color, newer versions use a darker, almost black color.

Before you begin, be sure you've set up your video card as specified by the manufacturer's instructions. Connect a video camera the same way you'd attach a VCR to it.

CAUTION

The manufacturer of your video card/TV tuner should provide instructions on how to connect a VCR, a video camera, or other input/output sources to the card. Be sure everything is installed properly before you attempt this procedure.

1. Run your television program and set it so you can see the video feed from your video camera. Place your video camera two or three feet away from the images you'll be capturing. Having a tripod for this purpose can help you. Adjust the camera so you can see the image clearly.

2. The ATI Multimedia Center has a video desktop feature that kicks in when you minimize the program window. When this feature is activated, the video feed will replace your desktop's wallpaper. You can also deactivate the Always On Top feature, so you can have more control over the actual size of the image being displayed by resizing the window and be able to place the TV feed directly behind the Flash program window.

3. The next step is to set up Flash so you can work with a transparent work area. Then you can see the video display directly through Flash's program window. Launch Flash and move the window to the side, so you can see the two program windows: Flash and the TV software window (see Figure 10-1).

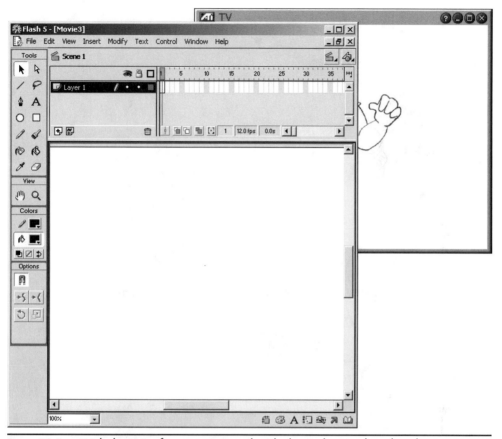

Figure 10-1   *With the TV software running, the Flash window is placed so that it overlaps the TV software window.*

4. In Flash, select Modify | Movie, and then click and hold your mouse on the color selection box. Don't let go of the mouse button! This turns your mouse cursor into the Eyedropper tool and enables you to select any color you see on your computer screen. Drag the cursor outside the program window and place it directly onto the video screen in the television software where the video feed is being displayed (see Figure 10-2).

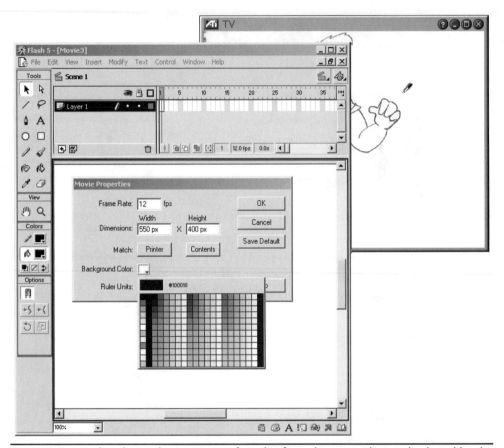

Figure 10-2   *Rather than selecting a specific color from the image being displayed by the TV software, Flash will grab the entire video feed and use it as a color!*

5. Let go of the mouse button and click the video display of the television program. You'll immediately notice the color selected is the actual video feed. Press the OK button and the stage background will appear transparent, enabling you to see the video feed directly underneath Flash's program window, as shown in Figure 10-3.

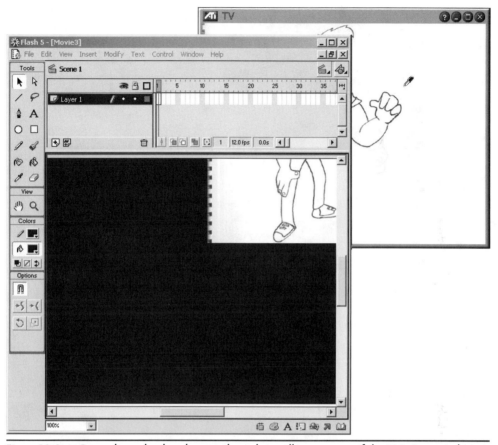

Figure 10-3   *Once the color has been selected, it will appear as if the TV picture is being displayed directly through the Flash stage.*

6. Adjust the TV program window at the center of your desktop and resize the screen as necessary. Next, you need to adjust the Flash program window so the video feed is properly aligned with the Flash stage, as shown in Figure 10-4.

Figure 10-4 *The two windows are centered so that the video image is displayed properly on the stage.*

7. With the image from the video camera now composited onto the stage in Flash, you can use the drawing tools to trace it and create a vector rendering of it. The thing to note here is that anything projected through your television program could be displayed onto the Flash stage (see Figure 10-5).

Figure 10-5   *You can even work with a live television signal and composite Flash animation with live footage.*

8.   When you finish tracing your image, you can move on to the next one by simply placing another drawing in front of the video camera and creating a new empty cel (Empty Key Frame) where you'll trace the next image.

Rotoscoping

One of the things that made *Snow White* such a remarkable film, aside from the fact that it was the first feature-length animated movie, was the beautiful, almost realistic way in which the human characters were animated. What many people don't know is that a lot of the animation performed in the film was created using a technique called rotoscoping.

Rotoscoping involves taking a live subject and having it perform an action on film. This is shown in these three frames of my buddy Luis walking on a treadmill so I can record the action on video.

The footage is then literally traced over by an animator, frame by frame, creating a hand-drawn version of the action originally performed by the actor. Shown here are the same three frames with the traced character overlaid, so you can see exactly what was rotoscoped.

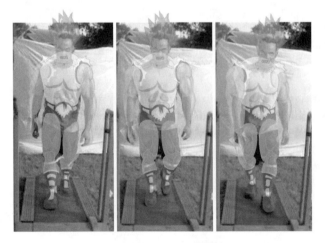

The end result is a realistic performance by the animated character. Here are the same three frames once the video images are removed, leaving behind only the animation.

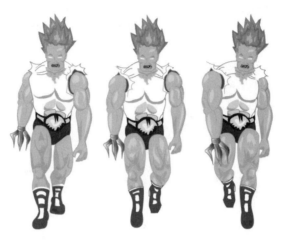

There are several ways of rotoscoping in Flash. A common approach would be to convert a segment of a video file into a sequence of individual images, such as a .jpeg or .gif, and then to import them into Flash where they are traced over on a separate layer.

An even easier approach is to take advantage of Flash's capability to import QuickTime video. By doing this, you eliminate the need for converting the video into a series of images, and instead you can jump straight into the tracing process.

When a QuickTime video is imported into Flash, it appears as if it were a typical sequence of images. If you extend the exposure of the cel that contains the QuickTime movie, you can scrub across the timeline and see all the frames contained in that video.

You then create a new layer and lock the layer that contains the QuickTime movie. Locate the frame where you'll begin tracing and, on the layer above it, create a new cel (Black Key Frame). Trace the character, and then move to the next frame. Use your own character to trace the action (the same way I did with the character and my friend Luis's video). In rotoscoping, you aren't out to trace the actor performing the motion. Instead, you're using the actor as a model for your character's motion performance. In short, you're tracing the character's actions, not their looks. Continue the procedure until you've traced the entire sequence.

When you finish, it's quite safe to delete the QuickTime layer and the video file itself from the Projects library.

Another method for rotoscoping is for you to play the video through your VCR or video camera one frame at a time by way of the television feed technique described earlier. This gives you the advantage of not having to deal with digital video files at all and jumping directly to the tracing process without the added processing strain added by using bulky images or QuickTime video files. The only drawback to this method is that most cameras and VCRs shut down after a certain period of being paused. So, if you can't trace the image within the time the frame remains paused, you'll find yourself surfing back and forth through your videotape trying to find the proper frame to continue tracing it.

Using Bitmaps

Once you start thinking about using more complex graphics in Flash animation, the issue of whether to use bitmaps in your animation comes into play. Using bitmapped images in Flash is often thought of as taboo. Using them, however, is often the better choice because, in many instances, bitmaps tend to be smaller in size and better looking than vector graphics.

For example, let's suppose you want to work with traditional oil-painted backgrounds in your cartoon. The complexity of the graphic when converted to vector art would lead to an extreme amount of points, lines, and curves, which will almost always result in the vector image being larger in size and heavier on processor strain than the actual bitmap.

Although the Trace Bitmap feature is perfectly capable of converting a bitmap image, such as a photograph, into a vector graphic, the resulting image always tends to be larger in file size than the bitmap itself when image accuracy is attempted. Reducing the quality and detail of the vector photograph greatly reduces the file size, but it comes at the cost of a great deal of distortion.

Shown here is a bitmapped image published at 100 percent .jpeg quality. The file size is a whopping 111Kb.

The same image is shown here at the default 80 percent .jpeg quality. Although the image itself has been slightly degraded, the file size has been dropped down to a sweet 21Kb.

With Macromedia Flash's Trace Bitmap feature, I traced the bitmap using the following settings.

The result is a vector rendition. Although the conversion took almost two minutes to process on a 1.2 GHz CPU computer, the end result looks worse than the original bitmap and weighs in at 165Kb.

Here's the same image once again, traced using the default settings, whose results are meant to be "web friendly." Although the image only weights in at 7Kb, it looks horrible and has been ruined beyond recognition.

In the end, it's always your choice whether you want to use actual bitmaps in your animation or vector renderings of them. The Trace Bitmap feature works best when what you're tracing is line work for cartooning. When it comes to using complex graphics that can't be created through vector means, however, I always recommend using bitmaps. This all depends on the look you're going for and whether you're willing to live with the file sizes resulting from either method.

Painting with Bitmaps and Creating Texture Effects

Bitmaps can be converted into paint fills for use in your animation. The process is simple.

1. Import a bitmap into Flash.

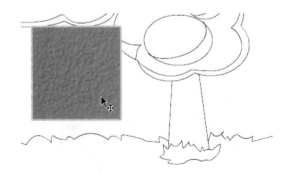

2. Break the bitmap apart.

3. Select the bitmap using the Eyedropper tool.

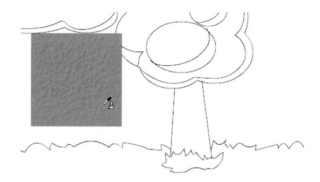

4. Paint with it, using either the Brush tool or the Paint Bucket tool.

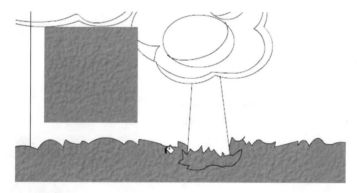

Here's a background painted using textured fill. The total file size when published at 80 percent .jpeg quality is 20Kb.

Modifying Textured Fills

After breaking apart a bitmap and converting it into a fill, you can modify the appearance of the texture, essentially creating an unlimited amount of texture effects based on the same bitmap.

1. Paint a shape using the texture and select it using the Transform Fill tool, which is a modifier for the Fill tool (the Paint Bucket).

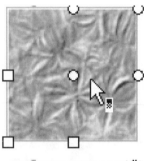

2. Once the fill has been selected, a series of stretch and rotation handles appear around the selected texture.

3. Just grab ahold of one and pull in any direction. You will notice the change immediately.

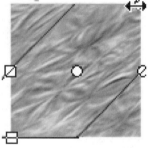

You can create an entire texture palette based on a single bitmap.

If you want to preserve the entire collection of modified texture fills, you need to convert it into a symbol. Anytime you need to use a certain variation of that texture, simply open the symbol and select the fill using the Dropper tool. You can then go back to the object you're painting and use either the Brush tool or the Paint Bucket to color it with the textured fill.

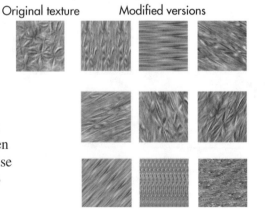

Original texture   Modified versions

As far as saving textured fill within the actual palette, Flash automatically grabs any bitmaps that have been imported into Flash and makes them available through the Fill panel. Follow these steps to save textured fill within the palette.

1. Import an entire collection of bitmaps (at least ten) into Flash. In the old days of web design, people used to use a tiled background to enhance the look of their web pages. Today, this practice is considered flat-out annoying. For our benefit, however, literally thousands of sites still offer these graphics as a free download. Tiled backgrounds make the best textures.

2. Once your textures are imported, delete them from the stage. Don't worry—the images will remain in the Projects library.

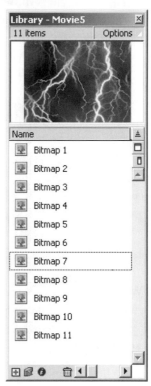

3. Open the Fill panel (Window | Panel | Fill).
   You'll notice you can use four types of fills
   (paints): Solid, Linear Gradient, Radial
   Gradient, and Bitmap.

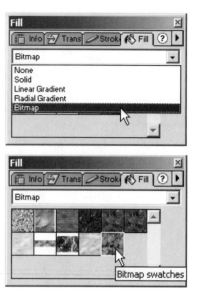

4. Select the Bitmap option from the
   pull-down menu and you'll see all the
   textures we imported into Flash appear
   in the palette window. Select one of the
   Bitmap swatches and move the Fill panel
   out of the way.

5. Using the Rectangle tool, draw a rectangle onto the stage.

6. The rectangle is drawn and painted with the texture you selected. By default,
   Flash makes the bitmap very small—only a few pixels wide and tall. To change
   the size of the texture, you need to select the
   Fill tool once again and use the Transform Fill
   modifier to adjust the size of the bitmap.

When it comes to creating textures for Flash, I recommend using tiled images no
bigger than 25×25 pixels. Remember, these are still bitmaps, and the larger they are,
the greater the amount of size added to your file. Using small bitmaps will hardly
make a difference, especially if you reuse the same ones over and over again.

Linear Gradients

The use of Gradient fills will add a good deal of processor strain to any movie file. However, when created and used properly, they're worth their weight in gold. These are the steps to follow to use Gradient fills.

1. Create a new project in Flash. Draw a rectangle on the stage and open the Fill panel. Select Linear Gradient from the pull-down menu.

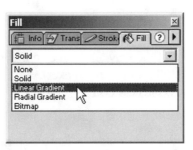

2. Click the first little lever and use the color selection box to choose a nice shade of blue.

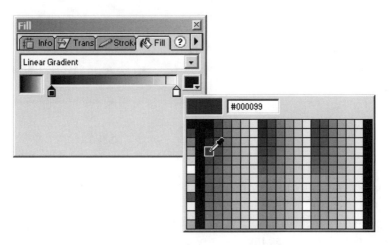

3. Click the second little lever—the one on the right side—and use the color selection box to choose an extremely light shade of blue.

4. Click somewhere directly in between the two little levers and a new level will be created. Use the color selection box to change the color to a nice purpleish color.

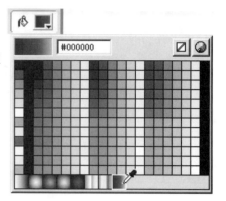

5. On the bottom right-hand corner of the Fill panel is an icon that looks like a diskette. Clicking this icon saves the color to your default color palette. Go ahead and click it and check your default color palette in your Tools panel. From now on, this color will be available for you to use whenever you need it.

6. Move the Fill panel out of the way and make sure you selected the new fill you just created. Using the Fill tool (Paint Bucket), click the inside of the rectangle you drew to paint it with the new color.

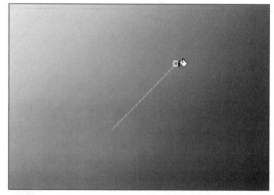

7. You can control the way the Linear Gradient is laid out by clicking-and-dragging the paint bucket across any given direction. When you let go of the mouse button, the gradient will be laid out according to the direction you dragged the bucket.

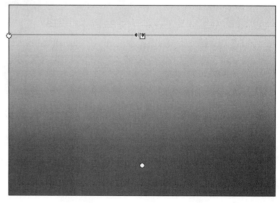

8. You can also use the Fill Transform modifier to alter the way the linear fill is laid out across the object. Use this tool now to adjust the fill, so the light blue area takes up most of the upper area, the purple area takes up most of the bottom area, and the deep blue area is barely seen at the bottom.

Save the project file using a unique name. Don't close it yet; we've only just begun.

Radial Gradients

As opposed to Linear Gradients where the colors are blended from one side to the other, the colors used in a Radial Gradient are blended radiating outward from the center of a circle.

1. Using the previous project file, create a new layer above the one containing the linear fill. Lock the layer below (the one with the linear fill), so you don't accidentally modify it. Next, select the empty key frame on Layer 2 [c(2,1)]. Now, on this cel, draw a white medium-sized circle. Draw it slightly below the rectangle.

TIP

To draw a perfect circle or square, hold down the SHIFT key while drawing with either the Oval or the Rectangle tool.

2. Pull up the Fill panel once again and, this time, select Radial Gradient from the pull-down menu. Once again, you're presented with a slider bar, a set of two sliders by default. The slider on the left represents the color closer to the center of the circle. The slider to the right represents the color closer to the outside of the circle. To the left of the slider bar, a little window gives you an idea of what your Gradient Fill looks like.

3. Although you can add extra color sliders to the color bar by clicking anywhere below the color bar, we only need the two default ones for this experiment. In the same manner you changed the color of the sliders when you created the linear fill, change the color of the left slider to a bright yellow. Also, change the color of the slider on the right to orange. Once you do this, slide the orange slider toward the center of the color bar.

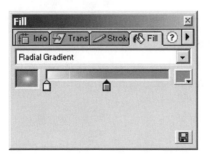

4. Save the color swatch to your default color palette by clicking the little disk icon, the same way you did with the Linear Gradient.

5. With the new Radial Gradient fill selected, use the Fill tool to paint inside the circle, replacing the white fill.

6. Use the Fill Transform modifier to increase the size of the gradient and adjust the center somewhere on the upper-left quadrant of the circle. The Radial Gradient makes the circle look almost three-dimensional.

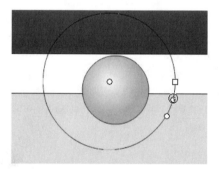

You've now learned how to create and modify Gradient fills in Flash. Don't close your project window yet, though. In the next section, you learn how to animate the Gradient fill within a shape.

Animating Gradient Fills

The animation of a Gradient fill is usually performed for lighting effects, but thousands of other uses exist for animated gradients. This procedure makes use of the Shape Tweening feature in Flash.

1. Go back to the project we've been working with. Just as a recap, we created a rectangle filled with a Linear Gradient on the first cel of Layer 1. On the first cel of Layer 2, we drew a circle that's filled with a Radial Gradient. Neither of these shapes has been converted into symbols or grouped in any way, shape, or form.

2. Go to frame 25 and select the two cels available for that frame by dragging your mouse across them. Once they're both highlighted, press the F6 key to duplicate the previous two cels.

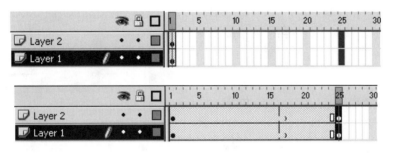

3. Select the top cel on frame 25. The circle contained on that cel will also be automatically selected. Use the UP ARROW to position the circle slightly below the top of the rectangle.

4. Select the Fill tool to reveal the Fill Transform modifier and to be able to use it once again to modify the gradient inside the circle. This time, modify the radial fill's size, so there's barely any orange on the circle.

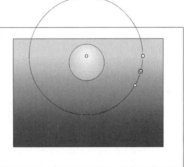

5. If you still have the first layer locked, unlock it, and then click the rectangle shape with the Fill Transform modifier.

   Be sure you're working on frame 25 before you click it. Adjust the gradient, so the fill is squished to the bottom, leaving most of the rectangle color light blue.

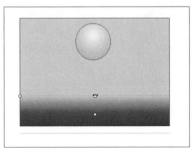

6. Focus your attention back on the timeline and select an area between the four cels across both layers. To do this, press and hold the CTRL key as you drag your mouse across any range between the cels.

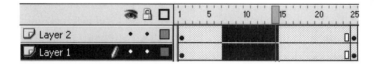

7. Release the CTRL key and right-click the highlighted segment. Use the right-click menu to bring up the Frame panel.

8. In the Frame panel, choose Shape as the Tweening option. You'll notice by the color change on the cel clusters (green highlight with an arrow across the cels) on the timeline that the tween was applied to both layers.

9. Press the ENTER key to preview your movie within the work environment or publish a test HTML page by pressing the F12 key. Shown here are a few selected images from the 25-frame animation.Because the only thing that changes in these shapes as they're tweened is the color, and not their actual form, the only thing that's tweened is the changes to the gradients themselves.

The end result is that of a dark sky becoming illuminated as a sun rises.

The Starburst and Anime Style Speed Lines Technique

Because of the nature of Flash, most animations tend to lean toward the limited style, rather than the classical frame-by-frame technique. One of the coolest effects developed by the anime style of animation is the starburst background, which has its roots in traditional comic book art. In this project, I'll teach you to use what you've learned so far to create a great-looking animated starburst background to add a bit of spice to your action sequences. Follow these steps to create the starburst background.

1. Modify your movie's properties to 400 pixels wide × 300 pixels tall. The background should be white and the measuring units in pixels.

2. Go to View | Grid | Edit Grid to pull up the Grid panel. We want the stage area to be divided into ten equal units in length as well as in height, so divide 400 by 10 and apply the result, which is 40 to the grid unit's width. We also divide 300 by 10 and apply the resulting number 30 to the grid unit's height. Place a check on both the Show Grid and Snap To Grid options. When you finish, click the OK button.

3. Your grid is now displayed on the stage and is evenly divided by 100 units.

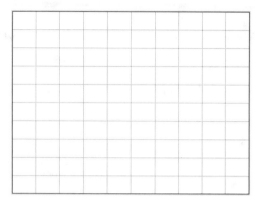

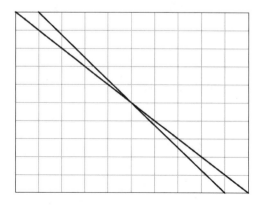
4. Make sure the Snap tool is active.

5. Select the Line tool and draw a line extending from the upper-left corner of the stage all the way to the bottom-right corner of the stage.

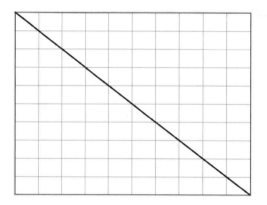

6. Go to the next notch on the grid and draw another line connecting it to its opposite one on the stage. The two lines should intercept at the exact center of the stage.

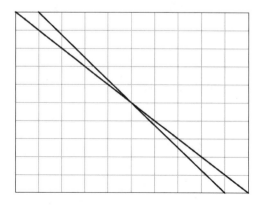

7. Continue to do this until you've connected each notch on one end of the grid to its opposite across the center of the stage.

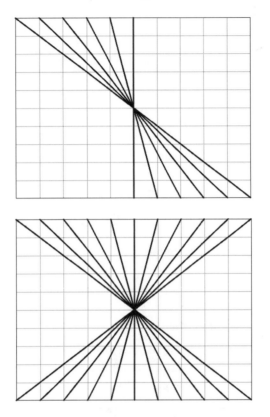

8. Connect all four outer corners of the stage, enclosing the entire work within a rectangle.

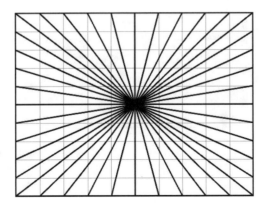

9. Now it's time to create a nice-looking Radial Gradient fill, so open the Fill panel and select the Radial Gradient option. Change the far-left slider's color to a bright yellow (almost white) color. Add as many sliders as you can to the color bar and space them evenly.

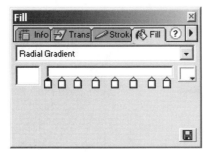

10. Change the color of the second slider from the left to a bright orange. Change the next slider from orange to yellow. And, from yellow to and from white-yellow, and so on until you run out of sliders. Play around with the colors and see what works best for you.

11. Click the Save icon on the Fill panel to add the new color to your default color palette. Before you begin painting with it, let's make sure the Lock Fill modifier is active.

12. With the Lock Fill modifier active, the same gradient pattern will be applied to all shapes painted with the fill. Paint only every other bar in your drawing, leaving one blank bar between each of the painted ones.

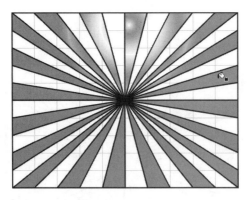

13. When you finish, unlock the fill by deactivating the Paint Fill modifier.

14. Paint one of the bars you previously left blank.

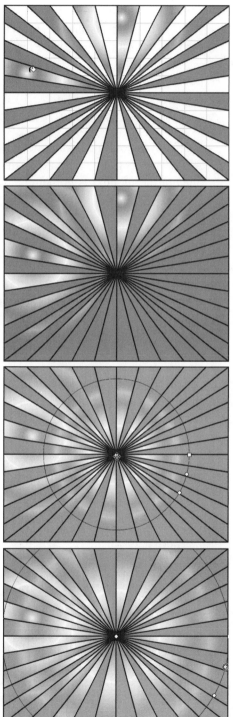

15. Lock the fill once again by activating the Lock Fill modifier, and then paint the rest of the blank bars. You will notice that when the fill color has been locked, the use of two different gradient instances is quite apparent.

16. Use the Transform Fill modifier to center one of the gradients directly at the point where all lines intercept.

17. After the gradient is centered, use the Transform Fill modifier to increase its size slightly.

18. Perform the same modifications to the second gradient fill. First, center it, and then increase its size. In this instance, though, you'll increase the size slightly larger than the first gradient.

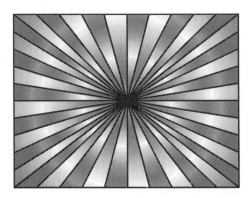

19. Select all the outlines using the Arrow tool. Simply double-clicking one outline should select them all because they're all interconnected.

20. Press the DELETE key to eliminate the outlines. If any rogue outlines exist that for some reason didn't want to be removed, select them individually and delete them. Your drawing should look like this illustration.

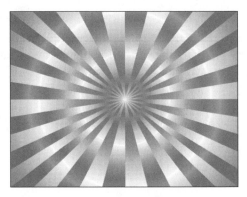

21. Now, let's turn our attention to the timeline where we'll duplicate the cel on frame 5 by way of the Insert Key Frame command.

22. On the new cel at frame 5, use the Transform Fill modifier to increase the size of both gradient fills once again. This way, when we shape tween it, the gradient colors will appear to travel from the center of the shape toward the outside.

23. Go ahead and perform the Shape Tween. In some cases, stubborn areas of the shape will retain their form as the Shape Tween is performed. To fix this, you can create shape hints between the two images using the option located at Modify | Transform | Add Shape Hints. Another way to do this, and much more convenient, is to draw straight lines (outlines) around the outer area of the shapes that are misbehaving. This tells Flash that those shapes are not supposed to be

morphed. You do this on both cels. Play it one time to see if Flash understands that you don't what those shapes to be modified. Once Flash stops trying to modify your shape, you can delete the lines you drew and Flash will no longer attempt to modify the form of those shapes.

24. Take your newly created sequence and convert it into a Movie Clip symbol using the Copy Frames | Paste Frames command. Name your symbol Starburst. Now that you have the symbol in your library, go ahead and remove the original sequence from your main timeline, leaving behind a single blank key frame (cel). On this empty cel, drag your new Movie Clip symbol from the library and center it on the stage (see Figure 10-6).

25. Create a new layer above the one holding the starburst layer and draw a cartoon character performing an action of some kind.

26. Publish an HTML page by pressing the F12 key and look at your movie. Because the Starburst symbol is a Movie Clip instance, it will play its five frames of film independent of the main timeline, which is only composed of one frame. This technique always adds a great deal of impact to any action performed by a cartoon character.

Use this technique to create other forms of action-enhancing backdrops, such as the infamous anime style speed lines that can be created using combinations of vertical, horizontal, or diagonal lines parallel to each other and Linear Gradient fills.

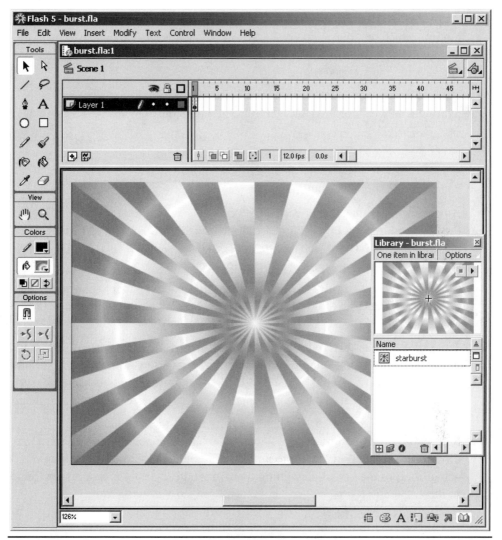

Figure 10-6 *The new Movie Clip symbol is placed onto the stage.*

Summary

Various import methods exist for converting a raster image into a vector-based graphic. The three most popular are by way of Adobe Streamline, Macromedia Freehand, and, of course, Flash's own Trace Bitmap feature.

▶ Make sure you properly ink your line work before you perform any type of conversion to the vector format. This is important.

▶ Rotoscoping is a technique employed by animators to create realistic character motion, which otherwise would be too complicated or too expensive to produce by hand. The process involves having an actor perform the actions on film and later tracing the actions, frame by frame.

▶ Using a live video feed can dramatically increase productivity by completely removing the need for a scanner or working with large amounts of digital images.

▶ The ATI Television Tuner software projects the video feed onto a special color in the same way Hollywood studios create Blue-Screen Imaging. Flash animators can also take advantage of this feature by outputting video projects that composite both live video and Flash animation.

▶ Any bitmapped image can be used to create a special textured fill, which can then be used to paint objects in your animation. Tiled backgrounds, such as those used in old-school web design, are perfect for the job. You can also create unlimited texture variations based on a single bitmap file.

▶ Cases occur when an animator will be better off using a bitmapped instead of a vector-based rendering. This usually happens when a photograph or complex image is used.

▶ The Trace Bitmap feature in Flash is great for converting properly inked line work to vector graphics, but when it comes to converting complex multicolored images, it's always better to use the bitmaps themselves. The vector-based version might not only be poorer in quality, but its file size could also be much heavier.

▶ Starbursts and speed line effects—used to enhance an action—are often quite difficult to create. By learning to animate Gradient fill without disturbing the actual form of the object containing that fill, you can easily create these effects in Flash.

CHAPTER
11

Cheating Your Audience
the Right Way

everal techniques used in animation can make your life easier regarding the amount of drawing you must create to sell an action effectively to your audience. The use of visual cheats is quite common in all forms of animation. In Flash animation, the use of these cheats—cycles, blurs, smears, and holds— are essential in keeping file sizes to a minimum.

This chapter tackles techniques like cycles, blurs, multiple exposures, and other visual cheats that not only can save you a lot of work, but can also make your work look much more professional.

Animation Cycles

Animation cycles are groups of cels that display a character or object performing some sort of motion. The motion will end exactly the same way it begins. When this sequence reaches the final frame, it's looped back to the first frame and continues to play. This gives the illusion of a never-ending uninterrupted motion.

In Chapter 9, we managed to get our hands on a simple walk cycle of a wrestler walking into an arena. Most cycles are done the same way in Flash. For the most part, cycles are encapsulated in the form of either a graphic symbol or a Movie Clip symbol. When placed on the main timeline, the sequence simply plays, looping over and over until that symbol's exposure is terminated.

As you study the following cycles, remember: many ways exist to draw your characters performing an action, especially because not all characters are alike. In all cases, a character's motion depends on his physical attributes, his individual mannerisms, his personality, and, largely, his body weight. I can only give you a basic outline of what a typical motion might look like, but it's ultimately up to you to create your character's motions to suit his physical characteristics and personality.

The Walk

Including the in-betweens, in a traditional environment, a typical walk cycle is composed of approximately 24 frames, but only a good 8 of these frames are key-frames. The rest are breakdown drawings and in-betweens. The following list takes you through a typical walk cycle.

► In the first key-frame of the cycle, a character can already be in motion, with the left leg extended all the way to the front and the right leg all the way behind him.

► The arms are also in full swing in opposing directions. If the right leg is in the back, then the right arm is swinging to the front.

► Only the heel of the right foot is touching the floor.

► In the second key-frame, he bends both knees, bringing his weight forward.

► The right foot is still planted firmly on the ground. Most of the weight is being shifted to the left leg, which acts as support for the entire body.

► The arms now begin to fall.

▶ With the weight of the body now entirely on the left leg, we come to what's called the crossover. The *crossover* is considered the high point in the walk cycle. The arms continue to fall.

▶ Technically, at this point, the arms are parallel to the body, although, for the same reason an actor doesn't turn his back to an audience while speaking his lines, the character's arms must not obstruct the view of the rest of the body (at least not in a key-frame). Notice in this image, I bend the character's arm so, as it passes over the body, you can still see the legs and the lower area.

▶ Most animators hyperextend the pose of a character to add more impact to the action. In this frame, the character has just passed the high point in the sequence, but the pose is extended a bit, making this the true high point in the sequence.

▶ In the frame that follows, the character brings the right leg down.

▶ The arms are again extended. The right arm, which was originally in the front, is now behind him. The left arm is opposite and the legs are virtually in the same position they were in the first frame. The difference is the foot that was behind him is now in front and vice versa.

▶ The first half of the step is now complete. For the step to be complete, you must bring the left leg to the front and take the right leg to the back, so you end up the same way you began.

▶ In the following frame, the character, once again, initiates a weight shift to whatever leg is in the front. In this case, it happens to be the right leg.

▶ The arms again begin to fall toward the bottom, so they can, once again, bounce back to their original positions.

▶ Once again, you go into a crossover step.

▶ Be careful that the right arm doesn't block too much of the action and the left leg can be seen being lifted toward the front.

▶ The left knee is hyperextended to the front, the same way the right knee was done earlier.

► The weight of the character was on the right leg, but it's now, once again, moving forward. At this point, he seems a bit off balance and the only way he can keep from falling is to bring his left foot down. The character can successfully accomplish this if you go from this frame back to frame 1.

Of course, in your work environment, your character doesn't really move forward. He simply mimics the action through the shifting of his weight.

To keep the walk consistent, it helps to pretend the character is walking on a treadmill. The *Onion Skin* feature also helps by acting as a form of virtual light box, enabling you to see one or two of the previous images and helping you maintain the character within registration.

Horizon line

Making the Character Walk Across the Stage

The recommendation for making the character walk across the stage is that you use graphic symbols rather than Movie Clip symbols in a cartoon production. This is because each frame in the graphic symbol will be linked to an actual frame in the main timeline and will only play when the movie itself is playing.

Creating the illusion of a believable walk doesn't end at animating your cycle. Much of this also takes place during the actual use of the symbol in the stage. Follow these steps to create a natural-looking walk for your character:

1. Create a new project in Flash with three layers. Name them from top to bottom as Registration Points, Main Character, and Scenery.

2. Create a walk cycle (or download the walk cycle file from the book's web site at www.osborne.com) and place your character on the first cel in Layer 1.

3. Take the symbol and place your character just outside the left area of the stage.

4. Draw a horizon line and place some scenery on the Scenery layer. Don't worry about being too elaborate. This simply gives you an actual background to work with.

5. Extend the exposure of both cels all the way to frame 50 by using an Insert Frame command at c(1,50) and c(2,50).

6. Right-click the Registration Points layer. From the right-click menu, select the Guide option. This places a special marking on the layer and prevents any contents from being published when you export a finished movie.

7. Make sure the first cel in Layer 3 c(3,1) is selected. Close in on the character and draw a small *x* near the heel of the left foot and extend the exposure of the Registration Points layer a few frames.

8. Notice if you press the less than (<) and greater than (>) symbols, the animation scrolls across the frames. If your symbol is set to graphic symbol, then the frames in the symbol also change, depending on how you're scrolling across the timeline. Apply an Insert Key Frame command at c(2,2). Now, notice as you look at frame 2 in the timeline, you're also looking at frame 2 in the graphic symbol. The character's left heel is no longer on the *x* mark.

9. Use the Arrow tool to adjust the character, so his left heel is once again on the registration point (the *x* mark).

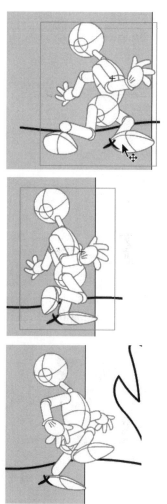

10. Insert Key Frame at c(2,3) and repeat the procedure. The new cel is created and you can adjust the position of the character, so his heel is once again on the registration point.

11. Continue to do this until the sequence reaches the frame where the left foot is about to be lifted and the right foot has been planted firmly on the ground.

12. Notice, for every frame you advance, the character is also moving forward.

13. At this point, the character is about to lift his left leg. You need to draw a new anchor point to help you keep the sequence perfectly synchronized to its surroundings.

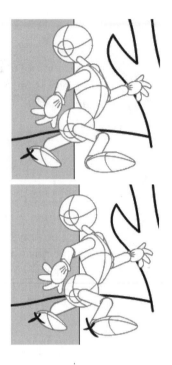

14. If you need to extend the exposure of the Registration Points layer, go ahead and do so. On that layer, draw a new registration point on the heel of the character's right foot.

15. Now, continue adding new cells (as mentioned in Chapter 9) to the Main Character layer and keep the character registered to the new *x* mark.

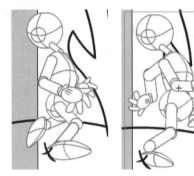

16. Once the character reaches the point where his left leg is planted firmly on the ground and his right leg is about to be lifted, draw a new registration point on the left heel, which belongs to the leg that's now going to be the stationary leg.

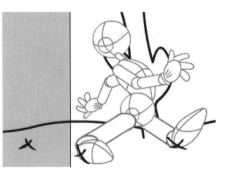

17. Continue to do this until the character has completely exited the stage. Test the movie by either scrubbing across the timeline or publishing a copy. The difference between this walking sequence and the one we created earlier (where the wrestler was simply tweened from one area of the screen to the other) is this: In this sequence, the character's footsteps and movements are made to conform to the laws of physics, rather than just having him waving his legs around at random and magically advancing from point A to point B. Although this takes a bit more effort on the animator's part, the results are far more gratifying and pleasing to the eye.

Believable Tracking

When you're tracking a character, you are basically focusing the camera on the character as he walks across the scene. The scenery element is what you're moving.

The procedure isn't that different than what we just did, but instead of animating the character from point A to point B, you're animating the background, making sure that if the character sets a foot on an area of the background, that area will stay attached to the character's foot. When you do this type of tracking, you can use areas of the background itself to keep the background registered to the character. For example, if in frame 1, a small pebble was by the character's foot, then the pebble should retain its position to the foot as he steps forward. Once he places his next foot on the ground, find another marker, maybe a tree, that could be directly behind the character. As the character steps forward, keep the tree behind the character until he places his foot down again to take a third step. At this point, you can find another anchor point to use as a reference. (This animated sequence is demonstrated below and continues on the following four pages.)

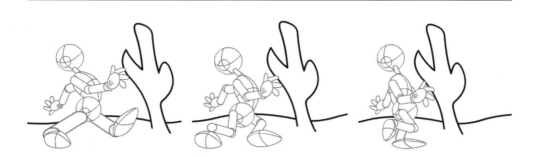

Running

Just because Flash lets you tween something from one point to another, doesn't mean that by taking the walk cycle and tweening it fast, you can make the character run.

In addition to moving faster from point A to point B, the character must look fast. His stride must be composed of larger steps. He must lean his weight forward more violently and, at the same time, he must reach with his legs not only to keep himself balanced but also, at the same time, to propel himself forward faster.

Cartoon animation isn't about creating realistic movement in a sense that the characters will move and behave the way people do. Realism in cartooning involves creating a sense of physics within their world, not ours, and making the audience believe it.

TIP

Frames have little to do with the actual speed at which a character is perceived to be moving or performing a motion. The secret to great animation is in the timing and the actual drawing of the characters. In some cases, running, or even walking, can be effectively pulled off with a mere two key-frames!

A typical cartoon run cycle will be composed of a good eight frames or so. Again, this depends on your character and the overproduction style.

▶   In the first frame of the action, the character is already drawn in motion. His body weight is shifted forward and his arms are in full swing.

► With his body weight continuing to fall forward, he bends his knee, so he can push against the ground to bring his body back up. This is the crossover step.

► As the character pushes against the ground, his entire body responds and he's once again lifted and thrust forward. He'll again need to prepare for the weight imbalance by bringing his other leg forward and preparing for it to catch him.

► As a cartoon, the character's movements are exaggerated. Nevertheless, the momentum is kept and he continues to prepare his left leg to receive the impact of the weight shift.

► The character's left heel makes contact with the ground. His body continues to fall off balance. The right leg is swung behind him.

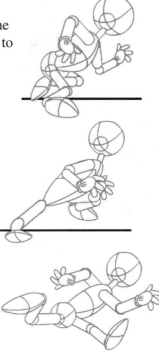

▶ As the body's center of balance continues to fall forward, the leg that's now planted on the ground is bent at the knee, preparing to once again spring his body up.

▶ He presses hard against the ground, and his body is once again thrust upward and yet still unbalanced. At this point, his right leg is prepared to receive the weight shift. The frame which follows this one is again frame 1, and the cycle will be complete.

Running Fast

By drawing the character running, rather than tweening him fast from one side of the screen to the other or increasing the frame rate as many amateurs do, you can bring the audience into the cartoon world. You can convince the audience that although cartooning might not be *the* real world, it is, in fact, *a* real world.

Sometimes a character runs faster than usual and, in such cases, that run is even more exaggerated than a typical run cycle. I usually create a fast run using only four key-frames.

▶ In the first frame, the character is drawn in full motion. In fact, he's running so fast that it isn't enough for the character simply to shift his body weight forward. He must look like he's carelessly diving into the air. His arms, fully extended forward, add to the illusion that the character is physically trying to maintain his momentum as far forward as possible. He's running so fast, he levitates off the ground. A shadow on the floor helps add to this illusion.

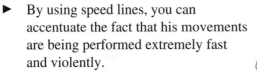

▶ By using speed lines, you can accentuate the fact that his movements are being performed extremely fast and violently.

▶ As the character thrusts his body forward, he arches his back to remain steady. His knee is thrown forward as far as it can go, preparing him to use his leg for the next step.

▶   Again, you are at the crossover step. This time, with the left leg about to launch the character forward, the right leg is preparing for the next step.

▶   After the four frames, the movie loops back to frame one and the cycle then repeats itself.

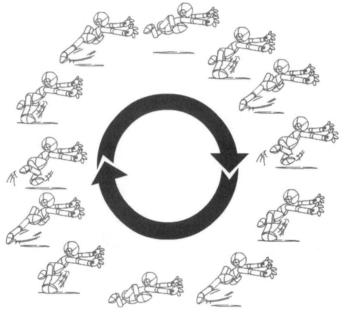

The Use of Cycles

Literally thousands of motions can be made into cycles. The best advice I can give you is to study the world around you and try to imitate the motions you see within the Flash environment. Think about the following, and then find other examples to help you.

▶ How many frames would it take to create a nice cycle of a ceiling fan spinning?

▶ Could you create a cycle of a bird in flight? How many frames would it take you to perform a seamlessly uninterrupted cycle?

▶ If your cartoon involves a chicken pecking on some corn, would you rather create an entire 100-frame sequence using individually drawn images of the chicken pecking or would you simplify your work by creating the same sequence using a four-frame cycle?

▶ Cycles don't only apply to motions like walking or running. Trees swaying in the wind, fire flickering at random, an angry relative waving her fist in hthe air—these can all be created using cycles.

▶ Study other cartoons on television and see if you can point out which sequences are created with cycles. You might be surprised to find out how much modern animation relies on this technique.

Special Uses of Cycles

One of the questions that I am often asked is, "How the heck do you draw things like fire and water in Flash?" Although these kinds of effects may seem difficult, they aren't.

Despite all the features available to you, such as multiple layering, masking, ActionScript, and so on, nothing can ever compare to a simple cycle, created using a few well-drawn frames.

A Single Flame

Creating a flame in Flash is probably the easiest thing you'll ever do:

1. Begin by opening Flash and create a new movie project named Candle.fla.

2. Go to the menu bar and select Insert | New Symbol. Create a new symbol named Flame. This time let's break my rule about avoiding Movie Clip symbols in animation and select Movie Clip as the Symbols property.

3. Draw a small teardrop around the midpoint of the symbol marker, which is the plus (+) sign on the center of the area.

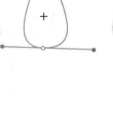

4. You can optimize the shape using the Molding tool (the white arrow) and reduce the shape to a mere two points.

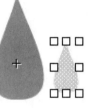

5. Use the Fill tool to color the shape a nice shade of orange.

6. Double-click the outline to select it, and then press the DELETE key to remove it.

7. Click the shape to select it and press CRTL-D to duplicate it. Move the new shape to the side and color it a nice orange-yellow color. Use the Transform tool to reduce the size of the shape to about half the original size.

8. Use the Arrow tool to relocate the smaller shape onto the larger one, slightly below the center.

9. Duplicate the cel three times by clicking it and pressing the F6 key three times.

10. The Movie Clip is now composed of three frames. On the second frame, modify the flame so it looks like it's swayed slightly to the left side. You can use the Onion Skin tool to help with the modification.

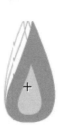

11. On frame 3, the flame will have bounced back into place, so we won't mess with it. Instead, go to frame 4 and modify the flame, so it looks as though it's swayed to the right.

12. The entire four-frame sequence should look like this, with the candle swaying to the left and to the right, and always reverting to the center.

13. Here's another comparison illustration that shows the flame's movement.

14. Go back into the stage and drag the Movie Clip symbol you just created onto the stage. As a visual aid, draw a candle supporting the flame.

15. Right-click the flame symbol and select Panels | Effect from the Options menu.

16. On the Effect panel, modify the candle's alpha state, so you can see the little candlewick well (80 percent is usually good enough).

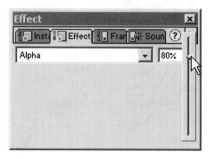

17. Because the Symbols property is set to Movie Clip, you won't be able to see the effect until you either publish the movie or test it using the Bandwidth Profiler (CTRL-ENTER). Go ahead and publish a copy of your new movie. You'll be amazed at how simple this effect is to create. Yet another great use for cycles.

18. If you want to give the flame a bit more of a glow, you might consider duplicating the flame symbol two more times. Reduce the alpha state of the two duplicates down to approximately 40 percent.

19. Now, place the two duplicates over the original in the same manner you did for the out-of-focus effect earlier in the book, by placing approximately two or three pixels on either side of the original.

Fire! Fire! Fire!

An actual fire works on the same principle. The only difference is, in a raging inferno, multiple flames are going at the same time. The movement of each individual flame is also more extreme, so much so that in many cases (but not always) when a flame sways to one side, it might even detach itself from the source and float away.

When creating fire, I recommend working with sets of three to five flames, as shown in this three-frame sequence:

The same sequence can then be duplicated, resized, and flipped horizontally to create the illusion of a blazing inferno. Throw a few independent flames into the mix and the result will literally be too hot to handle.

Simple Water Streams

You can create the illusion of flowing water a million ways in Flash. Here, I offer you a simple way of creating a water stream.

1. First, begin by creating the shape of your water. In my case, I'm creating a water stream flowing from a fountain. Create a linear gradient using shades of blue and white, and fill in the various shapes, as I did in this drawing.

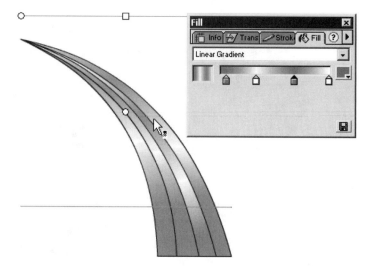

2. Animate the gradients in the direction the water is flowing. A five-frame sequence is good enough. You can animate the gradients either frame by frame or by creating a shape tween, as we did before with the starburst effect.

3. Remove the outlines and convert the animation into a symbol. If you plan to use it in a cartoon, give the symbol a graphic instance. If the animation is for a web page, give the symbol a Movie Clip instance, so it will play independent of the timeline.

4. The water creates a series of foamy splashes when it hits the base of the fountain. You can easily replicate this by creating a second cycle of the splash. A four-frame sequence is fine for this. Normally, I'd create the form of the splashes first by laying out a structure composed of circles and ovals.

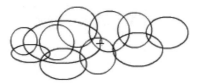

5. The unnecessary lines are then removed and the shapes are colored.

6. Shading and highlights are then added.

7. Go back into the main movie and place the newly created foam symbol at the base of the water stream. Adjust the size of the foam, so it's not too large compared to the stream.

8. You can give the water stream that diffused look by applying the same out-of-focus technique discussed while working on the flame. Duplicate the original symbols and flip them vertically, and give them a light alpha property to create a nice reflection. For the actual pool of water, you can also create a motion tweened gradient using the same color you used for the water.

9. You can add ripples to the water by simply tweening a series of ovals, increasing and decreasing them in size. Or, you can create a masking effect, which you learn in the following segment.

Water Ripples and Distorted Reflections

For this tutorial, download the water fountain project from this book's web site.
You can download it from the Chapter 11 directory.

1. When you first open the file, you'll find the animation I just created, laid out
    on Layer 1 (see Figure 11-1).

2. You need to create two more layers above it.

3. Right-click the graphic and select Copy.

4. Next, lock Layer 1, and then click the cel on Layer 2 to activate it.

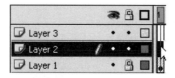

5. With the cel now active, right-click anywhere on the stage and select Paste In
    Place. A copy of the graphic is now placed exactly where the original one was.

```
Cut
Copy
Paste
Paste in Place
Select All
Deselect All

Scale
Rotate

Rulers
Grid              ▶
Guides            ▶

✔ Snap to Objects

Movie Properties...
Movie Explorer
Scenes
```

6. Use the Transform tool to increase the size of the graphic now residing on
    Layer 2 by a few pixels. Also, drag the layer a few pixels to the side. This way,
    the two graphics are no longer placed at exactly the same spot. Right-click the
    area where Layer 3 is labeled and select the Mask option.

7. When the mask is created, the labeling changes for the two layers. The layer with the arrow icon pointing down will be the actual mask. The layer with the purple icon and the arrow pointing to the right is the object being masked. By default when this action is performed, both layers will become locked.

8. Unlock Layer 3 and draw a series of ripples around the foam and the base of the statue using the Brush tool. The color you choose doesn't matter.

9. Go to frame 5 and, on Layer 3, insert a blank cel by right-clicking it and applying the Insert Empty Frame command. (You can also simply click the cel and press the F7 key.)

10. Extend the exposures of the cels in Layers 1 and 2 all the way to frame 5.

11. On the empty cel you created at c(3,5), again draw another series of ripples. You'll shape tween the contents of this layer, so draw them so they appear to be flowing away from the ones you originally drew. Using the Onion Skin tool helps with this procedure (see Figure 11-2).

12. Lock Layer 3 and notice most of the image in Layer 2 has disappeared. Again, this is because it has been masked. This image is only seen through the ripples you drew on Layer 3 and, because the images in Layer 1 and Layer 2 aren't identical in size or shape, the overpicture appears distorted in the areas where you drew the ripples.

13. Publish a copy of your movie and check it out. Pretty cool, eh? Not only do you get some nice water ripple effects, but also the ripples themselves cause the reflections to become distorted as they pass over the water.

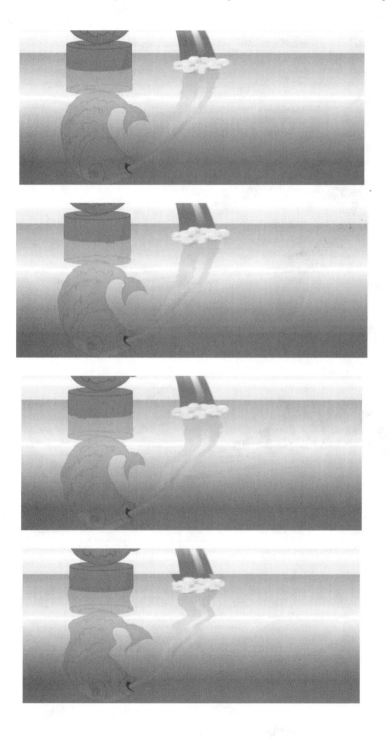

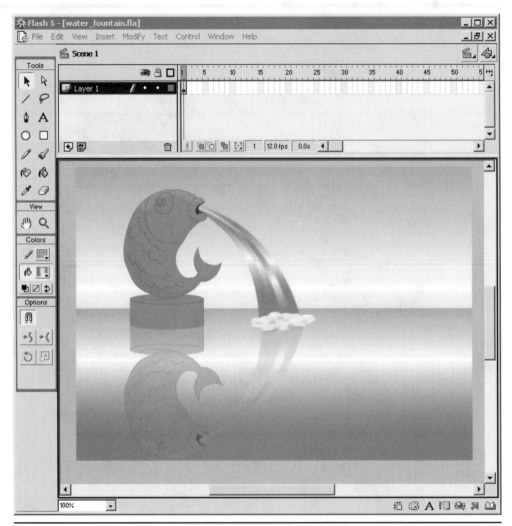

Figure 11-1 *Download the water fountain project from the Chapter 11 directory.*

Rain

Creating a rain effect using vector graphics isn't entirely impossible; it's simply unreasonable. The amount of lines and the combination of alpha channels won't increase the file size of the file, but it will render a file that no CPU known to

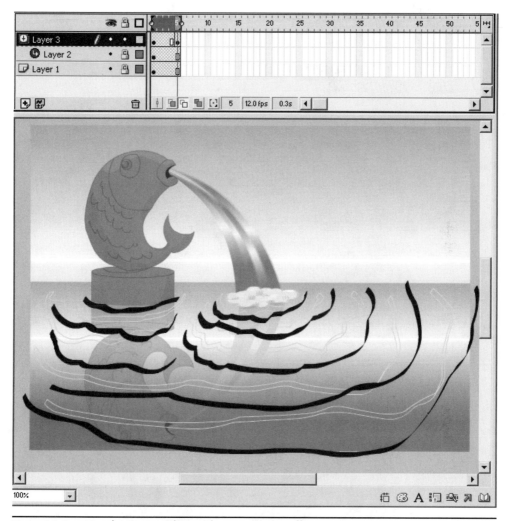

Figure 11-2   *Use the Onion Skin tool to create the effect you want.*

man could handle. Trust me, I've tried it. This is one of those instances when using bitmaps is the best option. That is, if you want to create some nice looking rain.

To demonstrate a rain effect, I'll use Adobe Photoshop 6 in conjunction with Flash, but you can use any software tool that enables you to apply a noise and a Motion Blur filter to any given image. Let's begin.

1. In Photoshop, create a project file with either the same or larger dimensions as your Flash stage. I'm fond of 288×216, so I'll go with that.

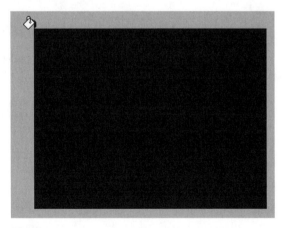

2. Grab the paint bucket and paint the stage black. (You could also have done this in the Settings panel, but I wanted to give you a hard time.)

3. Activate the Noise filter. A good setting for this filter is 100 percent, Gaussian, Monochromatic, as shown in the following illustration:

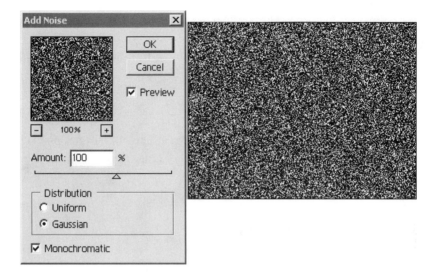

4. Next, go to the filters again and apply a Motion Blur. Set the degree to the direction in which you want your rain to fall toward. For this example, I set it at a 45-degree angle. As for distance, go with however fat or skinny you want the rain to look.

5. Select the entire area and copy the content to your clipboard.

6. Open a new Flash project (if you haven't already done so) and right-click the stage. Select Paste and you're good to go. Close Photoshop and don't worry about saving the .pdf file. You won't need it anymore.

7. Go to Flash and convert the bitmap into a Movie Clip symbol. For this example, we're only making a one-frame movie, and we want to see the animated rain when we test it. Name the symbol Rain and go to Edit In Place mode by double-clicking the symbol.

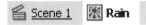

8. Once there, increase the size of the symbol to at least five or ten pixels larger than the actual stage. Using the outline feature helps so you can see the stage. This isn't an exact science, so just guesstimate.

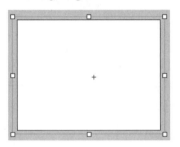

9. Duplicate the cel at frame 2 by applying the Insert Key Frame command. Position the image in frame 1 to the left of the stage and the image in frame 2 to the right. When this movie clip plays, it will create a left to right and back again motion.

10. Return to the main timeline and publish a test file by pressing the F12 key. The file will be launched in your default browser. The effect is not complete yet, but you can get an idea of how the rain will animate. Let's go back to the program file and reduce the alpha state of that symbol to a low number—something between 10 percent and 20 percent, depending on how gloomy you want this rainy day to look.

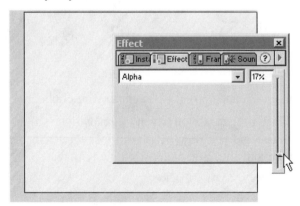

11. Create a new layer and drag it under Layer 1, so the rain can be on top. Throw in some images (perhaps a character walking or running in the rain) on the layers below and export another test movie.

12. You can enhance the rain effect by randomly placing water droplets splashing against the ground and on objects.

More Cheats Than Meet the Eye

Animation, whether full frame by frame or limited, will always make use of cheats in one form or another. Here are some of the most popular cheats among animators. Learn them. They can make your life much easier and your work a lot better.

The Blur

The *Blur* is created when a character is moving at an incredibly fast rate. Rather than drawing a part of the character moving fast, a blurred effect can be created by speed lines. In Flash, you can also reduce the alpha of the blurred area (which is usually a symbol) to spice up the effect.

Using bit maps in moderation can also add a great deal of quality to an animated sequence, especially when a Motion Blur filter is applied to the in-betweens.

The Smear

The *Smear* gets its name from the way the in-betweens are drawn. A quick and dirty way to do a Smear is by distorting the symbols in the in-between frame using the Transform tool. In the following sequence, the wrestler has to turn himself around.

Rather than drawing the action, the smeared in-between is created by manipulating the symbols, so they allow a sort of visual flow from the first frame to the third.

The action is so fast that the audience doesn't notice the actual details of the distortion. To them, it should look like a fast, yet smooth, movement.

Let's look at a more extreme Smear. In this sequence, the character needs to make a quick entrance.

▶   We begin with an empty area.

▶ All of a sudden, a distorted head appears.

▶ The elements continue to stretch, as the character moves to his location.

▶ He's now in full view.

When the movie is published and played back, the sequence appears as a smooth, almost liquid, motion. No one sees the actual distortions, only the smooth flow of the character from one place to the other.

The Smear can be applied to almost any movement. If you're a fan of the show *Johnny Bravo,* take a moment to study his quick and snappy movements as he takes out his comb to comb his hair, point at an object in midair, or karate chop his way into a secret military installation. The show makes full use of the Smear technique in nearly every action Johnny performs.

But remember, although the Smear can be well executed by modifying the symbols that make up a character, nothing beats drawing a smeared frame. By drawing the image, you can provide a smoother flow from one image to the other and your illusions will register much better with the audience.

Multiples

The *Multiples* effect is often created in conjunction with speed lines. It involves duplicating the object in motion (as a symbol) and animating multiple instances of it around the same area.

The effect can also be used to enhance slow-motion sequences or to add a bit of zest to an action shot.

Stretch and Squash

Stretch and Squash is perhaps one of the most widely used techniques in animation. This technique is grounded in this idea: The matter that makes up a cartoon object is rubbery in nature and is affected by the laws of gravity. For example, take a bouncing ball.

This normally would be a boring sequence to look at if it were tweened along a motion path. While the motion is there, you don't get a sense of any physics.

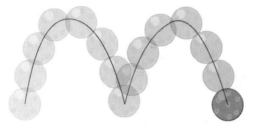

You need to give the impression that some kind of force is acting against the ball to make it bounce. When the ball impacts the ground, it will be squashed.

Because of the rubbery nature of the ball (for pretty much all cartoons, for that matter), it then causes itself to pop back into its normal form. This causes a force against the ground and, because the ball is so lightweight, it bounces away from the ground and toward the direction the momentum is taking it.

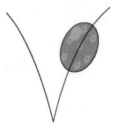

At the height of the action, the only force acting against the ball is the momentum. Gravity wins in a little bit and begins to pull the ball down again.

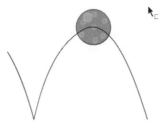

As the ball falls, gravity causes it to stretch a bit in the direction it's falling.

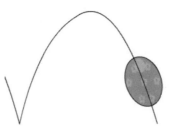

When the ball hits the ground again, the cycle continues. This motion is much more pleasing to the eye than a static object just floating around.

Slow In and Slow Out

In Flash, there's a setting for tweened objects called Ease In and Ease Out. This works along the same principle as the *Slow In and Slow Out* technique used in animation.

As less force is placed on an object in motion, that object slows down or maybe even stops. The greater the force acted upon the object, the faster it moves.

As you learned earlier, to create an object moving faster, you need to use less frames to animate its motion. By the same token, the slower an object is to move, the more frames are required to create that motion.

As the ball travels toward the ground, it generates more momentum because of the gravity pulling on it. As the ball ascends toward the sky, it gradually loses its momentum until the point where gravity wins and it begins to fall again. Knowing this, you can draw more frames in the areas where the ball is slowest, as well as determine which areas of the sequence will be composed of less frames. In the following illustration, you can see the sequence is composed of 15 frames. The areas where the balls are closer to each other are the Slow In areas, which require more frames to create. The Slow Out areas, or the areas in the sequence where the action speeds up, are created using less frames.

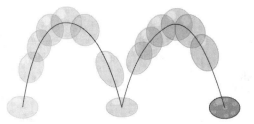

Don't think Slow In and Slow Out applies only to bouncing balls. When realism counts, this technique should apply to nearly anything you animate. Frogs leaping, an airplane landing, a character turning her head in one direction, a woman lifting a child in the air, a guy running—virtually any motion you can think of benefits from this technique.

Summary

This chapter discussed the creation of animation cycles not only to reduce the workload performed by the animator, but at the same time to create movies whose file sizes are incredibly small and web friendly.

▶ Almost any motion can be made into a never-ending cycle. The trick is to draw the sequence in a way so it ends the same way it begins.

▶ Formulaic cycles like the standard walks, runs, fast runs, and such are only guidelines for how to animate your own characters. Ultimately, animating your characters' motions is up to you, and should be based on their individual mannerisms, physical traits, personalities, and moods.

▶ When realism is of great importance, keeping your character's motion in register with the scenery is important. If a character takes a step and a pebble is next to her foot, make sure that pebble stays in the same location in relation to her foot as she takes her step until she lifts her foot. At that time, you can choose another point in the scenery to help you maintain your character's movements along a plane that's registered with the scenery.

▶ By studying motion and the way physics affects objects in motion, you can gain a better understanding about the world around you and apply your observations to your animations.

▶ Cartoon animation isn't about re-creating real-world motion. Cartoon animation is about drawing your audience into your cartoon environment and making them believe it's real.

▶ Water effects, such as flowing water and ripples, can easily be created using a combination of tweened gradients and masking effects. When a symbol needs to look diffused or blurred, a good technique is to duplicate it twice, reduce the alpha states of the duplicates, and place them on top of the original. Then place approximately two or three pixels on either side of the original.

▶ Flames and fires can be created using three- to four-frame cycles. The motion of the flame is always the same left to right movement. In a blazing fire, the flame's movements are more violent. In some cases, a flame can detach itself from its source and float away.

▶ Creating the illusion of believable rain within Flash can be a real nightmare. A Noise-Filtered and Motion-Blurred bitmap sequence always produces a better quality effect. In the case of rain, the creation of a similar effect using vectors would create a file that not only takes forever to render, but would be extremely CPU-dependent.

▶ Visual cheats, such as Blurs, can easily be created using vector graphics, as well as bitmaps. There's no wrong way to do this because each way has its benefits.

▶ Smears can be created by deforming your symbols using the Transform tool, although much better results can be achieved when you draw the figure being smeared.

▶ Speed lines and multiple exposed images can greatly enhance an action sequence. While speed lines create the illusion of an object moving at very high speeds, multiple exposures of the same element with a frame can add a bit of spice to any slow-motion sequence. Using multiples in conjunction with blurs creates awkward, almost clumsy, speed effects that can dramatically improve the humorous or comedic sequences.

▶ Stretch and Squash works under the principle that cartoon characters and objects are made out of a rubbery material and, when affected by the forces of nature and physics, they react accordingly.

▶ Slowing In and Slowing Out is a technique used to animate an object's momentum. As an object speeds up, it takes less drawing to animate the action. As an object slows down, it requires more drawings. Flash also has a feature called Ease In and Ease Out, which can be applied to tweened objects. Ease In and Ease Out works along the same principles as Slow In and Slow Out.

CHAPTER
12

Cartoon Talk

One of the most common ways for a cartoon character to communicate is simply to talk. Contrary to popular belief, cartoon speech isn't just a matter of having a mouth open and close while words magically appear out of thin air. Cartoon characters are actors and they must not only perform what they're saying through physical actions, they must also make the user believe the words being said are coming directly from their mouths. In this chapter, you learn the proper techniques for character lip-synching and creating cartoon speech, as well as how to draw character mouth actions. You also learn how these techniques are being applied in Flash.

Exposure Sheets and Lip-Sheets

In Chapter 9, you learned that in animation it takes a lot of cels to make up a finished film. Many of these cels are shot stacked on top of each other to achieve a complete single frame. Because of the different numbers of people who handle these drawings, an organizational tool was developed to help keep track of the drawings and their placement in relation to the film. In regular cel animation, each drawing is named individually according to the level and frame number it is going to reside on.

The exposure sheet, also known as the *x-sheet* or *dope sheet,* is a tool that allows animators to keep track of individual cels. And the exposure sheet is also a great tool for planning the timing and synchronization of your sound track to your character's mouth actions and lip-synching throughout the film. Figure 12-1 shows you what a generic, over-the-counter exposure sheet looks like.

If you approach the Flash timeline from an animation standpoint and learn to identify where the cels are placed in relation to frame and level number (see Chapter 9), you can see that Flash does a fairly decent job of paralleling an animation x-sheet. Many things are missing from the Flash timeline, however, that can only be overcome if you return to the good old pencil-and-paper approach. One of these things is the capability to lip-sync as you work with audio files and sequence your animation.

You can purchase x-sheets at any animation shop or order them through various catalogues, available both online and offline. You can also make your own, which can be tailored to include only the necessary information you need. Making your own is my recommendation because, unless you plan to draw each image by hand, and then vectorize to Flash, chances are you won't have any paper drawings to keep track of. Obviously, if you're working in Flash, you also don't need things such as a column for camera instructions because in Flash there is no camera.

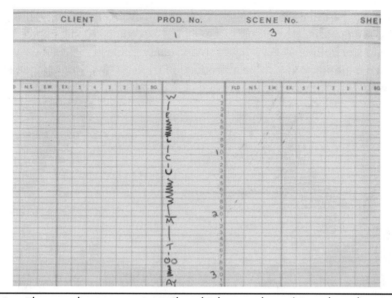

Figure 12-1   *These x-sheets come in pads, which cost about $2 each and contain about 50 sheets per pad.*

Flash also enables you to create unlimited layers, which means you might not be satisfied working on a standard x-sheet that only allows you to work with the traditional five levels over a background. Instead, you might want to create a custom x-sheet, which lets you work with ten layers, or maybe even more!

Lip-Sheets

When I work on Flash animation, I use exposure sheets primarily for lip-sync purposes. So, I decided to create my own version of an x-sheet, which contains only rows and columns specifically for the lip-synchronization process. I call these modified x-sheets, *lip-sheets*. All they are is a large table with rows and columns, which can be printed on regular 8.5" by 11" paper and organized in a three-ring binder. Again, these sheets are nothing more than a custom x-sheet, which contains only the stuff I need for lip-synching.

My particular lip-sheets contain a header with five fields for writing down production-related information. You can always create your own lip-sheets, custom-tailored to your own specific needs, but for this book I recommend downloading a copy of my lip-sheet from this book's web site (www.osborne.com).

I strongly suggest that when you work on story-driven animation, you work on a scene-by-scene basis. If you don't know what a scene is, read Chapter 13 on scripting and storytelling to get a better understanding. Flash makes it easy to insert and organize multiple scenes in your production by using the Scene panel, shown in the following illustration, which is located at Window | Panels | Scene.

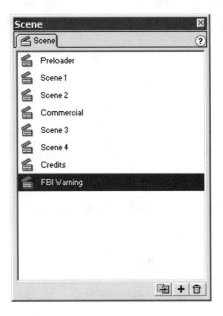

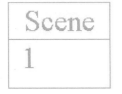

Use the first field of the lip-sheet to jot down the scene number or name of the scene (as in the name given to the scene in Flash).

The frames per second (fps) field is where you write the number of frames per second at which your Flash film will play. This is to remind you that if your movie is 12fps, every 12th frame marks exactly one second of film. Each row (except for the headings) on the table indicates a single frame. If your movie is 24fps, then it'll be each 24th row in the table that indicates one second of film.

Production
The Most Dangerous Brain

The name of the production is written in the production field. I try to keep separate sheets for every character in my animation. This helps keep everything organized and easy to find. But you can use the same sheet for all the characters in your story, as long as their dialogue doesn't overlap. The character field is for jotting down the name of the character(s) that will be speaking throughout those lip-sheets.

Character
Angie

If you're going to have multiple characters in the same sheets, I suggest writing their dialogues in different colors, so you can tell one character's dialogue from another.

Sheet Number
2

The last field in the header is the sheet number. Because each sheet enables you to work with only 48 frames at a time, you'll definitely need more than one sheet per film or scene.

The work area of the lip-sheet has five columns, as shown here:

Frame	Time	Audio File	Lip-Sync	Words

▶ The Frame column contains the actual frame numbers. Each row indicates a frame of film, so you use this column to number each frame in question.

Frame
1.
2.
3.
4.
5.
6.
7.
8.
9.
10.
11.
12.
13.

▶ The Time column is used to enter time values relative to the film. For example, if you already know your movie will play at 12fps, you can fill in 00:01:00 at frame 12, 00:02:00 at frame 24, 00:03:00 at frame 36, and so on. Remember, at 12fps, every 12 frames equals one second of time. Because your characters probably won't speak continuously throughout the entire timeline, however, chances are you'll only need to catalogue certain frames at a time, while completely skipping over others that contain nothing but dead air.

Time
00:01:00

▶ The Audio File column, I think, is one that's unnecessary in most cases. I use this column only when I work with multiple voice files, which is rarely. In most cases, I recommend a single voice file for the entire scene. Nevertheless, this is a column you can use to mark which files are being used in your Flash movie and at which frame they play.

Audio File
loaded.mp3
\
/
\
/
\
/
\
/
\
/
\
/
\
/

▶ Only nine basic mouth actions exist that a character can perform as she speaks. All other mouth actions are either a combination of the basic nine or a hybrid of two basic mouth actions (you learn about mouth actions later in this chapter). In the Lip-Sync column, you write the mouth action being performed in that particular frame.

Lip-Sync
W
E
L
K
U
M
\
/
T
O

▶ The Words column is where you write the actual words being spoken by that character. In the Lip-Sync column, everything is written either phonetically or by the actual name of the mouth action being used in that frame, so trying to read the content as dialogue can be quite disconcerting. Having a "dialogue" or "words" column enables you to place the actual words and to be able to read them back more easily.

Words
Welcome
\
/
\
/
\
/
\
To
\
/

Basic Cartoon Phonetics and Vocalization

Just as people use their lips and tongues to generate words when they speak, animated cartoons have been developed to mimic these actions to create a more realistic and satisfying experience. The act of making a cartoon character speak goes far beyond simply having them open and close their mouths. The character must give an honest performance and sell the audience the illusion that she is talking, not some actor doing the voice-over, while the drawing moves its mouth. Remember, everything in your film should try to coax the audience into your world, rather than making it obvious that what they're watching is simply a bunch of drawings and a voice track.

Although ventriloquism works perfectly well with hand-manipulated dummies, in animation the public doesn't want to believe some man is behind the curtains. We, as an audience, want to believe the characters are alive and the words they speak are their own. Because of this, over the years, cartoonists and animators have narrowed cartoon phonetics into nine basic physical mouth actions.

The Vowels

Five vowels are in the English language (you don't need me to tell you that). Look at yourself in a mirror and pay attention to what your mouth looks like when you pronounce each of the five vowels.

▶ Notice that when *a* and *i* are pronounced, your mouth basically looks the same. Your mouth is wide open, and your teeth show nice and large. In the back, you can see your tongue resting on the bottom of your mouth.

A–I

▶ When *e* is spoken, your mouth becomes wide and your teeth are even more pronounced. Sometimes the teeth will touch but, in most cases, a slight aperture exists. This depends on which pronunciation of *e* you're using. For example, if you're using the *e* mouth action in a word such as "Hector" or "set," where the *e* sounds more like "eh," the teeth tend to be slightly farther apart. When you're using it in words such as "see," "me," or "deer" where the *e* sounds like "ee," though, you might want to draw the teeth a little closer to each other and the mouth a bit wider.

E

▶ When the vowel *o* is pronounced, your lips take on a circular form. In most cases, it starts with a wide circle and slightly decreases in size. You don't usually see any teeth or tongue when the vowel is spoken.

o

▶ The vowel *u* is similar to *o;* however, when *u* is pronounced, an extra amount of stress is placed on the lips, making the circular shape itself even smaller and the lips protrude further outward.

u – o

Consonant Sounds

In many cases, there's no set way to represent a consonant by itself phonetically because, for the most part, the phonics behind a consonant (in a cartoon performance) are largely dependent on the vowel that immediately follows it. For example, take the letter *k;* by itself it makes a "kuh" type of sound, as does the letter *c*. When used in actual dialogue—as in the words "kid," "corner," or "can"—your mouth takes the shape of the vowel being pronounced immediately after the consonant. In the word "kid," for example, the first mouth action to be performed is the sound generated by the letter *i*. In this instance, this sounds more like "ee" rather than the usual "eye" sound. An important thing to know is, in animation, all dialogue is treated phonetically instead of grammatically.

Consonant sounds only create five distinct mouth actions. If you know of any others, they're probably created by using a hybrid of any two basic actions:

▶ The consonants *m-b-p* require your lips to be pressed against each other before any vowel can be pronounced. This action is usually drawn with pressure being applied to the lower lip by the upper lip. Words that make use of this action include "macho," "blue," or "potato."

M–B–P

▶ Next are the consonant sounds created when the letters *w-r* are pronounced. The letter *w* creates a sound like "whu" and the letter *r* makes a sound like "ruh." Both of these sounds cause your lips to form a circle while, at the same time, the top and bottom lips are forced outward and apart from each other. In some cases, this action is also used to indicate the sound produced by the letter *g*.

W–R

► Three consonants cause your mouth to open and make use of your tongue by pressing against either the roof of your mouth or the bottom of your upper teeth. These are the letters *l-n-d*. This mouth action can be clearly seen when you pronounce words that make use of these consonants, such as "lady," "Sylvester," "Nadine," and "nirvana."

L-N-D

► To create the sound produced by the consonant *f,* you must force air from your mouth, while pressing on your bottom lip with the upper teeth. For the letter *v,* the process is basically the same, except you focus on forcing the airflow to create a vibration between your teeth and your lower lip. In both cases, the mouth action being performed is basically the same.

F-V

► Last, but not least, is the mouth action for the letters *t* and *s.* When these consonants are spoken, the teeth are clenched together. The lips are spread apart and the mouth is stretched wide, looking almost like a smile. This mouth action is also shared by the consonants *z* ("zee"), *c* (as in "cell"), and, on rare occasions, the vowel sound of *e,* as when tugging an extra "ee" might be necessary.

T-S

Dependent Mouth Actions

Many consonants, such as the previously discussed letter *k,* have no mouth action of their own. Although they do produce a phoneme when spoken, the actual mouth action created isn't a direct result of the consonant, but of the vowel which immediately follows it. These types of consonants can be referred to as being *dependent* because, without the vowel, a cartoon character would be unable to sell the word properly that's being spoken.

NOTE

A phoneme is the smallest phonetic unit in a language that is capable of conveying a distinction in meaning, as the m of "mat" and the b of "bat" in English.

Dependent mouth actions include the letter *c* when it's used with the *k* sound in words like "cancer" or "corner." The letter *g* is often referred to as a dependent consonant because words like "gate" or "goal" can easily be performed by extending the exposure of the first vowel action a couple of frames, rather than drawing an action for the "guh" sound. In some cases, the *w-r* action is used to represent a "guh" sound.

"GATE"

The letter *h* is also dependent for the same reason. By extending the exposure of the mouth action created by the vowel, you can perform words like "hot" or "hairy."

The consonants *j, k,* and *x* are also dependent on vowel mouth actions.

Crossover Actions

Crossover mouth actions are actions that can be performed as both vowels and consonant sounds. For example, the same action used for the vowel *u* can also be used for the consonant *q,* which is why this action is usually referred to as *u-q.* Try enunciating these sounds in front of a mirror and you'll see how your mouth looks the same whether you say *q,* which is pronounced "cue," or *u,* which is pronounced "you."

Practice, Practice, Practice!

Study the mouth actions in Figure 12-2. Learn them. And then try to apply them to your own characters.

Practice drawing the mouth actions using as many different angles as you can and learn to draw them to the point where they become second nature. Get used to drawing them in profile view, 45-degree view, and front view. These are the most popular cartoon poses.

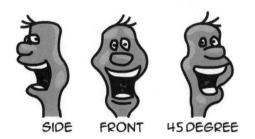

SIDE   FRONT   45 DEGREE

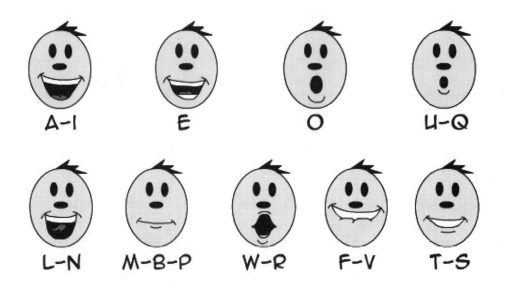

Figure 12-2 *The nine basic mouth actions*

The mouth actions are always the same, no matter what your character looks like. Try to avoid the generic mouth actions and, instead, use your character's own lips and mouth to perform the actions.

Some characters are more complex than others, so you need to get used to that. As long as you know how the mouth should look, you can easily make any character perform the action you require and have it sell. Animators usually keep a small mirror handy, so they can use their own faces as models for facial expressions and mouth actions.

NOTE

In showbiz, the term sell *is a slang word that means "to make the audience believe." Pro wrestlers, for instance, train hard to learn how to sell a punch or a fall effectively, so the audience will go crazy trying to figure out how any person could take so much punishment. (Yes, kiddies, wrestling is a performance and the wrestlers aren't out to kill each other. They're actors hired to entertain you with their athletic skills.)*

Don't rush this process. Take a few weeks or a month to develop this skill. Heck, take as long as you need. Forget about Flash, forget about the Web, and forget about coming up for ideas for cartoons. You'll have plenty of time for that later. For now, do something for yourself and teach yourself how to draw characters performing mouth actions.

Create a character and have him perform the nine actions in what would appear to be his normal tone of voice. You'll soon discover you can express the same mouth action in more than one way.

A-I (HAPPY)

Draw the same character again but, this time, have him perform the same nine mouth actions as if he's angry or even yelling.

A-I (ANGRY)

Take your character and give him the blues. Draw the character performing the mouth action as if he's sad or disappointed. Remember, in cartoons, the mouth is the window to the soul, so you need to teach yourself how to express an emotion or a feeling while, at the same time, enunciating a phoneme.

A-I (SAD)

Making Words

You create words by combining mouth actions. The basic nine are typically used as key cels in animation. Once the lip actions have been properly timed to the sound track, an inbetweener or an assistant animator is usually hired to create and in-between them, so they make the transition from one action to the next appear much more smooth and natural. In Flash, as in many forms of limited animation, key-frames are well accepted without the need for breakdown drawings or inbetweens. As a Flash animator or, as I prefer to call it, a Flash filmmaker, you can easily get by in life relying on the basic nine mouth actions alone.

To make a word, you must first break it down phonetically. Take, for example, the word "Flash." Only after you break the word "Flash" down phonetically can you begin to determine the vowel and consonant mouth actions used to create it. Phonetically, the word "Flash" sounds like "Fuh-lash." The *F* sound is strong, which means you'd most likely have to add special emphasis on the *F* action. This can be easily achieved by extending the exposure of the *F* action a little longer than you would for any of the others. Then, there's the "lash" part of the word, which is clustered together. Nevertheless, I can spot the *l* and the *a,* which are heard quite distinctly. The *s* and the *h* come together to form a "shhh" kind of sound, which can easily be performed with the standard action for the consonant *s* being held for a longer period of time than usual. When put together, the word "Flash," performed by a cartoon character, looks like this:

"FUH – LASH"

Let's try another word: "animation." When broken down phonetically, "animation" sounds something like "ah-nee-ma-shon." Remember, we aren't trying to perform the word according to the letters used when it's spelled properly. Instead, we're interpreting it phonetically.

AH   NEE

MA

SHON

"animation"

Here are two more words for you:

"elephant"

"cartoon"

Notice the use of tugs in the previous word cartoon. Tugs should preferably involve the entire face. Because the medium is somewhat less involved than traditional animation, however, when it comes to regular speech, a partial tug (a tug involving only one part or the body, such as the mouth) is an acceptable enhancement to otherwise boring-looking speech.

Practice with random words pulled from a dictionary. Break them down phonetically and practice performing them using a character of your own design. Create entire phrases and have your character perform them. Remember, performing dialogue involves more than only synchronized mouth action. Get the entire body involved. Make use of body language and lines of action to make your character seem alive as she speaks.

Preparing Sound for Flash

When it comes to web design and development, the use of multiple short audio files and loops is perfectly acceptable. In fact, this is highly encouraged. When it comes to filmmaking and storytelling, though, a scene should be a complete little story in itself with a beginning, a middle, and an end, which should never be broken. Keep your scenes in mind when you record and edit your sound files, and try to create a single uninterrupted audio file for each scene in your film.

The reason for this is, unlike the act of building a web interface, you're creating a work of content, which will play along a specific timeline. You not only want the sound perfectly synchronized to your cartoon's actions and speech, but you also want the file to play and stream smoothly from the Web, without having to stop in the middle of a scene to buffer a new instance of a sound file, which is what usually happens.

Suppose I create a cartoon where each of the phrases my character speaks is set up as an individual audio file. Let's say there are ten audio files in all. Whether your sound clips are set to play as event sound or as streaming audio doesn't matter. If the user's connection isn't fast enough, the movie will probably stop playing every time a new audio clip is reached, so it can either download the event sound in full or buffer a portion of it, in case the audio file is set to stream. Of course, you could always preload the entire thing before letting the user see your film, but that defeats the purpose of using Flash as your animation tool. The object of streaming media is for the content to start playing as soon as possible before the file has downloaded entirely, so the audience doesn't have to wait. If you can make the file stream and play smoothly over the user's connection, she won't ever be aware of the actual size of the movie file, whether it's 100K or 100MB. (Of course you'd have to be crazy to make any .swf file larger than 30MB.)

When it comes to using multiple sound files throughout the movie, only once the sound has loaded completely (in the case of an event sound) or buffered enough (in the case of streaming audio) will the movie resume its playback. If the entire voice track is timed properly, however, prior to importing it into Flash and saving it as a single uninterrupted audio file, you've drastically increased the chances for proper playback over the Web. All sound buffering should take place at the beginning of the movie and shouldn't interrupt the viewer, who might otherwise be immersed in the experience, in the middle of a scene.

In the event of multiple scenes, any buffering should always take place at the beginning of every scene and not in the middle of it. If you keep your scene structure as described in Chapter 13, this process will go completely unnoticed.

If you can mix the *sound track* (the music to enhance the mood) in the same voice track prior to importing it into Flash, then you'll only have a single file to buffer prior to playback. Thus, your Flash film will start faster and, perhaps, perform better.

However, I recommend your sound track file be a separate audio file, which will play alongside your voice track. This means you'll have two audio files buffering at the beginning of each of your scenes, which might make your movie take a little longer to start. The benefit to doing this, though, is you can take advantage of Flash's simple audio-editing features to enhance the user's experience.

Here's an example: At certain points in the film, you might want the music to play loudly to enhance an action scene. In other scenes where dialogue is important, you might want to increase the volume of the voice track and reduce the volume of the music and ambience, so the dialogue can be clearly heard. You can also play around with Flash's "pseudo surround sound" feature, which lets you tinker with the way speakers sound by fading the output from one speaker to the other. Having the two audio files, a voice and ambience track, playing independent of each other gives you more options as far as presentation and audio control. Remember, each of the two tracks should be a single, uninterrupted audio stream.

Having said this, it's important to know that although Flash lets you use simple editing functions to work with audio files, it's recommended you use more robust tools for your voice-editing and audio-mixing needs. Analog audio tools are usually the best way to go if you can afford them, but many digital solutions are also available which enable you to record and work with audio directly in your PC.

Recording Your Voice Track

For professional audio quality, a little microphone connected to your PC simply won't do. If you have a garage or basement, consider turning it into a sound studio. Line the walls with cardboard, old mattresses, thick wool sheets, or any combination of these. These can help soundproof your studio, so you don't annoy your neighbors (as much) and help absorb the sound to prevent undesirable echoes and feedback.

Throw away that little PC speaker. Go to the music shop and buy yourself a real microphone, perhaps even a microphone stand. This way, your voice actors can use a single microphone without having to grab it with their hands and pass it around when they say their lines. You might need a mixer so you can plug your microphones into it. And, you might want to use other special devices, such as voice-altering pedals or musical instruments.

TIP

Most music stores sell a package of three decent quality professional microphones for as little as $50.

If you'll primarily use a software-based solution for your sound recording and editing, you might also want to purchase an adapter for your new microphone. This will enable you to connect your microphone directly to your sound card and, thus, process your recording directly into a sound software, such as Cakewalk Pro. Remember, your PC's fan and hard drive tend to make all sorts of funny sounds and the microphone will tend to pick up those sounds. If possible, give the PC a sound-absorbing casing, such as a cardboard box filled with pillows or blankets. Also keep the PC as far away from the microphone as possible.

Avoid running any appliances during your recording sessions, such as air conditioners, fans, microwaves, televisions, radios, and politicians. They emit unpleasant noises that you don't want captured in your recording. Yes, the absence of fans and air-conditioning is terribly unpleasant, but that's showbiz: learn to deal with it.

CAUTION

Try to leave some breathing room for your PC's exhaust to make its way outside the box. The purpose is to drown the PC noises as much as possible without causing your PC to overheat.

For the best and most efficient results, consider an analog solution. Many of the larger music stores, such as Mars Music, carry personal recording studios, which cost anywhere from $300 to $700. What these machines do is let you record, edit, and mix your sound on high-quality tape, which is much faster and easier to edit and manipulate than on a PC.

Using personal recording studios, which were designed for musicians to record their own music tracks, you can edit your entire voice tracks and ambience/sound tracks prior to importing them into your PC. Then, if you want, you can further enhance the sound using sound-editing software, but this isn't usually necessary.

Importing Your Audio Files into Flash

You can import your audio files into Flash by selecting File | Import and browsing through your PC until you find the audio file you want to import. Flash enables you to import sound in various formats. Please check the help files provided with your version of Flash for the information on all the different file types that can be imported into your version of the software.

Since the release of Flash 5, the software has been capable of handling the direct import of files formatted in the MP3 format. Take advantage of this because it can make your life 99.9 percent easier. In the olden days, prior to version 5, it wasn't uncommon to work with a source file that weighed in at well over 80MB because of the .wav files you were using. Currently, the capability to import and use .mp3 files internally lets us work with source files whose size is kept down to a couple megs. Logically, this makes managing, backing up, and rendering your .fla files a lot faster and easier.

TIP

If you can't or don't want to convert a room in your house or part of your garage or basement into a personal recording sound studio, you can always rent one. Sure, if you have the big bucks, you can always buy studio time at a local recording studio, but the best places for recording stuff on the cheap are rehearsal spaces for bands. These spaces have already been soundproofed, and they have plenty of electrical outlets and lighting. All you need to do is take your equipment and plug it in. You can find rehearsal spaces in the classified section of your local urban-style newspaper (every major town has one). In some instances, I've found they charge as little as $30 a day and some charge as little as $50 a week. Give this a try. It can save you some manual labor and it won't cost much.

Lip-Synching

Whenever you animate, always animate your action first and worry about physically placing the characters' mouth actions onto their faces well after the scene or the entire film is complete. In other words, animate your story focusing on your characters' physical interpretation of the words being spoken, use body language to accentuate the words, and do this without using a single mouth on their faces. The actual animation of the characters' mouth action should always be among the last things you do.

Lip-synching and animating mouth actions are two different processes. *Lip-synching* is a process that can be done way before any actual animation is ever created. If you use a lip-sheet, such as the ones I use, or maybe a standard set of x-sheets to lip-sync your animation, by the time you're ready to animate the mouth actions, you should have a road map of all the mouth actions you're going to need and at which exact frame they'll be used. This is achieved by knowing the exact moment at which a certain mouth action will appear.

A simple formula exists for this, but it requires you first decide on the actual frame rate at which your film will be playing.

How to Predict the Future: Determining Playback Times and Frames of Specific Mouth Actions

To determine the actual time at which a frame will be displayed, you must divide the number of the frame by the number of frames per second.

Frame/fps = time in seconds

For example, if you're trying to determine the playback time of frame 136, and your movie will be set to play at 12fps, then you divide 136 by 12.

$136 \div 12 = 11.33$ seconds

Frame 136 will occur at exactly 11.33 seconds into the film. This is 00:11:33 in the actual clock timeline. If your movie will be playing at 24fps, and you want to determine at what time frame 136 will be displayed, then you use the same equation. This time, though, instead of dividing it by 12, which was the previous fps, you divide it by 24.

$136 \div 24 = 5.66$ seconds

At 24 frames per second, frame number 136 would actually appear at 00:05:66.

Let's say you want to figure it out the other way around. Perhaps you have a sound file you know will start playing immediately from frame 1 of your movie and you want to determine the frame at which a certain sound or word would first be heard. To do this, you have to know the time at which the event will play. For example, suppose your file has a phrase somewhere in the middle that begins with the word "hello." You determine the word "hello" first appears at exactly 02:30:00. Now you have to convert that time into a number of seconds (at least that's what I do). Two minutes and thirty seconds translates into 150 seconds. To determine the frame number, multiply it against the number of frames per second.

Time in seconds × Fps = Frame number

For example, if my desired fps is 12fps, then my equation would be $150 \times 12 = 1,800$. The word "hello" would first be heard at frame 1800 in my film.

Pop Quiz

Determine and fill in the estimated time of playback for the following frames, according to the various frames per second:

	12fps	24fps	29fps
#386			
#1895			
#2654			

Determine the frame number at which an event occurring at the specified time will play depending on the frame rate (answers are at the end of this chapter):

	12fps	24fps	29fps
03:32:00			
16:50:00			
00:40:00			

Most audio-editing software will tell you the exact duration of an audio file. If it doesn't, then you can always set it to play while you use a stopwatch to time it.

Just Lip It!

My lip-sheets are made to be printed on regular 8.5"×11" paper. They only let me work with 48 frames of film per sheet.

To begin synchronizing, you need either a trusty stopwatch (and a lot of patience) or some kind of waveform editor that enables you to view the waveform and display the actual time at which the current piece of sound is played (this is the preferred method).

Right here is where you must listen to the file for the words being spoken. Determine at what time each word begins and at which point it ends. If, for example, the character begins to speak at 00:30:00 seconds into the voice track and if your movie will play at 12fps, then using one of the previous equations you can determine that 00:30:00 will play at frame 360.

Because the character begins to speak at frame 360 into the movie, there's obviously no reason for us to worry about frames 1–359. The first frame we'll catalogue in our lip-sheet is number 360.

One technique that can help you speed the lip-sync process is to determine and catalogue entire sentences first, and then localize individual words within those sentences.

Suppose the sentence being spoken by a character is, "Wow, this is great!" You already know the sentence first began at frame 360, so you have to determine at which frame the last word in that sentence will end. Now suppose the sentence only lasts for approximately three seconds and ends at frame 396.

This means the sentence would be heard across 36 frames. Each word is composed of one syllable each. And, because there are four syllables to work with, each syllable in that sentence will have nine frames available for mouth actions.

In the Words or Dialogue column of the lip-sheet, you'd write the word "Wow" at frame 360 and fill in the remaining eight frames with a squiggly line. This squiggly line indicates a held cel or a held action and, because the word "Wow" is being spoken from frame 360 all the way to frame 368, that's how far the squiggly line will travel.

Frame	Time	Audio File	Lip-Sync	Dialogue
360	00:30:00	Great.pm3		Wow
361				
362				
363				
364				
365				
366				
367				
368				

At frame 369, you write the word "this" and mark the remaining eight frames as being held. (A total of nine frames for that one syllable word as well.)

369	00:30:75			this
370				
371				
372				
373				
374				
375				
376				
377				

The word "is" will begin at frame 378 and will last for another eight frames, just as the others did.

378	00:31:50				Is
379					
380					
381					
282					
383					
384					
385					
386					
387					

Finally, the word "great" will be written on frame 388 and will be marked as lasting all the way to the final frame, which is frame number 396.

388	00:32:33				Great
389					
390					
391					
392					
393					
394					
395					
396	00:33:00				

That was the easy part. Now you have to determine which mouth actions will be used at any given frame between frames 360 to 396. To do this, you must now interpret each word phonetically. The first word on the agenda is the word "Wow," which is already as phonetic as it's going to get. By looking at it, you can already determine you're going to need an instance of the *w-r* action, followed by the *o* action, and then followed once again by the *w-r* action.

These are three distinct mouth actions, which have to be displayed over a period of nine frames. Taking into consideration the timing of the sentence, you might want to place special emphasis on the first *w* and a small pause or held sound after the last *w* action. You might decide the first *w* action will be displayed for a period of three frames, the *o* action perhaps for a period of two frames, and then for the remaining four frames, you will display the last *w* action. This gives you a rather nice timing, which places a bit of emphasis on the slight pause that occurs between the word "Wow" and the word "this."

Frame	Time	Audio File	Lip-Sync	Dialogue
360	00:30:00	Great.pm3	W	Wow
361				
362				
363			O	
364				
365			W	
366				
367				
368				

The next word in our sentence is "this." Phonetically, "this" can be translated to something along the lines of "dees" or "des." By looking at the interpreted version, you can see you'll need to use the *l-n-d* mouth action, followed by *e,* and then *t-s.*

Again, you're faced with setting up the proper timing for this one-syllable word and the process would continue one syllable at a time until, in the end, you've transcribed and properly timed the mouth actions for every syllable in your sentence. Once this is done, you then move on to the next sentence and start the process all over again.

Frame	Time	Audio File	Lip-Sync	Dialogue
360	00:30:00	Great.pm3	W	Wow
361				
362				
363			O	
364				
365			W	
366				
367				
368				
369	00:30:75		D	This
370				
371			E	
372				
373				
374				
375			S	
376				
377				
378	00:31:50		EE	Is
379				
380				
381			S	
382				
383				
384				
385				
386				
387				
388	00:32:33		R	Great
389				
390			U	
391				
392			A	
393			T	
394			E	
395				
396	00:33:00			

By mastering this technique, you can effectively lip-sync your entire animation well in advance without having to draw a single cartoon or to open Flash. The lip-sync process is something you can do yourself at anytime either before or after the animation work has been performed in your film. Ideally, though, it's recommended that an additional person be responsible for determining the lip-sync, while someone else works on the actual animation of the film. This lets your film move along faster, and because more thought and concentration has been placed on the characters' lip-sync, it lets you deliver a superior quality product. Just remember, when you animate your film, you should animate your characters without mouths, at least during the periods where you know they'll have to talk. Because Flash filmmakers tend to be one-man studios, I recommend you teach yourself this method of lip-sync first. Then, develop it to the point where you don't have to write anything down and you can just as easily place the lips on the characters by listening to the audio packets on each frame of your Flash movie. When sound is set to stream, your audio is broken down into packets and each packet is associated with a specific frame.

Once you're ready to add the mouths to your characters, you can set up a new layer where you will place the mouths on and lock the other layers, so you don't accidentally place the mouths on the wrong layers or modify the other graphical elements on the stage.

Each mouth action you'll use can be converted into Flash graphic symbols, thus creating a reusable library of mouths. Because you created lip-sheets that tell you which mouth actions will be displayed at any given frame, placing the proper mouths on the characters is a simple drag-and-drop operation.

TIP

Because only nine basic mouth actions exist, you should create a set of actions for every character that will speak in your film. If your character will speak while in profile view or, perhaps, in 45-degree angle view, then you should also anticipate this. Create mouth action sets that can be used whenever those types of angles are performed by your characters.

Be a Pro: Don't Sabotage Your Own Work

One of the worst things you can ever do for an animated cartoon is to cheat the lip-synchronization process. Many amateurs (and even some pros) believe they can cheat their way around lip-synching by placing objects, such as a microphone or a piece of jewelry, in front of their characters' mouths or perhaps even a cast shadow so dark it's impossible to see their lips moving when they talk. They also have their characters speak with their backs toward the *fourth wall*. They draw their characters in angles so wide you can't make out their faces—much less their mouths—and they even create special aerial views, so all we see is the top of their characters' heads as they speak, all so they don't have to do any lip-sync.

NOTE

The fourth wall is referred to in showbiz as the wall behind which the audience watches the action unfold. When you go to the theater, there's a wall at the back of the stage, a wall on the left side of the stage, and a wall on the right side. An imaginary fourth wall is at the front of the stage. If this wall were a physical wall like the other three, we couldn't see the action that takes place on the stage. Therefore, this fourth wall is invisible and we, as the audience, sit behind it, watching the actors and the characters go about their business. On occasion, you see instances on television where a character directs his dialogue toward the audience rather than to the other characters. This is called breaking the fourth wall.

These techniques should be avoided at all cost. Arguably, in some instances, many of these techniques, such as the cast shadows or wide angles, might be used to create some sense of dramatic tension, but they should never be used for the purpose of avoiding lip-sync. The only thing this tells the audience about you is you're either too lazy to lip-sync your work properly or you simply don't know how. Well, my friends, now you have no excuse!

Anime Dialogue: The Art of Getting Away with Terrible Lip-Sync

In *anime,* a form of Japanese animation designed to be created under extremely low budgets, cartoon dialogue is spoken by way of three mouth actions, which are sequenced in a way that makes the characters look like they might be saying something in a foreign language. Because we subconsciously believe the original language was something other than English, however, we don't expect anime cartoons to be properly synchronized to the dialogue any more than we expect the dialogue from an old Jackie Chan movie, which has also been dubbed to English, to be in sync.

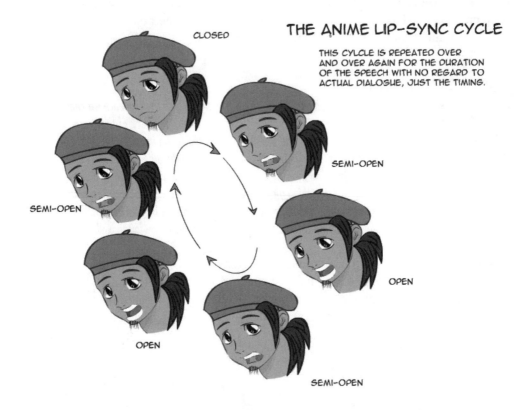

CLOSED

THE ANIME LIP-SYNC CYCLE

THIS CYLCE IS REPEATED OVER AND OVER AGAIN FOR THE DURATION OF THE SPEECH WITH NO REGARD TO ACTUAL DIALOGUE, JUST THE TIMING.

SEMI-OPEN

SEMI-OPEN

OPEN

OPEN

SEMI-OPEN

Anime-style lip-sync is rooted in the theory that translations into other languages will be made much easier and, by not having to pay someone to lip-sync, production cost can be kept to a bare minimum. No importance is ever really placed on the actual words the characters are supposed to be saying. Because these animated cartoons will be dubbed into other languages, having synchronized mouth actions is the least of worries for the animators.

This makes me wonder if the dialogue in the Kung Fu movies I grew up with was ever really recorded using real Chinese or Japanese dialogue or if the actors simply move their mouths at random during their "speaking" parts, so dialogue could be translated and dubbed over later. Hey, it's a thought.

The anime lip-sync technique is something you might want to consider whenever you're working with an extremely low budget and you want to deliver your product faster than usual. If your animation style happens to fall under the anime category, then by all means feel free to use this technique. There's no penalty. Because of the high popularity of anime and our constant exposure to foreign programming dubbed to the English language, we've become conditioned to the whole "dubbed over chop-saki flick" type of dialogue. This isn't a technique you should employ when the overall quality of the film is of major importance, though. You should always strive to lip-sync your cartoon to its native language.

Sound in Flash

Last, but not least, I feel I should mention a little something about sound in Flash. Only two types of sound settings are used in Flash for cartoon purposes: event sounds and streaming sounds. *Event sounds* are sounds that are required to download in full prior to playback. In cartoon animation, the recommendation is that event sounds be kept to a minimum and only be used for Foley purposes.

NOTE

Foley *is a procedure named after its creator, Jack Foley, and applied to film during postproduction to enhance many visual effects with sounds. Perhaps a character moves his hand real fast and you want to enhance that action with a quick "Zip!" type of sound. Perhaps your character punches a guy and you want to enhance it by adding the "swoosh, pop, crack!" sound to that action. When you're performing Foley work on a film, you're basically applying little sound effects here and there that make the action on the film pop out. The creaking of a door, footsteps, a bell ringing when a light bulb lights up above a person's head, fire burning, rain falling, water dripping — these are all forms of Foley work. Keep all your Foley effects as small in size as possible and be sure to preload them in full before your film begins to play. The Foley procedure should be the last thing on your mind, so finish your film first, and then worry about all those wonderful little effects.*

Any other sound should be presented in the form of streaming sound. When you set your sound to stream, you're basically attaching the sound to the timeline. Depending on the frame rate of your movie, your sound will be broken down into extremely small packets of audio that literally are attached to every single frame in your film.

As a frame is reached, the packet of audio attached to that frame will be played back to you. This not only allows for near-perfect audio/video synchronization, but it also lets your film start playing even though the entire audio file might not be fully downloaded. Being able to render a file as it downloads is known as *streaming*.

Any voice tracks, sound tracks, or ambience tracks you use in your Flash film should always be set to streaming. Even if your interest isn't in making the files stream over the Web, you should do this to ensure a decent A/V sync.

NOTE

A/V is showbiz slang for Audio/Video. It refers to combining a video sequence with multiple audio tracks.

Summary

▶ Exposure sheets are basically blueprints that tell you where everything in your film is—from the actual cels to the mouth actions performed by your characters' dialogue. X-sheets can be modified to suit your own particular needs or they can be bought in a generic format for use in any type of production.

▶ Lip-sheets are a type of modified x-sheet, which contain only the bare essentials for organizing and creating your characters' lip-sync.

▶ When characters speak, they must perform the dialogue in the same manner that would be expected if a live actor were speaking the words. Cartoon phonetics are based around nine basic mouth actions. These nine actions can be combined with each other to create more complex sounds and entire words.

▶ Tugging a mouth action involves taking a mouth action and stretching and squashing it across the face to enhance the way a certain sound is performed.

▶ To stream a file means the file will play as it downloads. When a sound is set to stream, that sound is broken up into small packets, which are bonded to individual frames. As a frame is reached, the small audio packet is played back. When you synchronize your character's actions to the sound track or voice tracks, you're synchronizing those actions to the audio packet assigned to any individual frame.

▶ Learn to draw the generic mouth actions and learn to perform those actions using your own original characters.

▶ To determine the time at which an actual event will occur, you must divide the frame number by the number of frames per second at which the movie will play. The result is in the form of actual seconds, which must be converted into clock time.

  Example: frame 360 ÷ 12fps = 30 seconds; 30 seconds = 00:30:00 in clock time.

▶ To determine the frame at which a specific moment occurs, you must first convert that moment into actual seconds. Then you need to multiply the number of seconds by the number of frames per second. The result is the number of the frame at which that event will take place.

  Example: 01:00:00 first must be converted into 60 seconds. Then 60 seconds × 12fps = frame 720.

▶ Here are the answers to the pop quiz:

  Determine and fill in the estimated time of playback for the following frames according to the various frames per second:

	12fps	24fps	29fps
#386	00:32:16	00:16:08	00:13:31
#1895	(157.92 secs) 02:37:92	(78.96 secs) 01:18:96	(65.34 secs) 01:05:34
#2654	(221.17 secs) 03:41:17	(110.58 secs) 01:50:58	(91.52 secs) 01:31:52

Determine the frame number at which an event occurring at the specified time will play depending on the frame rate:

	12fps	24fps	29fps
03:32:00	#2544	#5088	#6184
16:50:00	#12120	#24240	#29290
00:40:00	#480	#960	#1160

► When it comes to lip-sync, avoid sabotaging your own work by resorting to cheap tricks. Always make an honest effort to synchronize your characters' mouth actions to their own dialogue. If all else fails, you can always resort to the anime-style lip-sync procedure.

► If you use event sounds in your film, use them only in the Foley process and always be sure to preload those sounds before your movie starts. That way, your film won't suffer any lag because of having to stop in the middle of the film to download certain sounds. Your voice track and your music tracks should be single uninterrupted files, which play from the beginning until the end of a particular scene.

PART

III

Production

CHAPTER
13

Scripting

Because of the close relationship among Flash, the Internet, and the digital world, when someone refers to the terms "script" or "scripting," the first thing that pops into people's minds is a bunch of mathematical gibberish with parentheses, followed by greater than or equal to symbols, and a dialect that might as well be written in Klingon.

In animation, any type of programming used is an unnecessary little commodity, which you can employ if you want to add any sort of interactivity to your projects. But animation is about telling stories visually. In any type of production—whether or not it's animated—a script is the most important part of the entire project. In this chapter, you learn about writing a script in the standard feature-length film format, also known as the *Master Scene Screenplay* or the *Submission Screenplay*. As you learn how a feature-length film is written, you can learn to apply those techniques on a smaller scale, such as Flash films or short films, and make your franchises much more appealing and profitable.

The Master Scene Format

Several script formats are in the media, but the Master Scene format is considered the standard and the most widely accepted format in the film industry. The script is written using a scene-by-scene process and follows a strict three-act structure in both the movie and each individual scene.

The Master Scene format, however, isn't the final script involved in the making of a film. In animation, for example, the director either creates or commissions someone to draw the storyboards based on the script. For many animators, storyboards are their version of a production screenplay, used as their final guide for animating the scenes.

In conventional filmmaking, storyboards are also customary, but their purpose is for the cinematographers to plan out how to perform a shot. In most cases, an additional script is created, which makes up the final blueprint for the film. This script is known as the *Production Script,* which is usually rewritten by the director and contains specific camera instructions, numbered shots, and any other directorial instructions that might be necessary. Most writers needn't worry about writing the production script, but instead focus on telling the story. They leave the shots and technical instructions for the directors. After all, the director's interpretation of your script usually dictates how a film is shot or animated.

Oh, the Book Was Way Better Than the Movie

The Great Gatsby, Lord of the Flies, The Chocolate War, and *The Scarlet Letter* all have the same thing in common: the book was better than the movie. At least that's the response when titles like these are discussed.

Creative people often argue that writing, or any other form of artwork, should ascend from the artist's soul and be created for the pleasure of the artist before anyone else. The sad reality is, in today's commercial world, which is the entertainment industry, the product is created to appeal to a targeted audience to make the most profit. Whether or not the ideas or the concepts themselves are derived from an honest artistic effort, any film, cartoon, animated short, or form of entertainment media put into circulation is a franchise created to entertain an audience, while making as much profit as possible.

People create cartoons, paintings, films, and write stories for as many reasons as there are stars in the universe. And, the idea of gaining some sort of profit from the work is among the top ten on the list.

The reason much of the work created by people we consider as true artists didn't become well known until after their deaths is no mystery. The artists created these works for themselves and, truthfully, public opinion was the least of their worries. Selling their work or even showing it to anyone was a rare occasion.

No one can teach you how to be an artist. This is something that often comes to you in the form of natural talent. Screenwriting is based around structure and formulas, which is similar to the art of cartooning, and it, too, can be learned and developed as a skill.

Writing Begins with an Idea

For you to be able to write something, you must first have an idea. To many people, ideas come with no effort whatsoever, while others, who aren't blessed with strong imaginations, have to research their subjects and organize their thoughts. Although having a great imagination is a valuable asset, with proper research and planning, anyone can develop and spin their own stories quite successfully, with or without the natural talent.

For an idea to have some sort of merit, it must revolve around a conflict. Conflict is what makes the world go round. A story with no conflict isn't a story at all, but merely a narrative.

Conflict

The first step in coming up with a solid idea to work from is to create a conflict. In short-form screenwriting, such as that done for cartoon animation like *Tom and Jerry, Ren and Stimpy,* and *Bugs Bunny,* conflicts are usually kept simple and straightforward.

Farrah Fawcett is in town for her cousin's party and Johnny Bravo has to meet her. The only problem is there's a guy who won't let Johnny into the party.

Sylvester the cat is hungry and knows of a little bird that was left behind by his owner while she went shopping. The problem is this: how will Sylvester get to the bird without getting mauled to death by the giant bulldog that was left in charge?

While structure and format are of great importance in screenwriting, the conflict drives the story and moves it forward. Conflict isn't always physical; it can also be emotional. In fact, emotional conflict often leads to physical conflicts and vice versa, which are great if your goal is to write complete feature-length films or series. Any good story is based on a struggle to overcome an obstacle or adversity or to obtain something that is desired. Without conflict, you have no story to tell.

Getting the Idea

Ideas are everywhere. If you ever suffer from writer's block, make the public library your first stop. Spend the day looking at ugly old microfiche. You're bound to find a million stories to work from as you spin your own tales.

All sorts of stories are available at your fingertips, in magazines, newspapers, and, yes, even on microfiche. These stories are bound to get your mental juices flowing. Think about the people and the situations. Find the conflicts and develop your story from them. Use your own characters and put them in that situation. A story developed from an idea can be anything from dramatic to comedic and, in the end, your story needn't have anything to do with the actual people who were originally involved in that conflict. Just remember, there's no such thing as writer's block, only the inability to commit to an idea.

Not too long ago, a little product named Napster made the headlines as the heavy metal band Metallica initiated a lawsuit campaign against the company alleging that the sharing of MP3 music was a copyright infringement. Bob Cesca, an independent Flash animator from Pennsylvania, was able to spin from that conflict a phenomenally rated parody called *Napster Bad!*

Ideas come from everywhere. They might come from a conversation you had years ago or from personal experience, or from a dream, a fantasy, a fear. Ideas can come directly from the pages of written history or you can create your own alternate future. Emotion-driven ideas are the greatest because they enable you to express your true feeling about someone or something: love, hate, anger, passion, desire for revenge.

Getting ideas is easy. If you have trouble coming up with ideas, remember the following steps:

▶ Search the Web, go to the library, or look through your books and magazines.

▶ Get a notebook and pencil, and jot down any ideas you find.

▶ Narrow your ideas to simple conflicts and think about how a character would go about overcoming that conflict. Would there be other characters to stop him or to support him? Does the character have a love interest or is his action driven by other motives, such as hunger or comfort? What should that character's reward be if he overcomes that conflict?

▶ Collect at least ten good ideas, choose one, and then stick to it.

Sensuality and Dramatic Action: the Yin and Yang of Filmmaking

Many advocates constantly fight against the use of violence in cartoons, film, and theater, but sensuality and violence in filmmaking doesn't necessarily imply that films and cartoons are created with gratuitous violence and hardcore porn in mind. Many people in the entertainment industry consider these elements passion and tension, romance and dramatic action, sensitivity and struggle, or flirting and slapstick. No matter how these terms are sugarcoated or to what extent they're applied to a story, sensuality and dramatic action are nearly the most important ingredients in creating anything with some kind of entertainment value.

In Disney's *The Lion King,* a young lion cub must not only see his father trampled to death by wildebeests, he must also struggle against all sorts of adversities as he grows up and away from his pride. He battles physiological violence as he comes of age, sexual tension with the female lion, and physical violence as he escapes the hyenas and fights his uncle to the death. Without sensuality and dramatic action, theaters might as well sell caffeine pills instead of popcorn at the snack bar.

Sensuality and dramatic action can be as innocent as Tom competing against another cat to see who can catch Jerry, so they can give him to the pretty girl cat next door and win her affection. And how about Droopy the dog, who must always compete against the giant pit bull character, so in the end, he can get a kiss from a pretty girl?

Sensuality and dramatic action needn't always be present at the same time to make a script effective. Most of the time, Bugs Bunny just beats his enemies silly in a humorous and entertaining manner. Poor Elmer Fudd, he never gets a break.

Chilli Willi, the penguin, is often motivated by hunger or cold weather. He won't hesitate to take a bite from your leg if he thinks it looks like a giant chicken leg. This little penguin has been known to beat a polar bear to the point of surrender, and then skin him alive, so he can have a nice little fur coat to wear.

Without sensuality and dramatic action, the driving forces behind human nature, there would be neither *Macbeth* nor *Romeo and Juliet.* There would be no *Lion King, Toy Story, Dracula, Pocahontas, Transformers, GI Joe, The Powerpuff Girls, Frankenstein*— heck, there wouldn't even be a Mister Rogers!

It doesn't matter if you're writing an innocent children's cartoon like *Woody Woodpecker,* an action-packed adventure like *Rambo,* or a psychological drama like *Twelve Angry Men.* Sensuality and dramatic action play an important role in the entertainment value of a product.

Writing on a Budget

Think about the budget that will be involved in making your film. Obviously, if you're writing a film you plan to create single-handedly, the cost of the film will be the actual time you're willing to invest making it. The complexity of the animation, special effects, and amount of detail must be considered when you write your scenes. Why would you write a film that requires 30 different settings when you might only be able to afford two or three?

If a live-action film is to be produced by a team with a limited budget, you must consider that you might not have enough money for certain special effects or be able to afford hauling around a cast and crew to different locations.

If the film is to be animated, the same rule applies. Will you have enough money in the budget or do you have the time to design all the backgrounds, props, and other graphical elements you'll need? Ambient music and sound effects also cost money. Can you produce all the required sounds yourself or can you afford to have a sound engineer make them for you?

What about voices? If your characters will talk during your film, can you hire professional voice actors or will you rely on friends for that task? Do you have the time to spend lip-synching the characters' mouths to the voice track? Can you afford to hire an assistant to do this? There's nothing wrong with nonspeaking characters. Tom and Jerry don't speak, so the studio saves a bundle by not having to synchronize voices to lips, and the nonspeaking characters can be seen by anyone in the world without translating the language.

In Flash animation, probably the most important part of writing within the available budget is understanding how complex the actions of the characters will be to animate. If your movie has many fight scenes, can you play them out convincingly by using and reusing graphic symbols or will you need a more complex form of animation that requires full frames to be drawn? Can you afford to go the full-animation route or will you have to restrain your characters' actions to those that can be reasonably animated by using Flash symbols in a relative short time?

Even if you're doing all the work yourself, there's still a budget involved in the amount of time you're willing to invest in your film. Look at your chosen idea and consider the amount of time and/or money you can invest in it, and then decide whether the idea is worth pursuing after all. If you decide to go through with your idea, keep your budget in mind as you write. Think about how complex the events will be and whether you can afford to have certain scenes. Think of alternative ways of performing an action. In short, always think of the budget involved to make this film and avoid writing anything you can't afford.

Anatomy of a Screenplay

All good films are composed of three distinct parts: a beginning, a middle, and an end.

To help explain the screenwriting process, I'm including the Episode One script for my series *Without You*. Feel free to turn to this script later in this chapter at any time as you work on your own writing. When I work on a series, my approach is usually to write the entire screenplay in feature-length format, and then break it down into several episodes. You needn't do this, but I find that laying out the entire storyline ahead of time enables me to concentrate on putting out the episodes faster and it helps me avoid having to write each individual script in advance. When you learn about structure and composition, though, you can apply them to your own films and animated stories, no matter what their length.

ANATOMY OF A SCREENPLAY

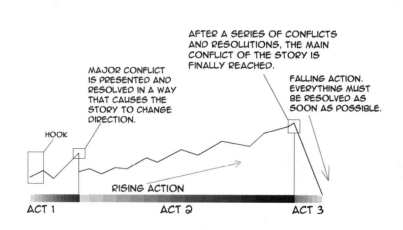

AFTER A SERIES OF CONFLICTS AND RESOLUTIONS, THE MAIN CONFLICT OF THE STORY IS FINALLY REACHED.

MAJOR CONFLICT IS PRESENTED AND RESOLVED IN A WAY THAT CAUSES THE STORY TO CHANGE DIRECTION.

FALLING ACTION. EVERYTHING MUST BE RESOLVED AS SOON AS POSSIBLE.

HOOK

RISING ACTION

ACT 1   ACT 2   ACT 3

Act One — The Beginning

Rent any popular feature-length film and grab some popcorn. Watch the first ten minutes of the movie, which include some of the most interesting and action-packed scenes you'll see for a while. The purpose of these scenes is to grab your attention as soon as possible and, literally, hook you, so you don't change the channel or walk out of the theater. These first ten minutes of film are known as the *hook*.

Act One is the beginning of the story. Aside from hooking the audience, the main purpose of Act One is to introduce all your main characters and establish the setting. Act One usually runs for the first 30 minutes of the film, during which a major conflict is presented, which will be resolved in a way that changes the direction of the story.

Now, rewind your movie and play it again. This time watch the film for 30 minutes. Remember the scenes involved in the hook and notice, for the remaining 20 minutes or so, the filmmakers try to give you all the information you need to know, such as locations and circumstances. They introduce you to all the main characters, including the villain, although they might not tell you who he (or she) is right away.

Filmmakers introduce you to all the main characters, so you can start getting to know and relate to them right away. During Act One, a film seems headed in a specific direction but, as you reach that 30-minute mark, something happens that causes the story to change directions completely.

The hero might be accused of a crime he didn't commit and sentenced to prison, where he must find a way to prove his innocence. Perhaps the father of a lion cub who was destined to be king is murdered. The cub is now banished from his homeland, and must grow up and adapt on his own.

Perhaps a young hacker named Neo, who apparently was on the run from the feds, will suddenly awaken and be told his world isn't real, but a Matrix. Neo must now deal with living in the real world, which has been overrun by machines. Talk about a drastic change in direction!

Whatever the change in direction is, it will happen sometime around the 30-minute mark—give or take a few minutes.

Act Two — The Middle

Act Two comprises the majority of the film's substance. By this time, you know all the main characters and all the important settings where the story takes place. Now, you can concentrate on what's really important: the story. At this point, the story also changes into the direction the rest of the film will move and a main conflicting force is presented for the hero to try to resolve.

Act Two consists of a series of events that eventually lead the hero(es) into coming face-to-face with the ultimate part of his (their) conflicting force. This confrontation leads to Act Three, which is the resolution.

Perhaps an innocent man, sentenced to life in prison, suffers through a series of adversities while, at the same time, he teaches himself the law. When he manages to get an appeal, he once again comes before the law to prove his innocence so he can be free.

The lion cub lives through a series of events and adversities, and forms relationships that mold him into a fully grown lion. Now he's ready to return home and take his rightful place as the Lion King, but not before facing his evil uncle and fighting him to the death.

After a series of events, Neo finally reaches the point where he's ready to accept that he's "the one." He decides to stand up against the agents Smiths and take back the Matrix.

The second act of every film is a series of events—some major, some small— but they all build up and up, until they finally reach that high point where the hero must face and resolve the main conflict.

Get yourself another bucket of popcorn and sit through the rest of the movie. Notice how every scene presents a new conflict; some conflicts are merely verbal discussions. Other conflicts involve violence, which must be resolved to move on to the next conflict. As the characters move from one conflict to another, they come closer to the final, ultimate conflict. Will the hero fail or will he prevail? One thing is for sure, one way or another, this conflict will be resolved.

Act Three — The Resolution

The third act of any good film is the shortest. Act Three starts immediately after the conflict is resolved. Its purpose is to close any loose ends and resolve any other subplot you might have left hanging around. Act Three is usually no more than ten minutes long (anything longer than ten minutes or so is considered dwelling and makes the film boring).

By the time you reach Act Three, all the tension is gone. The conflict has been resolved and everyone either lives happily ever after or they don't. Period.

If a film takes too long to explain what happens to the people during the aftermath, chances are you are watching one of the sorriest films ever made.

If our hero manages to prove his innocence, he gets to go home, perhaps to his wife who has been patiently waiting for him. We don't care whether he lives to have grandchildren, or learns a new trade, starts a business, and all sorts of stuff that will require another hour of film to show. We've watched him prepare himself to beat the system for nearly two hours and now that he has, we're satisfied and happy for him. He has beaten his demon and let's leave it at that.

The lion cub has grown up and defeated his greatest adversary. In Act Three, he has become the Lion King. He captures the heart of the girl lion and they have a baby cub. We don't care what happens to the baby cub when he grows up. All we care about is that our hero has finally defeated his enemy and taken back his land. The end.

Neo has also defeated the agents in *The Matrix,* which is the reason we sat in the theater for 120 minutes. Neo has served his purpose and there's nothing left they can possibly show you to interest you in sitting there for another 120 minute or even 12 minutes. We don't care how Neo goes about awakening the people, we don't care how long it takes, and we don't care if he goes on to have nine kids with Trinity. All we care about is that the conflict is resolved and, now that it has been, it's time to go home.

Act Three must instill a sense of closure within the audience and it must do so in as little time as possible. The audience must know everything was resolved and be left with a sense of satisfaction. This way, the memories the audience takes with them are of our hero's struggle to overcome his adversities, not the boring aftermath.

A Quick Note on Short-Form Screenwriting

Short films, episodic cartoons, and cartoon shorts all follow the same structure as feature films, only in a more compressed format. Act One begins with a hook, presents you with main characters, and gives you all the information you need within the first minute or two. A typical first act for a short-form script goes a little something like this:

"The city of Townsville . . . IS UNDER ATTACK!" Bam, with no hesitation on the animator's behalf, a giant green blob appears in the middle of downtown and is destroying the town. Here come the Powerpuff Girls to save the day. They defeat the monster, but the supervillain responsible for putting the monster there has zapped one of the girls into a frog, kidnapped the mayor, and gotten away.

Act One is over. The cartoon began with a major event that hooked the audience into wanting to watch the rest of it. The main characters were presented. Then, the story changed direction because the villain kidnapped the mayor and transformed one of the girls into a frog. The Powerpuff Girls must find a way to restore their sister back to her human state and to rescue the mayor.

In Act Two, the girls go through a series of trial and error until the opportunity arises for them to face the villain. They will defeat him and, perhaps, even restore their sister back to human form.

Act Three consists of a quick breakdown of the aftermath. Perhaps the girls realize they didn't rescue the mayor after all and we'll see him on an island somewhere, being chased by a group of female Amazonian headhunters. The girls will share a quick anecdote relating to their experience and assure us the cartoon is over. The end, period.

No matter how short your film is, always be sure to include all three acts. Otherwise, despite how much effort you put into the characters and their design, the end result is a waste of time for you and for your audience.

Scenes

Scenes are complete screenplays in and of themselves. Scenes, too, are composed of a beginning, a middle, and an end. They always contain a conflict and rising action, which leads to the characters taking the conflict head-on and resolving it. Once the conflict is resolved, the scene is over and we move on to the next scene.

A typical scene in a movie revolves around characters being presented with a conflict. For example, "Dude, where my car?" The characters in this scene find themselves with no car and have no memory of where they might have left it. The conflict is trying to remember where they left the car. Eventually, they realize they can't remember, but they decide to put themselves in the same state of mind as the night before and try to locate the vehicle. Once they agree on that plan, the conflict for this scene is resolved. Then, we can move on to the next scene, which also presents the characters with another conflict.

"Man, I don't want to walk. Let's hitchhike." In this scene, they're faced with the conflict of trying to get a car to stop and pick them up. Nobody does—in fact, they get run over a few times. They give up. "Dude, I think we'd better walk." That conflict is resolved, and then we can move on to the next scene.

In a typical cartoon, a scene is often referred to as a *gag,* but not always. A typical gag goes something like this: The coyote has yet another opportunity to capture the roadrunner. He sets a trap, thus creating a conflict for the roadrunner. The roadrunner uses his speed and agility to turn the trap against the coyote. This resolves the conflict and allows the next scene or gag to begin.

Think of a scene as a brick on a house. Each of these bricks is a complete little story by itself. Writing a screenplay is like building a brick house because you're stacking a bunch of independent bricks on top of each other, making them form an even bigger structure.

Laying Out the Foundation

I decided I want my story to be about a young couple and their struggle to stay together, despite their differences. These are conflicts that deal with human emotion, which are almost always well received by the audience. This is why I write the type of stories I do. However, the conflict is pretty vague at the moment, so I have to make it more precise. How are these people so different—racially, socially, intellectually? Why not all of the above? Let's make them as opposite as they can be.

My idea is for a story that's loosely based on a personal experience of mine, which is the easiest type of story to write. But, just because a story is based on a true event doesn't necessarily mean it must be an autobiographical account.

What about a poor guy and a rich girl? She can be a college graduate, while he's a high-school dropout. Perhaps the guy works hard to support his family, while the girl has been handed everything on a silver platter all her life. Let's go with something like this.

The Premise

The *premise* of a film is the idea put into as few words as possible—one or two lines at the most. The premise should capture the entire essence of what you're about to create.

After a few weeks of playing around with the idea in my mind, I decided the premise to my story would be as follows: *One man's struggle to overcome social barriers and be with the woman he loves.*

Determining the premise of your story is one of the most important steps in its development. If you don't know what your story is about, how can you write it?

Above all, I want this film to be a love story. Everyone has felt love at some point in his or her life, so I want to use that emotion to my advantage. Also, because much of the work on the Web is on the wacky side, I think this type of story will be refreshing to a more contemporary audience.

TIP

Artistic integrity aside, remember, a film is a franchise, and if a profit is to be gained from it, then you must have a target audience in mind. And that isn't all. If you want to maximize the potential revenue to be gained from this "product," then you must create it so it can appeal to the majority, not a small niche of cult followers. If you're only making your film for personal entertainment or as a hobby, cult followings are great, but nine times out of ten they don't pay the bills.

I still have to decide on the degree of violence I want to have in my story. Although I love action films, I feel a story should have a decent plot and not just a bunch of gratuitous *chop saki* or placing a bomb on a bus, just so I can have a bunch of cool chase scenes, loud explosions, and maybe a building on fire.

Balancing the Sensuality to Dramatic Action Ratio

As I previously stated, I love action films when the violence itself isn't the driving force. One such film, which immediately comes to mind, is *Crouching Tiger, Hidden Dragon*. While the film itself contains many beautifully choreographed and intense fight scenes, these are merely props used to enhance the storytelling. *Crouching Tiger, Hidden Dragon* is a beautifully told love story and a great example of effectively balancing the elements of sensuality and dramatic Action.

Other films, such as *Bloodsport,* choose to make violence their driving force. The guy wants to win a tournament, so he will battle to the death against other guys who want the same thing. Sure, he may meet a girl along the way and, perhaps, fall in love with her, but in this case the sensuality element is merely a prop and is nearly invisible. The story could just as easily be told without the girl. Most animated cartoons also raise their violence levels to overpower the sensuality element because it's easier to win over a mainstream audience with violence than with sensuality. In Mister Rogers' neighborhood, something terrible is always happening in the land of the puppets (dramatic action) and rarely do you see any form of romance or displays of affection (sensuality).

Animated cartoons are more often about someone saving the galaxy from a supervillain, about physically defeating or eluding an enemy, or about a character going through a series of physical challenges to reach his or her goal. Few cartoons choose to emphasize the sensuality element and, even when they do, they still have a healthy portion of violence somewhere in there. *Popeye* is a great example of this because, in most cases, the emphasis is placed on the attraction between Popeye and Olive Oyl. In many instances, Popeye competes against Bluto for Olive Oyl's affection or to keep her from being harmed.

Some forms of programming choose to focus strictly on the sensuality element to such an extreme that violence is almost nonexistent. *Ally McBeal* is a great example of a show revolving around sexual tension. Any form of violence on the show is usually either on an emotional or intellectual level, played out in a courtroom and resolved though verbal discussion.

I've decided I'll go with the sensuality over violence approach but, because I'm a big fan of action films, I do want my characters involved in a physical struggle occasionally. In fact, I want my main character to be either a boxer or a kickboxer. Whatever I choose, I'm making a commitment at this point that, for this film, I won't let the violence overshadow the love story (the sensual element).

Determine Your Main Characters

Although it's important to know your characters as well as possible, it isn't necessary to write a ten-page report on every character like many people want you to believe. In fact, I normally start with figuring out who and what will be the key players in the story, and then worry about their personalities later.

One technique I use is to imagine my friends and other people I know as my characters and write them in to the story, with a few minor embellishments and exaggerations. I'm also not good with names, so one technique I use is to find first and last names at random in phone books (this technique is more common than you might think). Many writers collect phone books from various locations they visit around the country. For example, if your film is based in Canada, you're most likely to find names a typical Canadian might have if you look in a Canadian phone book. In the United States, the population is so diverse, you're likely to find unique names that are indigenous to specific regions of the country. Need a name for someone native to Louisiana, New York, or Missouri? Look in the phone books for those states and you'll see a clear difference in people's names (for the most part) because a good 75 percent of the people are native to the region.

Another thing that personally influences the way I create a character for this kind of film is I hate the stereotypical image Hollywood has created for Hispanics. I'd love to write something that portrays my culture in a more positive light, so Number One on my list is to make the main character and his family Hispanic. I'll name the hero of my story Odesio—Spanish for Odysseus—who was the hero in one of my favorite books, Homer's *The Odyssey*.

Any good hero needs a confidant. This applies to any story-driven film. He needs someone he can talk to; otherwise, we have no way of knowing how he feels. I'll give him a lifelong friend, someone he can talk to and bond with. The friend's name isn't too important now—only his purpose is important. Perhaps I'll also use this character as comic relief.

Of course, I need to think about the leading lady as well. At this point, all I know is she's some rich girl, way above Odesio's social class. I don't do much as far as her initial character development because I'll mold her character based on a type. Basing a character on a *type* is the easiest way to create a character. For example, if the character is a short boxing promoter, you might consider a Danny Devito type. If the character is a nerdy guy with a terrible sense of humor and an annoying speech pattern, you could refer to him as a Woody Allen type. In this case, my leading lady will be based on a Soleil Moon Frye/Melissa Joan Hart type, whom I'll call Elena.

Our hero needs an adversary. In my case, I find his true adversary is his blind desire to achieve wealth, but that doesn't mean he can't also have a physical adversary or rival. I'll make this rival Elena's ex-boyfriend. This way, they can have a mutual objective to fight over.

I continue to create my characters concentrating on their relationship to each other, rather than their specific habits or mannerisms.

Minor characters don't require as much thought. If they're necessary, just slap them on to the script and give them a name from a phone book. If they need a personality, then develop it as you go. Most actors are pretty good about developing a character's personality into something unique, so a good deal of that personality comes from the voice-over artist or the actor's performance.

Once all the initial work is done, my main cast list is as follows:

▶ Odesio is a 25-year-old high-school dropout, who works to support his family as a taxi driver. He lives with his grandmother Maria, a housekeeper, and two nephews, a set of twins named Julio and Cesar. His best friend is a black male named Robert, but everyone calls him by his nickname, Taco. At this point, I'm also considering starting him off in the story with a girlfriend, whom he later dumps.

▶ Elena Watkins, the heroine, lives with her wealthy parents. Elena has a brother named Chris, who is the best friend of Sean.

▶ Sean is Elena's rich ex-boyfriend who wants her back. Sean is the son of Alice Romano, a powerful business magnate, who is an associate of Elena's father.

I continue to see how all my characters can relate to each other and, once I'm satisfied, I move on to my next step, which is to plot my story.

Setting Up the Framework

As mentioned earlier, a screenplay is a story composed of three acts. Each act is composed of a number of scenes, and each scene is once again composed of three individual parts, which makes them complete little stories by themselves.

Once you develop your premise, determine your main conflict, and create your characters, you've laid out the foundation. The next step is to set up the framework. Why does this sound like we're building a house?

When you set up your framework, you're writing a synopsis of your entire film. I use the screenplay anatomy as a guide and remember the three-act structure. I'm also thinking about the conflict and how it will be resolved. Another thing I think about is the hook I'll use to get the audience interested in watching the film. To do this, I write my story within the span of a page or two. This is usually referred to as writing a *synopsis*. The point of a synopsis is to tell your story in as few words as possible, thus pinpointing all the major events to take place in your film. This, too, can take me a couple weeks to complete if I'm writing a feature-length film, but it's time well spent if the audience likes the story.

If you're writing a short animated cartoon, you can usually finish this in one day and, most likely, you can do it within a single page or less.

After a few weeks of planning the structure of my story, I put it onto paper, and Episode One reads as follows:

```
FADE IN


        EXT. KEEMAH, TX / DAY

        Tourists and locals alike are enjoying this beautiful
        summer day. A unique taxicab, fashioned from an old
        Mustang convertible, steals the scene. Its driver is a
        25-year-old man named ODESIO. Flirting with the tourists
        as he searches for his next fare, ODESIO comes up to a
        small lunch wagon parked by the beach and honks his horn
        at his best friend, TACO, a 23-year-old man who tends to
        his customers.


                        ODESIO
                Hey, buddy!


                        TACO
                Qué onda, loco!
```

                    ODESIO
        Hey, you want to go see about getting
        in on some of that action tonight?

                    TACO
        Sorry, no can do, grizzly. Kind of
        swamped right now. Besides, I spoke with
        RAUL this morning and he said you're in.

                    ·ODESIO
        Did he say how much?

                    TACO
        Nahhh. You know him. Dude's got
        more tricks than a 12-toed monkey.
        I say we ask first before we commit
        to anything.

                    ODESIO
        So, where's it going to be?

TACO walks up to the car and speaks in a more
subtle tone.

                    TACO
        Are you sure you want to do this? Been
        quite a while, bro.

                    ODESIO
        Don't worry about it, got it all under
        control. Besides, I'm already two months
        late on the rent.

                    TACO
        Hey listen, TONEA is going to want to
        go, too. You want me to pick her up on
        the way?

                    ODESIO
        Yeah, sure.

Two very attractive female tourists walk up to the cab.

> LADY TOURIST #1
> Excuse me. Are you on duty?

> ODESIO
> Sure, ladies. What can I do you for?

> LADY TOURIST #2
> We need to get back to our hotel. Can
> you take us?

> ODESIO
> Hop right in.

> TACO
> Dude, can I come?

> ODESIO
> No way, cubby. I thought you said you
> were busy. You should have got in when I
> told you to.

ODESIO drives away, honking his horn, which plays
"La Cucaracha."

> TACO
> Why, you doity rat!

> CUT TO:

INT. WAREHOUSE / NIGHT

The run-down warehouse is packed with people.

A 45-year-old sleazy, short, and fat bookie, RAUL
walks around. RAUL walks along with a more
distinctive elderly man, JACK HANNA, and a 24-year-old
woman named TONEA who doesn't appear to be having a
good time.

                         RAUL
          So where the heck is he? Is he coming
          or what?

                         TONEA
          TACO's helping him warm up, in the back.

WAREHOUSE / BACK AREA

ODESIO is getting ready. TACO is there, wrapping his hands
and helping him prepare by acting as a shadow-boxing
partner. TACO uses his hands as targets for ODESIO to hit.

                         TACO
          Don't let this corn-fed dude fool you, bro.
          He's got some heavy punches. But if you
          check him out, his footwork sucks, so as
          long as you keep moving, he won't even
          touch you. You're way faster than him.

WAREHOUSE / MAIN AREA

Two young men, HECKLE and JECKLE, between the ages of 25
and 32, talk among the crowd.

                         HECKLE
          Doooode! You're crrrrazy! I'm telling
          you, this guy's good. I've seen him
          fight before.

                         JECKLE
          Yeah, I've seen him, too. He got his butt
          kicked by VICTOR WILDE about two years
          ago. Dude ended up in the hospital with
          some kind of head injury or brain damage
          or something.

                         HECKLE
          Well, I don't know about all that, but
          I've seen that dude whip some serious
          butt. That other dude ain't got nothing
          on him.

                              JECKLE
                    So, why don't you bet on him?

                              HECKLE
                    Man, I'm tapped out.

                              JECKLE
                    Well, I'm not betting on him! All I
                    got left is the rent money.

                              HECKLE
                    Doooode! He's going to double your money.

WAREHOUSE / BACK AREA

A man wearing a cheap referee shirt walks into the room.

                              REF #1
                    All right, ladies, you ready?

WAREHOUSE / MAIN AREA

                              RAUL
                    Here they come. MR. HANNA, you just keep
                    your eyes on this kid, okay?

                              JACK HANNA
                    RAUL, you better not be wasting my time.

TONEA'S eyes light up and she cheers as she sees ODESIO
entering the "pit." The ref checks both opponents for
foreign objects or weapons and gives them a quick rundown
on what little rules they have.

The fight begins with ODESIO taking a punch to the face
and falling flat on his butt. He waves his hands at his
opponent, as if saying, "Hang on, man! I wasn't ready."
People laugh. Many of them are already sorry they bet
on him. MR. HANNA looks on as ODESIO rises from the ground
and they once again go at it. Their fighting style is very
raw and undisciplined, but their punches are hard, fast,
and furious. ODESIO dominates the match. Onlookers cheer
him on. Just as he's about to finish off his opponent,

ODESIO is pulled away by his grandmother, MAMA MARIA, who somehow managed to get in there. Grabbing ODESIO by the ear, MAMA MARIA drags him away.

>   MAMA MARIA
> So this is what you've been doing, huh?
> Do you have any idea how long I've been
> out searching for you?

>   ODESIO
> Ow! MAMA, what the heck are you doing?
> That's my @#$%& ear!

>   MAMA MARIA
>   (slaps him on the mouth)
> Don't you swear at me, boy!

>   ODESIO
> MAMA, you're going to get hurt. Let me go!

>   MAMA MARIA
> What's wrong with you, boy? Didn't you
> learn your lesson last time? Do you
> want to end up in the hospital again?

>   ODESIO
> No, MAMA, but, but, but...

>   MAMA MARIA
> Oh, shut up, and get moving.

TACO is somehow caught along the way with no place to hide or run from the furious old lady.

>   TACO
> Hi, MAMA.

>   MAMA MARIA
>   (grabs him by the ear as well)
> I knew you had to be around here, too.
> Get over here! Wait till I tell your
> mother what you've been doing!

As MAMA MARIA approaches the exit, she's intercepted by
RAUL and MR. HANNA.

> RAUL
>
> Hey, lady, what're you doing? We're in
> the middle of a fight here!

> MAMA MARIA
>
> Ah, ha! So you're the one responsible
> for this. I should have known it. Get
> out of my way before I give you a fat lip!

As MAMA MARIA gestures with her hand, TACO flees before
she can grab hold of him again. All of a sudden, RAUL is
intimidated by the threat and crosses his arms. Using his
eyes and part of his hand, he gestures toward MR. HANNA
as if pointing out the guilty party.

> MAMA MARIA
> (to MR. HANNAH)
> You no good weasel. Why don't you get
> a real job? Ah ha! So you're the one
> who's responsible!

> JACK HANNA
>
> I'm sorry, Ma'am. I'm just a guest here.
> I was invited.

> MAMA MARIA
>
> Who invited you?

Just as MR. HANNA is about to place the spotlight back
on to RAUL, RAUL cuts back into the conversation.

> RAUL
>
> He's a guest of everybody. Ha ha. We all
> invited him.

> MAMA MARIA
>
> I don't have time for this nonsense.
> Get out of my way!

The old lady heads toward the exit once again,
pushing through the crowd and still dragging ODESIO by
the ear. A JIVE-TALKING DUDE yells a taunt.

                       JIVE-TALKING DUDE
        Ha ha! We should have bet on the old
        lady. How come no one told me she was
        going to be on the card?

Hearing this, ODESIO breaks away and lunges at the
JIVE-TALKING DUDE, but before ODESIO can get to him,
MAMA MARIA grabs hold of him once again and yanks him
toward the exit.

                       ODESIO
        Ow! MAMA, you gonna tear my ear off!

                       MAMA MARIA
        Shut up!

                                     CUT TO:

INT. NIGHT CLUB / NIGHT

ELENA WATKINS (LANEY), a wealthy 22-year-old woman, has
just come back from school in New York. Her brother CHRIS
and her rich ex-boyfriend, SEAN, have taken her out to
celebrate her return. Chris's girlfriend JENNA is also
with them. They make their way to a table and sit down.
A waitress brings them their drinks.

                       CHRIS
        This place is fantastic!

                       SEAN
        This is nothing. You should have gone
        with me to Vegas. That was the life!
        The food, drinks, entertainment.
        Heck, I'm going back next month. I mean,
        if that's okay with you, of course.

> CHRIS
> That's a good one! The owner of the company asking his employee if he can take some time off.

They all laugh.

> SEAN
> (to LANEY)
> I think your brother's still coming to terms with the fact that he's the one who's really in charge.

> CHRIS
> Oh, listen, did you remember to fill the nomination ballot for the...?

> SEAN
> Yeah, yeah, don't worry. I faxed it over to your secretary right before I left the office.

> JENNA
> Come on, guys, LANEY just came back from New York and all you guys can do is talk business. We're supposed to be celebrating.

> CHRIS
> You're absolutely right, my dear. Come on. Let's dance.

They go to the dance floor, leaving LANEY alone with SEAN.

> LANEY
> So, did you do any gambling while you were in Vegas? Any luck?

> SEAN
> Of course! Actually, I made off with well over half a million dollars.

> LANEY
> Wow! That's a lot of money. That's what I call "luck."

                    SEAN
Luck has very little to do with it.
If you want to win big, you got to
spend big. Take chances. Just part of
being a natural-born winner.

                    LANEY
Well, congratulations, SEAN. There are
those who have it all.

                    SEAN
No, not everything.

                    LANEY
What do you mean?

                    SEAN
Well, love for example.

                    LANEY
What's the matter? Won't that special
someone return your affections?

                    SEAN
You should know.

                    LANEY
Me?

                    SEAN
If I remember correctly, before you left for
college, you and I had a good thing going.
At one point in our relationship, we even
spoke about marriage. Now that you're back,
you seem to be giving me the cold shoulder.

                    LANEY
Oh come on, SEAN, that was years ago. I
was practically a little girl. I didn't
know what I wanted, I still don't.

                                SEAN
            Is there someone else?

                                LANEY
            No, SEAN, there's no one else. Can we
            change the subject?

                                SEAN
            I guess that's your way of telling me
            there's no longer a possibility
            between us, is there?

                                LANEY
            SEAN, aside from our fathers' lifelong
            partnership, and now your business
            relationship with my brother, there's
            always been a great friendship between
            our families. That's really all I feel
            for you, SEAN.

                                SEAN
            A great friendship.

                                LANEY
            Yes.

                                SEAN
            I suppose only time will tell. But you seem
            to overlook the obvious.

                                LANEY
            And what would that be?

                                SEAN
            I'm a natural-born winner, my dear, and
            sooner or later, I always get what I want.

LANEY: Extremely uncomfortable, she slowly takes a drink. Lots of
tension. SOUND: Impending complication fills the air.

FADE OUT

Writing the Film

Writing a script in the Master Scene format is a science all its own. You must become accustomed to standard formatting rules and vocabulary.

One Page Equals One Minute of Film

The most important thing to know is this: for every page of script you write, one minute of actual film is produced. A script, which is 90 pages long whether it's all action or all dialogue, always results in a production that runs for approximately 90 minutes.

If you're planning a three-minute cartoon, which is quite typical for the Web these days, make sure your script can effectively be written using a beginning, a middle, and a satisfactory ending within those three pages of text. If you can't do this, then it won't matter how beautifully you designed your characters, the quality of the animation, or the attention to detail you placed on your backgrounds. Your film simply won't work.

The seven-minute short film format, however, is a more widely accepted format within the industry because it not only conforms to being presented on television, while leaving room for commercial breaks, but it also is a format that can easily and feasibly be created in Flash for web distribution purposes. A seven-minute short film also requires seven pages of text to be written.

The Difference Between a Cliffhanger and Garbage

In the popular television series *Quantum Leap,* Dr. Sam Becket traveled through time solving all sorts of dilemmas. He would overcome the conflict of the day, and then everyone would live happily ever after. The audience watched Dr. Becket struggle to overcome his conflict, so in the end he would triumph and we could have closure. The only problem was, as he said good-bye, Dr. Becket was transported to his next adventure, where he, once again, found himself in an unpredictable dilemma, which he must resolve.

Quantum Leap was a great example of proper use of the cliffhanger. On the one hand the writers satisfied us and gave us closure, while on the other hand they spiced up the closing, so we became interested in the next episode of the show.

For some reason, many of today's Flash filmmakers believe the Internet is so different that the quality of our entertainment must be equally different from the quality of the entertainment in shows such as *Quantum Leap* or *Dexter's Laboratory.* Nothing could be farther from the truth.

I hate to single out a specific work because, quite honestly, much of Flash animation is, to date, treated the same way. However, *The Seventh Portal,* by Stan Lee Media, is a great example of terrible filmmaking in general. Sure, the art is dazzling, the voices and sound are clean, and a lot of attention was paid to the amount of detail in the artwork. But the storytelling was absolute garbage. I don't necessarily attribute *The Seventh Portal*'s failure to bad writing because the script in its entirety was rather well constructed and the story was somewhat interesting. The way the script was presented is what killed it.

In most cases, what was referred to as an episode or a *webisode* wasn't even a complete scene but instead an unfinished thought. A typical *Seventh Portal* webisode would set up its characters and present a conflict. Then, just as the conflict arose, the webisode reached its designated time limit and the audience was left hanging, rubbing its collective head and wondering, what the heck was that?

The Seventh Portal, as with many works of Flash filmmaking being produced to date, is created with the mentality that the Web is so constricting, a three- or four-minute time limit should be on every cartoon presented over the Web. What usually happens is the script for the webisode is chopped up to meet those time requirements, even if this means cutting the continuity of the story right in the middle of a scene.

This is a terrible thing to do. Cliffhangers are great, but there's a definite distinction between applying a cliffhanger to an already complete episode and leaving your thought unfinished and your audience hanging.

Flash animation is already low in file size. Add to this that the animation itself can be streamed while it plays. You, as a filmmaker, shouldn't worry too much about how long the running time of your film will be or even its file size. The average web surfer doesn't mind waiting to download or preload something when they know the wait will be justified by the quality of entertainment. I always say, if people will sit through a 20-minute download of a 30 second video, why wouldn't they sit through a two- or three-minute preload of film that promises to entertain them for an entire ten minutes or more?

In the previous segment, you read Episode One for the storyline in my animated series, *Without You.* Feel free to reference this script as you work on your own scripts. Study the formatting and the scene construction. Notice how every scene forms a complete thought, with a beginning, a middle, and an ending.

Once my original script was completed, I found myself holding an 80-page screenplay for a feature film! If I break this screenplay up into a series, I could effectively keep myself busy for at least an entire year creating and presenting the series in the form of periodically released episodes. The greatest advantage to this approach is I already have the scripts to every possible episode in the series, so I won't be making the story up as I go. Instead, I'll be concentrating on the actual production and presentation of each individual episode.

If I did my job well as far as writing complete scenes, I should have no problem in picking any point in my film where a scene ends and another one begins. I should be able to split up the film into a series of episodes that will leave the audience satisfied with the episode they've seen and, at the same time, keep them wanting to see how the overall story will unfold.

My target is for each episode to be approximately seven minutes long, so I started counting pages, seven pages to be exact. On page seven, I looked for a place where one scene ends and another begins. In my case, page seven is a page that's in the middle of a scene, which started early on page six, so I decided to keep the scene and follow it to see how far it extends.

I've determined Episode One; now for Episode Two. Starting with the next scene, I count seven pages and again have to decide whether the scene on that page should be kept as part of Episode Two or carried over and made the first scene of Episode Three.

This process continues until I no longer have any additional pages to work with and have effectively split up my script into what, someday, will be a 12-episode series presented entirely in Flash. The final episode is a bit shorter than the others, but I'm not too worried because its scenes still make the episode conform to being self-standing, which will bring closure to the overall story.

In using this seven-minute approach, not only am I leaving my franchise marketable over the Web but, because its time format conforms to standard TV segments, this can make targeting other markets, such as cable television, easier. Also, once the entire "series" is complete, I could easily splice the series back together into a full-blown feature-length film that can be distributed offline, through CD-ROM, video, DVD, and whatever other media format I can get my hands on.

In conclusion, try to stay away from incomplete thoughts and always structure your writing using complete scenes. Stay away from webisodes and, instead, strive to create real episodes. This way, even if you choose to present your Flash film on a scene-by-scene basis, you will always instill a sense of closure and satisfaction in your audience.

Script Formatting

The language of filmmaking and screenwriting is similar to HTML in that certain formatting conventions are also followed as it uses its own set of proprietary tags, which instruct filmmakers on how to go about interpreting your screenplay. I say "interpret" because, as is often the case, the writer has little to do with the way the director chooses to produce the script. In most cases, the final product is the director's interpretation of the story, rather than the writer's original vision.

TIP

It's considered bad form to tell the director or the actors how to go about doing their jobs. As a writer, stick to telling the story as best you can, and leave the camera and special effects for the director to decide. Always avoid telling the actors how to do their jobs or say their lines. They are professionals and will, in most cases, interpret the lines better than you could have ever imagined. Of course, if you happen to be a one-man studio and do the film entirely by yourself, then go crazy. After all, you're the boss, and you rock!

Sluglines

Because time is of the essence on every page, you don't want to write unnecessary descriptions to places and settings unless they're absolutely crucial to the story. A *slugline* is where all the necessary information about a scene's location and setting is written. Sluglines are composed of three district parts.

The first part of a slugline tells you whether the scene takes place indoors or outdoors. You only have two options for this—interior and exterior—and they are written as INT. or EXT.

The second part of the slugline gives you the name of your locale. For example, CHUBBY CHEESE PIZZA or THE DOCKS.

The third part of the slugline describes the time of day. In film, only two options exist for this—DAY or NIGHT—because day and night are the only two time periods that can be told apart on film. Asking for dawn, morning, or afternoon wouldn't work out because, through the camera, they all look the same. Many amateurs make this mistake, so try to avoid it and only consider whether or not there's daylight outside.

Typical sluglines look like this:

```
INT.   JANE DOE'S HOUSE / NIGHT
EXT.   JOHN DOE'S BACKYARD / DAY
INT.   - SPACESHIP - NIGHT
EXT.   - THEME PARK - DAY
```

Action

Once you set up your slugline and establish your setting, it's most likely followed by either action or dialogue. *Action* is the description that tells you what's taking place at the specified setting. Once action is added below a slugline, a typical screenplay looks like this:

```
INT. STARSHIP CALYPSO BRIDGE  / NIGHT
```

```
KRUT can no longer control the ship by himself. It continues to
SHAKE as if it's going to fall apart. He looks at MOJO standing on
the other side of bridge picking his teeth.
```

Writing your characters' names in all capital letters is customary the first time they appear. This makes it easy to go through the script and to count the number of characters in the film. Most writers currently write the names of the characters in all capital letters when they appear in your action throughout the entire script because it's easier to tell which character is doing what.

In the action previously described, you can tell Krut and Mojo are both characters in the scene. Also notice the word "shake" is in all capital letters. This is because I want to bring special attention to the shaking of the ship. Do this whenever you want to specify specific sounds or actions that are crucial to the story.

Dialogue

Normally, *dialogue* is written in a format which makes it easy to read and easy to tell who is saying the lines. When characters speak, their names are written approximately 40 to 45 spaces from the left margin. Wherever you put the names, be sure the placement of any future character names remains consistent throughout the rest of the screenplay.

The dialogue itself is written in a sort of block format, which is constrained to about 25 spaces from both the left and right margins. Once dialogue is applied to your script, it looks something like this:

```
INT. STARSHIP CALYPSO BRIDGE  / NIGHT

KRUT can no longer control the ship by himself. It continues to
SHAKE as if it is going to fall apart. He looks at MOJO standing
on the other side of the bridge picking his teeth.


                         KRUT
               Mojo, take control of the ship. I'll try to get to
               the warp core and see if I can manually stabilize it.


                         MOJO
               Sure, no problem, man.

Mojo takes the station and the ship begins to spin out of control.
```

> KRUT
> Dude, what are you doing? Haven't you ever
> driven a hyperspace intergalactic warship before?
>
> MOJO
> I drove my parents to drinking. Does that count?
>
> KRUT
> Dude, you're a moron!
>
> MOJO
> No, I'm not! I'm a Catholic.

CUT TO:

Notice, on the last line of that sequence, the words CUT TO appear justified to the right side of the page. This is a transition device, which is used either to change to a different shot or to change to a new scene.

If you read the script for Episode One, you'll also notice the words FADE IN at the beginning of the episode and the words FADE OUT at the end of the episode. FADE IN and FADE OUT should only be used once for each individual film to mark the beginning or ending. They should never be used as a transitional device from one scene to another.

The Lingo

You should become familiar with many terms if you're going to write your own scripts.

Term	Description
BG	BG is short for BACKGROUND.
CONTINUOUS	Normally, when you place a new slugline, it implies you're starting a new scene. However, many scenes often require multiple setups or locations. When this happens, we place this tag as a fourth element in your slugline. This isn't necessary unless you're writing the production script.
CU	A CLOSE-UP is a camera instruction, which places the camera on a character, so you can see him or her from the chest up.
CUT TO:	CUT TO: is a term used to change from one scene or shot to another. This is the most widely accepted transition device.
DISSOLVE TO:	DISSOLVE TO: is yet another transition device and there are a million of them. Stick to using CUT TO: and you should be fine.

Term	Description
DOLLY	A DOLLY SHOT is similar to a zoom; however, when you perform a DOLLY SHOT, you physically move the camera in and out. This creates a nice three-dimensional feeling and gives a shot a sense of depth of field.
ESTABLISHING SHOT	This is a dinosaur term, which has been replaced with WA and is used to establish the setting.
EX CU	An EXTREME CLOSE-UP focuses the camera on a specific object or part of a person, such as the face, eyes, hands, and so forth.
EXT.	EXTERIOR is part of a slugline, which describes a scene's location.
FADE IN	A FADE IN marks the beginning of your film. It begins with absolute darkness and fades into a visible image. This instruction should only be used one time in your script. It tells the director this is where the film begins.
FADE OUT	A FADE OUT takes your image and fades it in to absolute darkness. This is the opposite of FADE IN and it, too, is used only one time in your script. FADE OUT tells us the film is finished.
FAVOR	FAVOR is applied when you want to imply a certain character should be favored over another in a shot.
FG	FG is short for FOREGROUND.
INT.	INTERIOR is part of a slugline, which describes a scene's location.
INT./EXT.	On a rare occasion, a scene takes place both indoors and outdoors. Try to avoid using these scenes.
MATCH TO:	MATCH TO: is a transition device used when you want an object in one scene to match an object in the following scene. A good example is a scene that ends with someone looking at a clock and the matching image in the next scene begins with someone looking at their wristwatch.
MEDIUM	A MEDIUM SHOT is normally applied to characters and shot from the waist up.
O.S.	OFF SHOT means a character is speaking, but isn't seen by the camera.
ODOR LINES	An animation term, ODOR LINES specifies that a smell is coming from somewhere. In animation, smells are drawn as ODOR LINES.
PAN	When you PAN a scene, you take the camera and move it along a horizontal or vertical plane.

Term	Description
POV	This is a POINT OF VIEW shot, which sees the environment through the eyes of the character.
SFX	SFX is short for SOUND EFFECTS.
SPEED LINES	In animation, when an object moves really fast, it usually creates SPEED LINES, which are visible to the audience.
SPIN	Another animation term, SPIN is used to imply a body part spinning so fast that all you see is motion blurs. Popular SPINS are HEAD SPIN, TAIL SPIN, and LEG SPIN.
TAKE	A TAKE or a DOUBLE TAKE is an action performed in cartoons when characters are shocked by something they've seen.
TILT	TILT is when the camera is placed in a nonmoving location, and the lens is tilted up, down, left, or right. This normally creates a nice distortion of perception.
TRACK	When you TRACK an object, you focus the camera on an object and follow it across the scene.
TRAVELING	This is another dinosaur term. It has been replaced with PAN, which means to move the camera from one place to another in a scene.
V.O.	VOICE OVER is voices or narrations, which are dubbed over a video sequence.
WA	A WIDE ANGLE SHOT is used to establish the setting and lets us see multiple characters in a single shot.
WALLA	An animation term, WALLA implies nonspecific jibber-jabber, which a group of characters might speak to add sound to the ambience.
WIPE TO:	WIPE TO: is also a transition device where the image is wiped from one side to the other as it's replaced with the new image from the next scene.
ZIP	ZIP is an animation term, which is basically a fast PAN. Because this is animation, motion blurs or speed lines usually accompany it.
ZOOM	A ZOOM IN is when you focus into an object by increasing the magnification of the image. A ZOOM OUT is when you focus on the greater image by reducing its magnification. Zooms are highly undesirable shots in filmmaking because they look fake or synthetic. A better approach is to grab the camera physically, and move in or away from the object being filmed.

Summary

The standard screenplay format is referred to as the Master Scene format because of the way it's created, one Master Scene followed by another. This format is also known as the Submission format.

▶ When a writer writes a screenplay in the Master Scene, he writes in a way that concentrates on the storytelling and leaves any directorial decision to the director.

▶ Although not everyone refers to sensuality and dramatic action by the same terms, these are usually the driving forces behind any storyline devised to appeal to a mature audience. While most cartoons are written with violence or dramatic action in mind, most serious productions are more sensual in nature. Learning to balance these two elements in any production can enhance the quality of your writing.

▶ Writing a screenplay, much like the art of cartooning and animation, involves the use of formulas that have been proven time after time to appeal to a majority audience. In the entertainment business, appealing to a majority audience is crucial to maximize the revenue-earning potential of the product.

▶ When you develop a story, always start by establishing a premise. Develop your premise into a synopsis, and then use the synopsis as a blueprint for writing your screenplay. For animation purposes, the storyboards are a most crucial step that visually aids the animators on how to go about animating the scenes. For live action, the storyboard is secondary. Often, a production-formatted screenplay is used as the guide.

▶ In writing for the Web, remember the following important point. Flash animation is a low-budget medium. The more scenery and backgrounds you use, the more expensive the production of the film will be.

▶ Production expense isn't only financial. In the case of a one-man animation studio, the expense involved in the production of a film is the amount of time it takes the filmmaker to create it. Before you write a script that involves 30 different locations, ask yourself whether you're willing (and able) to create backgrounds for all those locations.

Screenplay formatting isn't that different than formatting a page in HTML. By using an established set of tags and formatting style, you can transform a typical story into what will someday be an actual film.

CHAPTER
14

The Production Process

I n this chapter, you learn about the entire production process involved in the creation of a web/TV commercial I made not long ago. Be aware that every animation house has its own procedures and policies about how the production work flow is approached. For this book, though, I followed a standard approach, which is common among most animation houses and studios.

Assessing the Project

Once the client reaches a stage where he wants to engage in a consultation with you to discuss his project, he's most likely already seen your work and knows what you're capable of, or you were recommended to him by someone else. His major concerns at this point are production costs, the time it will take to create the product, and how you're going to go about creating it.

At this stage, the client also has several other animators in mind, so don't think this means you already have the gig. The client will normally ask questions about your work and what you do, your experience in the field, and how you go about getting the job done. Be prepared to answer these questions honestly, but don't mistake this conversation to be some kind of job interview because this interview isn't about getting the contract. It's about learning as much as you can about the project and whether you want to, or are able to, take on the project. During this interview, you are running the show, interviewing the client, and assessing his needs, so you can get a better idea of what he wants and whether you can give it to him. You should always ask your clients four questions when you assess potential projects.

What Production Time Frame Is Your Client Looking At?

By traditional standards, a 30-second commercial takes 6–8 weeks to produce (sometimes faster, depending on your staff). Flash animation isn't that different if you're going for traditional quality. Although the software makes it easier for a one-man studio to provide the same type of service to the client, you must also take into account that, as a Flash animator, you're not only doing the work of the animator, but you might also be responsible for the sound, the backgrounds, the storyboards, and, in many cases, the scripts, the voices, the Foley editing, and everything else. So, for a one-man studio to provide a product that can rival one produced by a big budget studio with a large staff and higher-end software, it'll still take you about the same amount of time. In many cases, you might find it more convenient to hire other freelancers to perform the other tasks, such as the coloring and backgrounds, which can enable you to finish the work much faster.

Making the client aware of your procedures is important because this can help you find a middle ground. Suppose the project is a three-minute piece, which must be done within a span of seven days. Obviously a client isn't being realistic if he or she expects you to produce something with the effect of the Trix rabbit or a Lucky Charms commercial and be finished within that time span. Toning down the quality of animation, the detail, the color, and reducing the complexity of the background will always be a major time saver, but it comes at the cost of the overall production quality. Lip-synching is also important and you could spend two or three days lip-synching the production for accurate lip interpretation of the words. Or you can stick in a symbol containing a generic anime-style lip cycle and be done within an hour.

TIP

When working freelance, always give the client what she wants. If the client wants an elephant in the background and a blue giraffe jumping up and down for no reason, don't argue — just do it. As long as the client gets what she wants, she'll be happy. If time and budget allow for creative changes that you personally suggest and the client approves them, then, by all means, go for it. Otherwise, though, stick to giving the client what she wants.

Many clients also have no idea what's involved in the production of an animated piece, so you have to inform them. I can't begin to count the number of clients who have approached me believing that Flash animation is a form of high-speed animation delivery, which means they can place an order for a ten-minute piece today and that I, as a Flash animator or filmmaker, can deliver it tomorrow. You need to make your clients aware that Flash is simply the name of the format. It has nothing to do with the turnaround time of the production.

Is There a Script?

Believe it or not, many clients who hire animators to do work for them have no idea what they want in the first place. They just know they want something cool for their web site or TV promo, or they have a vague idea for a spec film they want to invest in, and they expect you magically to produce it.

Here's an actual posting I took from a Usenet newsgroup from a client looking for someone to create a little animated promo in Flash:

> "I'm looking for someone to create a short flash animation that I can use for marketing purposes. It needs to be humorous, clean and professional. While I'm looking for animation, three video samples are on my site at http://www.xxxxxxx.xxx.xx/xxx.htm while I'm looking for animation these videos have the type of fun theme I like. Joecartoon.com's work, while not quite my taste, he has the right humorous style."

This is a typical client, who comes to you with absolutely nothing more than they want something cool. Although some animators do have a natural talent for writing humor, most animators don't. You need to inform potential clients that you need a solid script to make progress.

When there's no script to work from, you or your client need to have one written (my preference is to have the client supply the script). In many cases, you can discuss the concept with your client and come up with a decent idea to work from, but I always recommend using a professional writer. Once your client is happy with the script, he can bring it to you and you can begin working from it.

TIP

If the client's concept is for a short film or commercial, which might be a few minutes or less, work with him to develop the concept, but don't write the script unless you're getting paid. It's hard for many clients to make up their minds, so unless your client is paying you to write the screenplay — and for every revision performed — don't let yourself get involved in the writing stage of a production that isn't your own. You'll get caught up in an endless sea of one revision after another.

What about the Budget?

Many animators usually ask this question right away and expect the client to have something in mind. Animators then use that number to balance out the type of work and the time frame they can deliver. Although there's no harm in this, I strongly advise against it. As an independent animator, you should have a set of rates available to your client. Instead of asking them "What kind of budget do you have?" a better approach is to show them what kind of work you can provide and at what rates. Also explain to them that the more complex the work is, the longer it will take. Leave it up to your clients to decide whether you fall within their budget. Most companies appreciate the fact that you aren't out to use every single cent in their budget. If they know what to expect from you as far as the work itself and the estimated cost, they'll be more inclined to go with your services.

What Does the Client Provide?

Sometimes the client will be another animator or an animation company who might provide you with everything you need, such as storyboards, x-sheets, sound elements, voice tracks, and so forth, and all you need to do is concentrate on the actual animation. Other times, the client is the owner of a small car dealership looking for a wacky commercial or the owner of a web site looking for some kind of virtual marketing thingamajig. In this case, the client might go as far as providing you with a basic script (maybe) and expect you to take care of everything else. When this happens, other things to remember as you assess the project are what your rates are for storyboarding, backgrounds, coloring, and so forth. I normally throw in the storyboarding as a freebie, so the client can get an idea of what to expect the product to look like and give him the opportunity to change things around before committing to the animation.

When time is essential, in most cases I hire a freelance background artist and a colorist to help speed the work along. If the project is big, I might even hire another animator to animate a scene or two.

Step One: Evaluate the Script

If you receive a script from another animator or a person involved in the entertainment and film industry, chances are it will already be formatted in the Master Scene or Production format. The average client's script, however, will require a makeover before you can determine how to proceed.

Here's the script written in the Master Scene format.

```
FADE IN.



        EXT. BIG BANG CASINO/ DAY

        WAYNE GAMBLE has lost all his money. He checks his
        pockets. Nothing.

                              WAYNE
                    This is ridiculous. I've got to try my
                    luck somewhere else.

                                              CUT TO:



        EXT. LUCKY DAY CASINO/ NIGHT

        Wayne heads toward the entrance of the casino.

                                              CUT TO:



        INT. LUCKY DAY CASINO/ NIGHT

        Wayne has entered the casino and likes what he sees. He's
        drinking a Long Island Iced Tea.
```

                              WAYNE
                    Hey, the drinks aren't watered down here
                    like they are at my old stomping ground.

          ANGIE passes by. We follow her across the room and pass
          by a sign that reads: "Lucky Day Casino presents Showgirls
          On Ice." PAN back to Wayne who's about to roll some dice.

                              WAYNE
                    And the showgirls are sure prettier
                    than at the old ball-and-chain casino.

          The dice fly into the air and land on a craps table where
          a dealer lets us know that he has won.

                              DEALER
                    Seven!

                              WAYNE
                    And you know what they say about the
                    other side of the fence: The grass is
                    always greener.

                                               FADE OUT.

At this stage, I evaluate the actions to be performed by the characters. I also think about cool ways of performing these actions in front of the "camera" and what type of camera angles and movement I can use to enhance the experience. The script itself is slightly under one page in length (if it's printed on 8.5"×11" paper). This tells me the production itself will be under one minute long. Here's a breakdown of what's happening as I read and evaluate the script.

FADE IN.

This is easy. To do a fade in, all I have to do is create a graphic symbol, which will contain a black rectangle and animate its instance, going from solid black to an alpha state of 0 percent.

          EXT. BIG BANG CASINO/ DAY

This scene takes place outside the Big Bang Casino during the day. This means, so far, this is one background I have to create.

```
WAYNE GAMBLE has lost all his money. He checks his
pockets. Nothing.
```

Nothing special here. Perhaps I could animate him walking out with his head hanging and looking disappointed that he's lost all his money.

```
                            WAYNE
            This is ridiculous. I've got to try my
            luck somewhere else.
```

Well, that's one line he says. I need to make a note for the voice actor who will lend his voice to the character.

```
                                        CUT  TO:
```

That's a transition. I think instead of the actual cut, I might use a fade. This way, it'll give us a sense that some time has passed. Although the commands FADE IN: and FADE OUT: are only used once to indicate the beginning and the end of the script, the use of FADE as a transitional device is quite common to indicate a sense of time-lapse or, perhaps, bring closure to a scene before going to a commercial break.

```
EXT. LUCKY DAY CASINO/ NIGHT

Wayne heads toward the entrance of the casino.
```

```
                                        CUT  TO:
```

It's just a shot of Wayne walking and heading toward the entrance of the casino. To get the overall idea in as short an amount of time and resources as possible, I think it would be wise to have an aerial view shot with Wayne walking toward the entrance. This way, I can pull off the entire shot with one background of the exterior of the Lucky Day Casino at night and a simple walk cycle.

```
INT. LUCKY DAY CASINO/ NIGHT

Wayne has entered the casino and likes what he sees. He's
drinking a Long Island Iced Tea.
```

Here's another background that must be made: the interior of the Lucky Day Casino at night. I have to find a way to show Wayne drinking his beverage and, at the same time, give the idea that he likes what he sees.

> WAYNE
> Hey, the drinks aren't watered down here
> like they are at my old stomping ground.

That was Wayne's second line. I have to make a note of this for the voice actor.

> ANGIE passes by. We follow her across the room and pass
> by a sign that reads: "Lucky Day Casino presents Showgirls
> On Ice." PAN back to Wayne who's about to roll some dice.

This action is pretty well described and self-explanatory.

> WAYNE
> And the showgirls are sure prettier
> than at the old ball-and-chain casino.

Note to self: this is Wayne Gamble's third line.

> The dice fly into the air and land on a craps table where
> a dealer lets us know that he has won.

> DEALER
> Seven!

I think it would be cool to shoot this entire sequence within a single shot à la *The Matrix*. Perhaps after the camera has panned back to Wayne, he'll throw the dice and we can focus on them as the entire scene revolves and we're on the other side of the room when the dice land. Then, we can pan back around to Wayne, where he'll say his fourth and final line.

> WAYNE
> And you know what they say about the
> other side of the fence: The grass is
> always greener.

> FADE OUT.

I guess that's the end of that, except the client also requested that the web version have a button at the end that lets the users play the animation again and another button that lets them e-mail it to their friends. No biggie there.

Step Two: Create the Production Script or Storyboards

In this step, you can either create a "shooting script," based on the Master Scene screen play, or you can go ahead and generate the storyboards, which you can use as a visual reference as you work on the project. The production script will have all the camera instructions, shot numbers, and any other production-specific comments or directions.

Here's the production screenplay for this project. Notice how the shot numbers are written on the sides of every new slug line to indicate a new independent shot. Directorial comments and instructions are also added.

```
        FADE IN.


1       EXT. BIG BANG CASINO/ DAY                              1


        WAYNE GAMBLE is WALKING out of the casino. He has lost
        all his money. He STOPS, checks his pockets. Nothing.

                            WAYNE
                    This is ridiculous. I've got to try my
                    luck somewhere else.


                                                        CUT TO:

2       EXT. LUCKY DAY CASINO/ NIGHT                           2


        AERIAL VIEW. Wayne heads toward the entrance of the
        casino. (Nothing complicated; just a simple overhead walk
        cycle will do.) Use fades to give a sense of passing of time
        in the beginning as well as in the end of the shot.


                                                        CUT TO:


3       INT. LUCKY DAY CASINO/ NIGHT                           3


        Wayne has entered the casino and likes what he sees. He's
        drinking a Long Island Iced Tea. FLASH: We can take the
```

symbols we used for the ice cubes and use them as dice
to keep file size down.

                              WAYNE
                Hey the drinks aren't watered down here
                like they are at my old stomping ground.

ANGIE passes by. We follow her across the room and pass
by a sign that reads: "Lucky Day Casino presents Showgirls
On Ice." PAN back to Wayne who's about to roll some dice.
Place an image of ANGIE on the POSTER as well so that we
can see that Angie is starring in the show.

                              WAYNE
                And the show girls are sure prettier
                than at the old ball-and-chain casino.

Wayne will roll the dice in his hand as he speaks. As he
finishes his last line he will throw the dice in the air.
As the dice fly into the air we track the action in the shot
similar to the special effects in *The Matrix* where the
entire scene will revolve around the object and land on a
craps table where a dealer lets us know that he has won.
The dealer will look down and raise his finger up in
the air to declare the winner.

                              DEALER
                Seven!

CU Wayne: Pulling a pile of chips toward himself.

                              WAYNE
                And you know what they say about the
                other side of the fence: The grass is
                always greener.

                                             FADE OUT.

   Many animation studios don't bother with production screenplays. They just
create the storyboards and work from there. As far as storyboarding is concerned, it
needn't be something overly elaborate. If you want to, you could do the storyboards
using stick figures as long as you get across the idea of how things are supposed to
look. If you print out your production screenplay, you could even draw little boxes
next to the action and doodle the storyboard there.

Here's what a typical storyboard for this project would look like. I recommend you have your client approve the storyboard before getting any actual animation done. This can protect you from having your client change his mind about how the production should be performed well after you start on the animation stage.

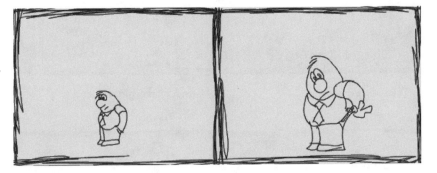

Wayne walks out of the casino.   Digs in his pocket. Finds nothing.

"Man, this is ridiculous..."   He's headed toward the new casino.

Drinks his Long Island Iced Tea.   "The drinks aren't watered down..."

"The girls are prettier…"   Sign for Showgirls on Ice."

Rolling them bones.   He shoots.

The dice fly across the room.   "Seven!!!"
Camera tracks.

"You know what they say…"   "…the grass is always greener…"

If you use a word processor program, such as Microsoft Word, you have the added benefit of being able to import your storyboard images and merge them with your screenplay. This enables you to create a much more functional storyboard/screenplay hybrid, which is, in my opinion, easier to manage and much more functional than a typical storyboard.

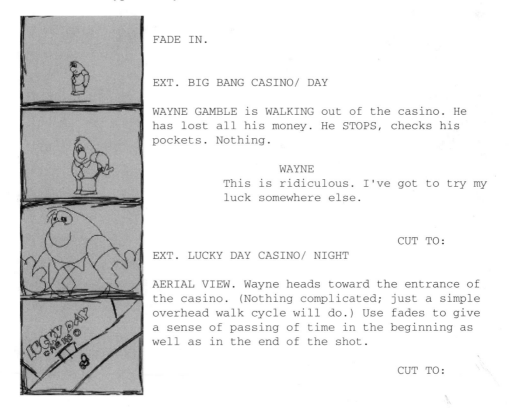

```
FADE IN.


EXT. BIG BANG CASINO/ DAY

WAYNE GAMBLE is WALKING out of the casino. He
has lost all his money. He STOPS, checks his
pockets. Nothing.

                    WAYNE
          This is ridiculous. I've got to try my
          luck somewhere else.


                                        CUT TO:
EXT. LUCKY DAY CASINO/ NIGHT

AERIAL VIEW. Wayne heads toward the entrance of
the casino. (Nothing complicated; just a simple
overhead walk cycle will do.) Use fades to give
a sense of passing of time in the beginning as
well as in the end of the shot.

                                        CUT TO:
```

INT. LUCKY DAY CASINO/ NIGHT

Wayne has entered the casino and likes what he sees. He's drinking a Long Island Iced Tea. FLASH: We can take the symbols we used for the ice cubes and use them as dice to keep file size down.

>   WAYNE
>   Hey, the drinks aren't watered down
>   here like they are at my old stomping
>   ground.

ANGIE passes by. We follow her across the room and pass by a sign that reads: "Lucky Day Casino Presents "Showgirls On Ice." PAN back to Wayne who's about to roll some dice. Place an image of ANGIE on the POSTER as well so that we can see that Angie is starring in the show.

>   WAYNE
>   And the showgirls are sure
>   prettier than at the old ball-
>   and-chain casino.

Wayne will roll the dice in his hand as he speaks. As he finishes his last line he will throw the dice in the air. As the dice fly into the air we track the action in the shot similar to the special effects in *The Matrix* where the entire scene will revolve around the object and land on a craps table where a dealer lets us know that he has won. The dealer will look down and raise his finger up in the air to declare the winner.

>   DEALER
>   Seven!

Close in on Wayne, who grabs a pile of chips and pulls them toward him.

>   WAYNE
>   And you know what they say about
>   the other side of the fence: The
>   grass is always greener.

>   FADE OUT.

Step Three: Vocals and Sound

At this stage, you would record all the voice tracks you'll need and, if possible, include any additional sounds, such as an ambience track or music track (if essential). If this were a multiscene production, it would be recommended that each scene be treated as an independent production and preferably animated by different people at the same time to finish the work faster. Once all scenes are finished, they can be cut-and-pasted together to form the entire production.

TIP

It's essential that all animators working on a single production become familiar with the characters and how they're drawn. Because every artist has their own unique style and way of drawing, adhering to instructions and guidelines provided in the production's models sheets are the best way to ensure everything will look the way it should.

This particular project, however, takes place within a single scene. The entire production involves three shots (they're numbered in the production screenplay). The voice actor for this particular project is my good friend Robert O. Smith, who is a talented voice actor, better known for his character voices in *Transformers*, *G. I. Joe*, and *Ranma ½*. After I explain what I'm looking for to Robert, he quickly goes to work, and the next day I get the voice files in MP3 format.

Because the film only has four lines, Robert decided to do them as four separate MP3 files. This is great because it gives me a chance to import them into Flash and play around with the timing.

Background music always adds a great deal of energy and enhances the mood of any production. Many companies specialize in sound production for use in multimedia, and you can purchase and download the sound files directly through their web sites.

Step Four: Animation

At this point, the biggest concern is how to get the animation done. Notice I said "animation," not coloring or background design, and not wasting time with props or unnecessary details. We're only concerned with getting our performers out there and having them perform the actions described in the script to the best of our abilities.

I decided that for this particular project, drawing the artwork directly within Flash would be better. This will save me a lot of time associated with having to capture artwork and convert it to vector art.

Let's look at some of the more important frames in the movie. Before we do that, though, notice the time code bar that appears at the bottom of every frame. Although the bandwidth profiler contains information about the length of the movie and the amount of frames, and it gives you important details about the file size being used at any given frame, Flash doesn't have a native time code feature for testing and editing animation to the effect of an actual video production–like device. I needed to know at what exact moment an event is happening and I needed a way to track and play a specific frame at any time with the click of a button or key press. So, I made my own drag-and-drop time code feature, which enables me to work with the movie as if it were a production rather than some clip art for a web page.

My particular time code bar is, for the most part, based on the equations covered in the lip-synching chapter. Its main use is to help me pinpoint at which frame or moment in time a specific sound is spoken without having to do that entire crazy math. It also facilitates references to actual frames or moments in time within my x-sheets. The first part, the fps, tells you the current playback speed, which is what all the calculations are based on. If you download the time code file from this book's web site (www.osborne.com) for use in your own production, be sure to change this number to reflect the fps rate to match that of your own movie. By default, the rate will be set to 12fps.

The *frame section* is composed of two parts: the current frame being displayed and the total number of frames in the movie.

The *secs. section* tells you the amount of time in seconds that have elapsed up to the frame being displayed.

The *time section* tells you the exact moment at which a frame is being displayed. Next to the time section is a text input field with a GO button. During a test publish of the movie, I use this field to type in a frame number. Next, I can either press the ENTER key or click the GO button, and it will immediately jump to that frame and play. By doing this, I can easily lock down exactly where a syllable is being spoken or an action happens where timing is of great importance. Rather than spend valuable time doing math, I simply make a record of any required data from the time code bar and jot it down on my x-sheet.

Now, let's look at some of the most important key-frames in this production.

On frame 1, Wayne is walking away from the casino. I made a walk cycle and converted it into a graphic symbol, so I can tween in a way that makes Wayne appear as if the camera is closing in on him.

TIP

When it comes to an actual cartoon, always avoid using Movie Clip symbols. Because Movie Clip symbols play independently of the timeline, it's impossible to synchronize them to anything. Movie Clip symbols also won't translate into video if you choose to publish your film directly to a video format.

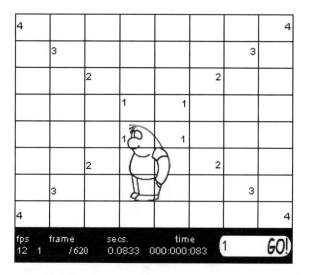

The sequence ends at frame 60. Wayne pulls out his pockets to show us he has no money.

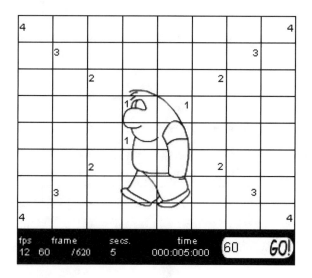

Frame 61 is a cheat. I used a blur to act as a transition between frames 60 and 62. Because the image is only displayed for 1/12 of a second, it won't be enough time for the user's eye to see that the drawing isn't an accurate drawing of Wayne Gamble. Instead, it's a similar mass that allows persistence of vision to be maintained within that area and to flow from one extreme pose to another as the frames change.

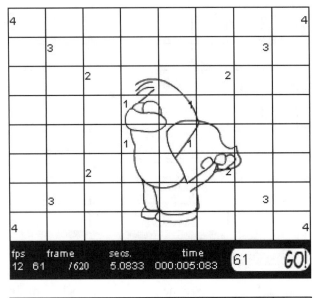

fps	frame	secs.	time	
12	61 /620	5.0833	000:005:083	61 GO!

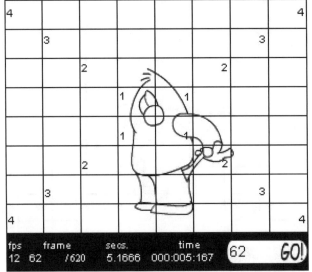

fps	frame	secs.	time	
12	62 /620	5.1666	000:005:167	62 GO!

Shot 1 ends right after Wayne says his line about wanting to try his luck somewhere else. According to the script, Shot 2 says Wayne is to be shot from an aerial view outside the Lucky Day Casino.

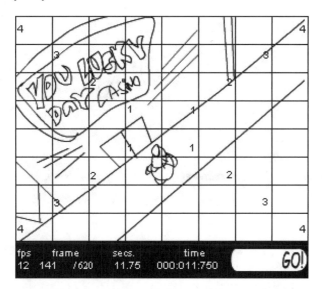

I won't put too much effort into this shot now because I want to concentrate on getting the entire production laid out first. I make a graphic symbol to imply Wayne is walking and I tween it, so he's walking in the path that the final version of the symbol will be walking.

TIP

Avoid embedding motion-tweened sequences within symbols. They create unnecessary file size and might not translate to video if you choose to export them as such. Tweening is perfectly fine if you keep it within the restraints of the main timeline.

It's not even an actual cycle—it's sort of a placeholder symbol—I'll come back and reedit later. The background is also a placeholder that I'll come back and fix later.

The next shot is the big one, and it takes place on the main floor of the casino. There's going to be some complicated camera movement here, but because I'm concentrating on the animation of the characters before anything else, I can go back and design the backgrounds and props later. That way, they'll conform to the camera movements taking place, rather than wasting time trying to do it all at once.

One particular section of the shot that intimidated me at this point was the sequence where Wayne rolls the dice and the camera spins around the room, tracking the dice as they fall onto the craps table. Once I got to that part, I found it was easier to do than I thought and I was happy with the results.

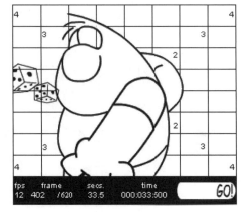

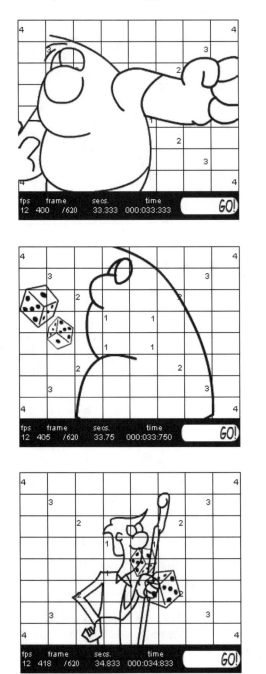

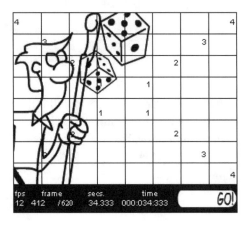

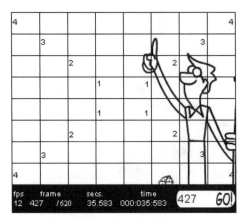

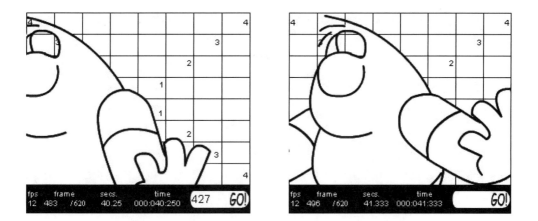

After the entire film is animated, I still have to go back and spruce up my line work, optimize it further, if needed, and fill in my placeholders, such as the overhead walk cycle and the temporary background of the outside of the casino.

The total time it took me to animate this commercial was two days. It would have taken several more days—perhaps even the entire week—to animate something similar through conventional animation practices. Because I used Flash, though, the work didn't have to be drawn on paper, inked, digitized, or to go through any number of pencil tests. Reusable graphics are also a great convenience and I made full use of them. If this had also been a standard animation gig, at this point I would also be finished with my part of the work (the animation) and the project would now move into the hands of a colorist. The backgrounds, which would be designed by someone else, would then be added to the production. And, finally, whoever was responsible for the sound would come in and work with the Foley. As an animator, I'd most likely already be working on animating the next project or, in the case of a multiscene project, I'd be working on animating a different scene. Unfortunately, this isn't the case here and, as a Flash filmmaker, my responsibilities aren't just those of an animator. In the coming days, I'm also faced with coloring, designing backgrounds, working with the sound, and, to a certain degree, even some programming.

Step Five: Color

At this stage, I have several options. I could go ahead and move into lip-synching, and then color, or I could work on the backgrounds, and then come back and color. For this project, however, I chose to make the coloring process my fifth step.

Many of my graphics are Flash symbols, so by coloring one of them, I'm actually coloring every single instance where that symbol appears.

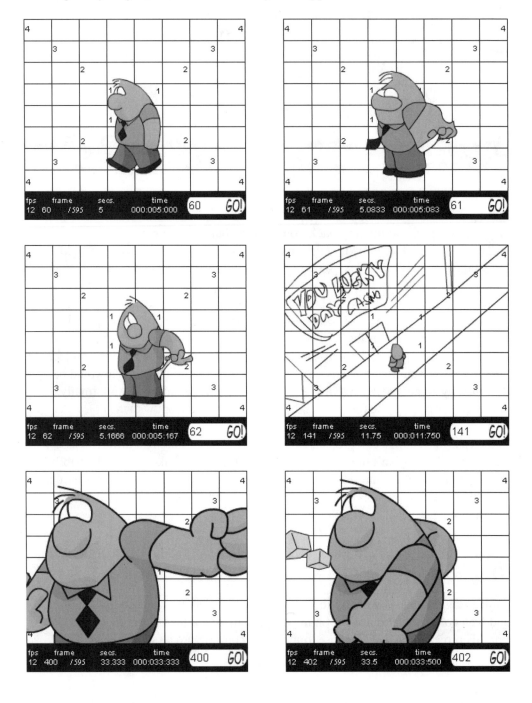

Step Six: Backgrounds

After coloring my characters, I usually go ahead and move into the background design stage where I study the camera movements performed in the sequences and try to visualize the best way to draw the backgrounds. I managed to save myself a great deal of time in the creation of the background for Shot 1: the exterior of the Big Bang Casino. I remembered that not too long ago I had created a background for a scene which took place outside a movie theater. I opened the source file to that project as a library and searched for the symbol. When I found it, I merely dragged and dropped it onto my stage and modified it to look like a casino, which needless to say saved me a great deal of time.

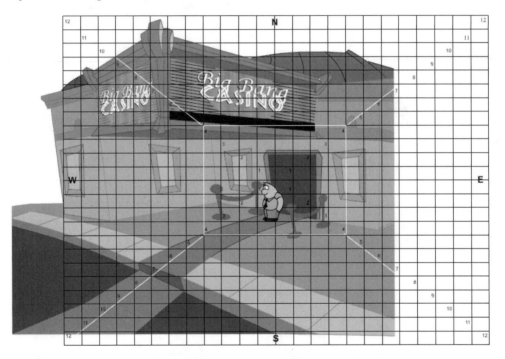

It's hard to tell where the field of view (the camera) is when a large object such as a background is placed over it. We can always turn the outline feature of the layer containing the large graphic so we can see the stage, or we can use a properly aligned field guide on a layer above. In my case, I prefer to be able to see the graphic elements in full. So what I did is simply moved my already existing field guide layer to the uppermost layer and, since my animation is a four-field animation, I use the four-field area to keep track of where my stage is.

For the second shot, I created a placeholder symbol to indicate where the background would be. Getting the background there was a matter of simply replacing the crude line sketches with a more polished graphic.

Here's the Shot 2 background as it looked before.

Here's what the finished background looks like once it was polished.

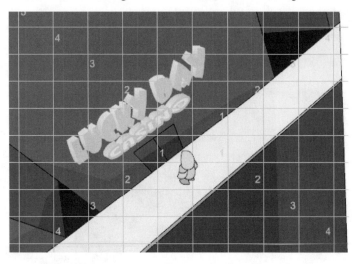

The final background was simple in design, but the important thing was to make it so it conformed to the illusion of time passing within a single shot. This shot required more than a simple background. It needed several extra elements to be put in and taken out at various intervals to give the illusion of Wayne Gamble going from one moment in time, where he's first having a drink, to a few hours later when he's gambling and winning. This all had to be done within a single shot and without the use of extreme editing or transitional devices, such as a cut or fades. Note, in the following sequence of images, I highlighted the four field areas of my guide so you could see where the stage is located and what the audience will see when the movie is published.

Here's Wayne Gamble sipping on his Long Island Iced Tea. The background will be panned left and right using various camera angles, so I placed it at what I call the *neutral position*. This neutral position isn't necessarily the center, but it's the area of the stage that lends itself to the different side-to-side camera movements.

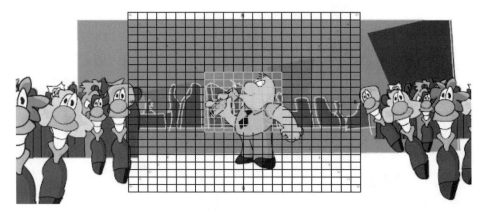

Angie (from my comic strip *Braindead*) comes into the picture. She plays a showgirl in this movie.

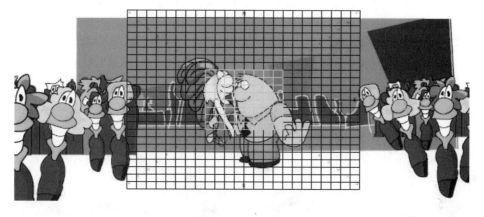

The camera tracks Angie across the room. Outside the field of view (FOV), a sign magically appears telling about tonight's performance.

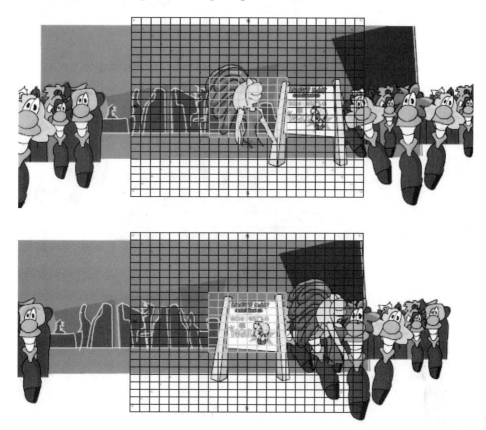

The camera stops at the sign, but Angie continues until she's out of the FOV. After giving the audience enough time to read the sign, we pan back to Wayne, who's now holding a pair of dice in his hand. The sign was sort of a prosthetic piece to the background; it was only needed for that little sequence. Once Wayne is back inside the FOV, it's no longer necessary, so I remove it to make way for the remaining part of the sequence.

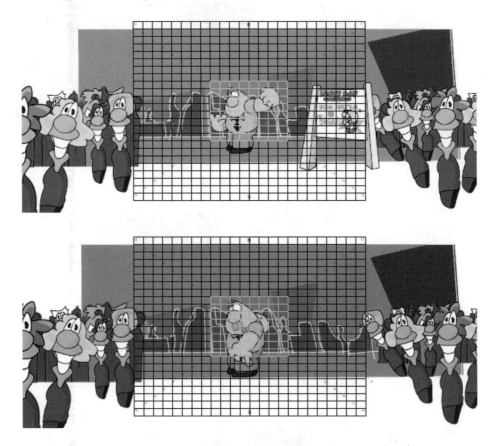

Wayne throws the dice and the camera revolves around him. Of course, this is only how it will appear to the audience because, as you can see here, the elements are being rotated around the camera, not the other way around.

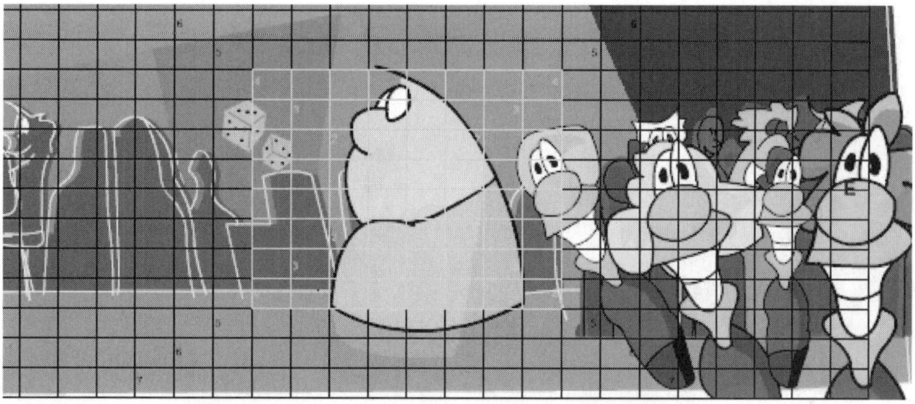

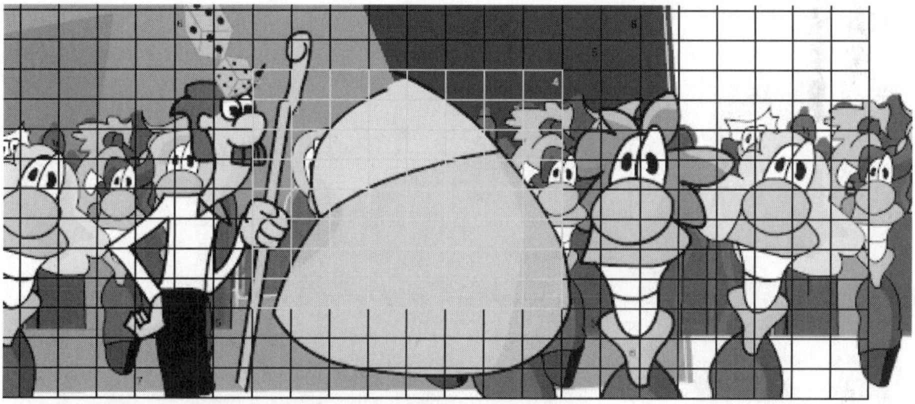

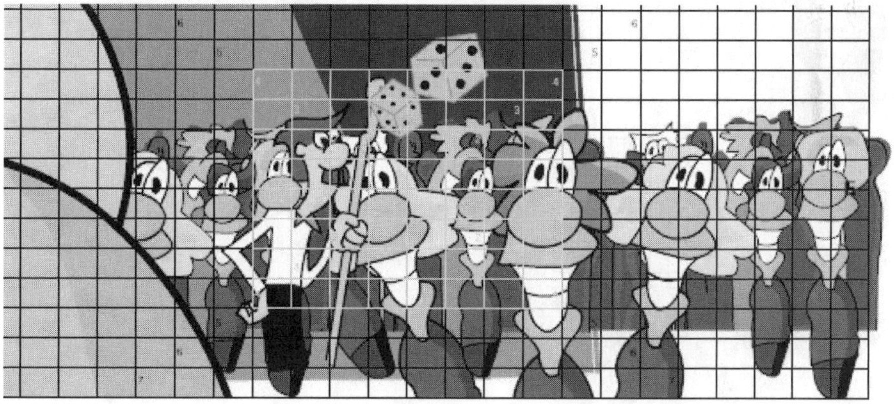

As the dice land on the table, the camera continues until Wayne is, once again, in the center of the FOV. The empty area of the background is now filled with extra people, who have gathered around.

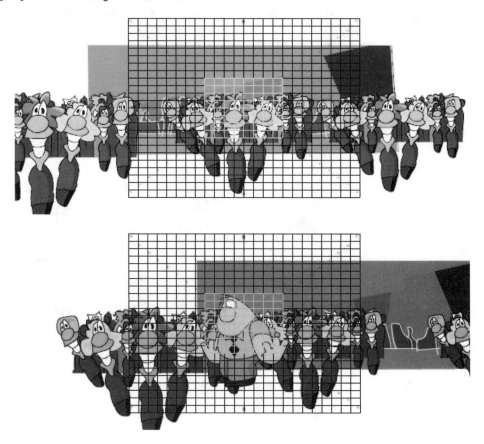

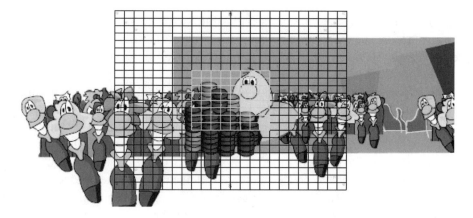

The last and final steps are adding lip-synch and Foley effects, if any. Cleanup and touchups usually consume a good 10–16 hours' worth of work but, in the end, it's all worth it. If you're interested in dissecting this project firsthand, I set up a series of source files for this project, including scripts, storyboards, and Flash source files, which show the entire project through various stages—animating the line work, color, backgrounds, and the final presentation. You can download the whole shebang at www.osborne.com.

Summary

This chapter documented the creation of a typical Flash project as approached by most animation houses and studios.

During the initial stages of the project, a script must be written to have something solid to work from. Not all studios work from an actual script, though, and, in a few cases when the production is a proprietary piece, many studios simply jump into the storyboard phase and use those storyboards as the basis from which to work.

The preference, however, is to have a script formatted in the standard submission format (Master Scene screenplay) and written before any action is taken in the project's development. The submission screenplay is written with all the important action and dialogue that takes place and should contain no directorial or camera instructions.

The director of the project is then responsible for deciding how the film should be shot and creates what's known as the production screenplay. The production screenplay is broken down and numbered shot by shot. It also includes any directorial instruction, camera movement, and special editing instructions required by the director.

It doesn't take an animator or a guru illustrator to create the storyboards. And, they also needn't be elaborate or cleanly drawn. Simple stick figures or rough sketches, along with a printout of the script, will do, as long as you can get a good idea what the final piece should look like.

Note, animation is animation. It doesn't include color, designing backgrounds, working with sound, or anything else. During the animation phase, concentrate on animating the characters' actions and on the overall performance of the film. The addition of backgrounds and color is secondary. They should be left until the animation is completed to save time.

If you don't have time to create a complete element during the production of a Flash movie, you can always create a basic symbol that you can animate and use as a placeholder. So when you're done doing all the important things, you can go back and modify it into the finished graphic.

The last and final steps are usually the addition of lip-synched mouth graphics, as well as any Foley effect that's necessary.

CHAPTER

15

Cinematography
in Flash

Achieving cinematic effects in Flash is often a major obstacle for many animators, who otherwise tend to settle for static or nonconventional approaches, which usually hinders their work rather than helps it. Talking heads are pretty boring and, sometimes, drawing your characters in the right poses and having them performing the action as best they can isn't enough.

Cinematic techniques—a combination of photography, choreography, and film editing—are key players in any successful animated cartoon. Often, those cinematic techniques enhance the overall production quality and make a piece stand out in a league of its own.

In this chapter, I let you in on some crucial technical knowledge that every animator should know, plus I teach you some of the most common cinematic techniques in filmmaking and how to perform them in Flash.

Lights, Cameras, Wait . . . Where the Heck *Is the Camera?*

Flash was originally designed to be a simple web animation tool to create cute little animations like spinning logos and text effects that could be used to spice up web sites, much like any other GIF animation tool. Flash was never directly intended to be used for actual production-oriented animation. Once people began seeing the value in Flash's scripting capabilities, the software itself became even less of an animation tool and more of a web design tool. Despite the overall improvement within the software itself, more animators continue to use Flash 4 simply because all the tools they need have changed little since version 3.

As far as actual animation goes, it's difficult to treat Flash as a tool for serious animation (the kind that goes beyond spinning boxes and moving text) when much of the workflow is performed in complete contrast to conventional animation practices.

This isn't to say that Flash doesn't measure up to the more robust tools. Although limited as it may appear, Flash does have the capability to enable you to perform cinematic effects comparable to the tools used by big-budget studios—if you take the time to learn about the conventional techniques and how to apply them within the constraints of the Flash environment. The most noticeable of all features is this: in Flash, there's no camera! The closest thing to a camera in Flash is the stage, which is where your graphical elements must be laid out if you want your audience to see them.

If an object is inside the stage, then it's within the camera's field of view (FOV) and the audience will see it. If the item is outside the stage, then it won't be "recorded" when it's published (it will be recorded, you just won't be able to see it).

Animating in Flash is like shooting a movie with a camera planted permanently on a tripod that won't budge. Sure, the camera works and it will record whatever you put in front of it, but if your scene takes place in another location, you can't just pick up the camera and go. You have to bring the location to it. You can't tilt the camera to the side. You have to tilt the world around the camera, so the camera can capture it. Instead of panning across a scene, you have to pan the scene across the camera.

This is horrible and we can only hope that in a future release of the software, animators can grab the camera and move it across the work area: up, down, left, right, in, and out, but until that happens we have to conform and work with what we have.

Manipulating the "camera" in Flash is definitely one of the most daunting tasks faced by animators. What can I say: it's the pits.

Setting Up Your Camera

A useful tool developed by the animation industry is the *graticule,* which is also known as the *Field Guide*.

Traditionally, a Field Guide is used to decide how an object should be filmed and where its location will be in relation to the background and the FOV. It allows the animator to draw an object on a cel (as mentioned in Chapter 9) and to communicate to the cameraman how the drawing should be framed by the camera, so it appears correctly on film.

The *FOV* (field of view) is the area of the film the audience sees when they see it on their television sets or computer monitors. The actual size of this area (the size of the stage in Flash) is known, in animation terms, as the *field size*.

In Flash, a Field Guide may aid in determining a proper field size to work with if your interest lies in creating animation that conforms to academy standards.

There is, however, no true standard, as far as creating animation for the Web. Although most web animators are free to choose any aspect ratio they desire, most professionals choose to create their work based on the 12- or 15-field traditional animation standard.

In traditional animation, no set size exists for what a field should be. This is mainly because so much depends on the cameras being used to shoot the animation and the projection format for which the production team will be created. For the most part, the animation industry tries to stay within the mainstream of NTSC (National Television Standards Committee)-based field sizes, mostly because so much of the animation being done is produced for distribution via television or another form of video distribution.

The 12-field and 15-field graticules are known as standard academic sizes. Each field is based on a 4×3 unit ratio, which is how NTSC is measured. Study the 12-field graticule pictured in the following. In fact, go ahead and download it from the Chapter 15 section of this book's web site (www.osborne.com). This is part of a template I created called NTSC TV 12.fla. It can help you properly format your animation, so it conforms to industry standards.

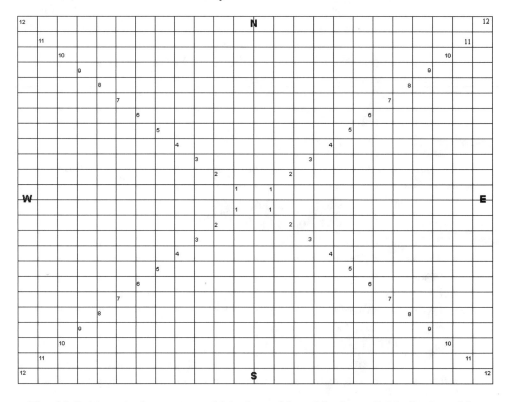

The 12-field graticule measures 12 inches wide × 9 inches tall. Notice how it's divided into four quadrants and the way it's uniquely numbered from the center outward.

A traditional graticule is printed on some form of acetate or clear vinyl. This lets the animator place it on top of the animation paper and be aware of where his fields are as he draws, so he can communicate his shooting requirements to the cameraman.

An animator can animate her drawing to any size she wants, as long as she stays within the 12-field area of the paper or is instructed otherwise.

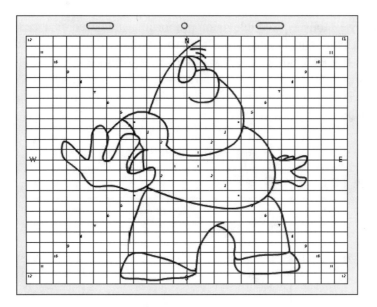

Shooting this image would be a breeze because it takes up all 12 fields. There would be no question about how the camera should be set up.

However, animators may also choose to stay within a certain area of the paper where the Field Guide will definitely come in handy when it comes time to shoot it to film. Take this drawing, which has been drawn somewhere on the upper-right quadrant of the paper. To shoot this image properly, we need to make certain adjustments to the camera.

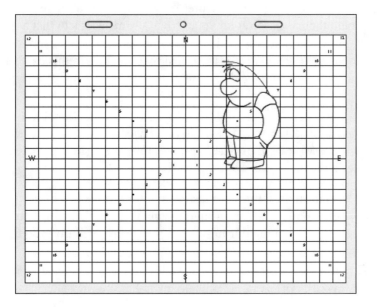

We already established that television proportions are based on a 4×3 unit aspect ratio, so each field is in an academy standard graticule. If you look at the image, you'll notice that each number appears four times. Animators rely on this to keep their FOV in proportion. A four-field structure, which is a typical aspect ratio for Flash films, can be determined by tracing the area around the four field areas labeled with the number 4.

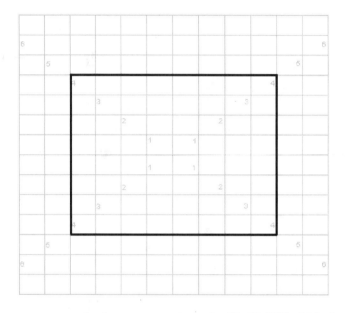

This gives you a rectangle that measures exactly 4"×3" (288×216 pixels). In Flash, you would then need to set up your movie's dimensions to that aspect ratio, so you can work within that area. This is the same concept behind shooting a regular animation sequence for television or theatrical presentation. In this case, the camera would be adjusted so the four-field area takes up the entire television screen.

NOTE

In Flash, the stage is the camera. Although you can adjust it to a specific field size, you cannot move the camera to the desired area in the Field Guide. Instead, you have to move the drawing inside the stage.

Adjusting an eight-field setting in Flash would be approached in much the same way. First, by determining the area around the number 8 fields, as the following shows, and next by adjusting your movie's dimensions to conform to that area.

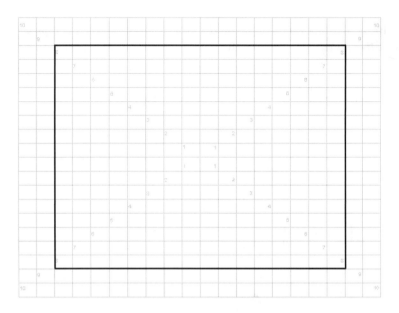

The naming convention for the field you're working with is based on the type of Field Guide you're using. For example, an 8-field setting based on a 12-field graticule is written like this:

The absolute center of the graticule is known as the *Field Center* (F.C.). Because this is a 12-field graticule, this would be referenced as (12 F.C.). If this were based on a 15-field graticule, then it would be referenced as (15 F.C.) in your notation.

NOTE

Field measurements are usually included in the appropriate fields within the animator's x-sheets, so the cameraman can read it and know how to set up the camera and shoot that particular sequence of frames.

Going back to our previous dilemma, you can see that our character is drawn way off course from the field center. When this image is shot on film, the cameraman would have to adjust the field to match the field the animator has requested. Suppose the animator is working on an eight-field setting. This is where his image would be if shot with the camera centered on the Field Guide's original center.

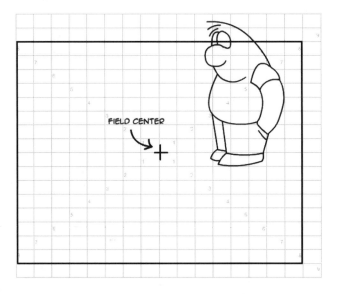

As you can see, the character is way off to the side of the FOV. In fact, if this image is shot this way, it would cut off a major part of this character's head. This is where the four directional reference points (north, south, east, and west) come into play. If we want our character to be properly framed, we would have to move the camera so it captures the character the way it should. This would place the Field Center two fields east and four fields north from its original location.

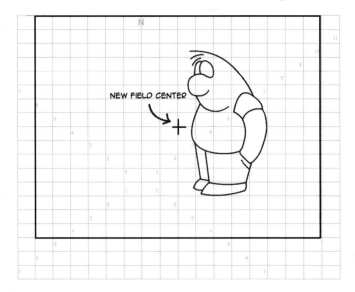

Now the image will be properly framed and the animator would provide the instructions for that sequence to be shot using an 8-field setting located two fields east and four fields north from the center of a 12-field graticule.

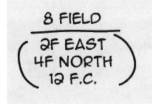

This is a convenient way to draw and shoot your work as far as standard animation practices are concerned. If the Flash animator were able to move the camera around the work area, he too could lay out his animation anywhere on the stage and simply animate the camera, or place the camera on the appropriate locations when applicable. Because Flash doesn't have a camera, though, the graticule's only form of function within the Flash environment is to help you set up your field size (stage dimensions) and to help you keep the backgrounds with the setup if you're drawing them outside the software the good old-fashioned way.

Choosing a Proper Field Size for Web Presentation

The way you format the field size of your movie can be largely dependent on the web design structure of your web site or the web site where the film is to be put on display.

Many web sites are designed to conform to certain monitor resolutions depending on their demographics. In most cases, people choose to design their sites to conform to a resolution setting of 640×480, although resolutions of 800×600 are rapidly becoming the new norm.

At a screen resolution of 640×480, the maximum decent-looking field size based on the standard academy sizes is a six-field setup. This creates a movie that is 6 inches wide × 4.5 inches tall (432×324 pixels); see Figure 15-1. Taking into consideration that the browser itself would normally take up a good part of the screen and that you're trying to keep the user from having to scroll down the page to view your movie properly, you would barely leave enough room at the side of the page for small amounts of advertising or other forms of web gibberish.

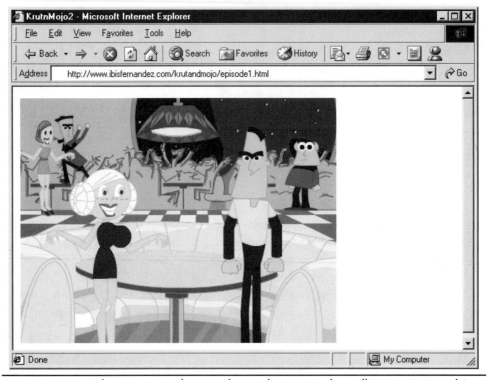

Figure 15-1   *A web page created at 6 inches wide × 4.5 inches tall (432×324 pixels)*

When the same page is viewed through a higher resolution, the movie appears much smaller (Figure 15-2).

If my web page was designed to be watched through a minimum resolution of 800×600, then, as you can see, I'd have more room to place all my advertising, buttons, links, and all those spanky web devices that would help people navigate through my site more effectively.

A four-field animation (288×216 pixels or 4×3 inches) seems do a great job at conforming to the rules, no matter what the resolution level is. It even gives you plenty of white space for advertising and displaying other web site features without the user having to scroll the browser in any direction (see Figure 15-3).

The three most common monitor resolution settings are 640×480, 800×600, and 1,024×768. The following table might help you decide on the field size to use in presenting your work to your targeted viewers. Remember, if you're animating based on an academic standard, it won't matter what the actual size of your work is created in. After exporting the movie, its size can always be altered to whatever field size you want. As long as you keep the 4×3 proportions, your movie will always look great.

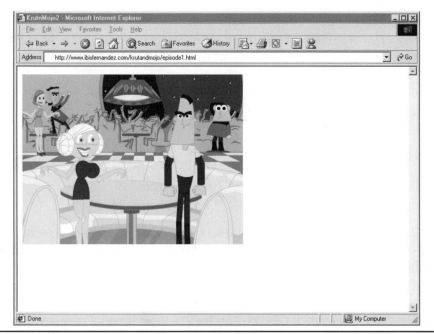

Figure 15-2   *The same page created at a higher resolution*

Figure 15-3   *A web page created at 4 inches wide × 3 inches tall (288×216 pixels), using a four-field structure*

I personally create most of my animation at 288×216 pixels (four-field structure). If the work is for web publication, the movie's dimensions can always be altered to a different field size.

Resolution	Maximum	Recommended
640×480	6 Field (12 F.C.)	4 Field (12 F.C.)
800×600	8 Field (12 F.C.)	6 Field (12 F.C.)
1,024×768	11 Field (12 F.C.)	10 Field (12 F.C.)

Any Flash animation created at a field size larger than 8 will have a greater chance of poor playback unless when it's published at smaller proportions. Although a monitor set at 1,024×768 enables you to view and create an animation set at a full 12-field size setting, I recommend this be done only if your animation will be strictly for video publishing. In any event, you'll most likely require a superior machine with a tremendous amount of CPU power, such as those used for digital video editing, to play back the film properly. So, unless you're creating cels for use in higher-end animation software or for the specific purpose of broadcast animation, stay away from anything larger than an eight-field setting.

Here's a list of all the field sizes based on a 12-field graticule, as well as their measurement in pixels.

Field Size	Inches	Pixels
1	1"×.75"	72×54
2	2"×1.5"	144×108
3	3"×2.25"	216×162
4	4"×3"	288×216
5	5"×3.75"	360×270
6	6"×4.50"	432×324
7	7"×5.25"	504×378
8	8"×6"	576×432
9	9"×6.75"	648×486
10	10"×7.50"	720×540
11	11"×8.25"	792×594
12	12"×9"	864×648

TV—Cut-Off and Titling

If all you're doing is formatting your work to be displayed in TV proportions, with no intention of ever converting it or having it seen on television, then you needn't worry about TV cut-off areas. If you feel there's a slight chance your film might someday end up on the video screen, though, then you should take special precautions in advance or be prepared to have the television mutilate a good portion of your work.

The first zone to consider when animating for television is the TV cut-off zone. This is the area of the screen that a typical television is more likely to cut off. Not all televisions are created equal, so establishing a TV cut-off in your picture often is the result of a pure and simple guesstimate. By academy standards, the TV cut-off area on a 12-field guide is approximately three fields smaller than the actual field size itself.

The dark gray area with rounded corners in the following illustration represents the TV cut-off area (1.5 inches from the left and right sides, while conforming to NTSC standards). It doesn't necessarily mean the television will cut that area off the image at that exact place, but your image will definitely be cut off at any point within that area, depending on the person's television. Most modern TV sets currently support a much broader FOV, so the TV cut-off area could, in fact, be much smaller.

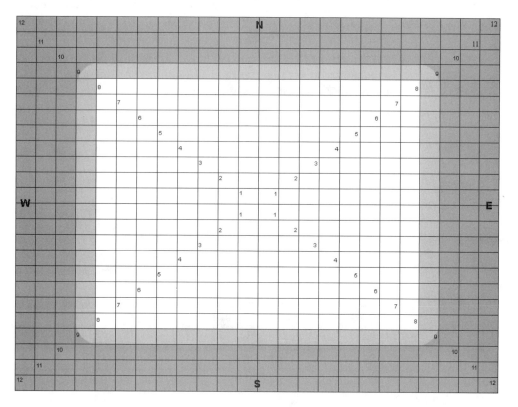

TV titling is done at .5" (36 pixels) away from the cut-off area. This is represented by the rectangular area in the center of the illustration and its purpose is to help you keep any type of lettering used in the film from becoming distorted by the curvature of the television screen or, even worse, from being cut off.

When you animate something that's purely for web or theatrical presentation, then there's no need to worry about where your TV cut-off zones and title-safe areas are. But, if there's any chance your work might end up in a video format of some kind, please take the necessary precautions to keep from having to rework your stuff when it comes time to do the conversion.

Camera Technique

In this section, I cover some of the most common camera and filmmaking techniques that you can put to work to enhance your animation.

The Pan

When the camera pans, it moves across the scene from one direction to the other. It can be from left to right, from right to left, from top to bottom, or from bottom to top.

You can't just grab the camera in Flash and pan it to achieve the effect you need to tween your scene elements across the stage. In this example, the camera is going to pan from left to right across a scene of a downtown street.

The symbol in the starting frame is positioned at the place where we want the action to begin. It helps to set the layers being panned as outlines. That way, you can see the camera's FOV.

The second step is to create a new cel (insert a key-frame) at a frame where you want the action to end and position the BG (background), so the ending location will be shown through the stage.

Finally, we perform a basic tween by right-clicking in between both key cels and selecting Create Motion Tween from the right-click menu. Remember, to tween an object properly, there must only be one instance of the symbol within a cel. If multiple objects are within a cel that's being tweened, the results will be unpredictable. If the sequence contains multiple elements, however, they must all be tweened at the same time, along with the background.

For the best cinematic feel, the closer an item is to the camera, the faster it will travel across the stage. A great example of a well-done pan can be seen in Mark Clarkson's short film *The Evolution of Modern Animation* (shown at the bottom of this page and the next), where the camera is made to pan across the basement of an old-school animation sweatshop.

This sequence, from Rick Rousses's *Frank Mallard: Duck Detective,* displays a well-done PAN-DOWN using multiple background elements tweened at different speeds.

Zoom

A *zoom* is when the image is enhanced in size. You can zoom in on an object to focus on a particular element on the screen or you can zoom out to show the audience the

entire picture. To zoom in on an object, you have to tween all the elements on the stage at the same speed, increasing in size. To zoom out, you must tween them, decreasing in size to show the overall picture.

If you absolutely have to use a zoom, use it as a way to help the audience focus on flat objects, such as images on a wall, a person holding a knife within a painting, or an apple as part of a fruit basket included in a mural on the wall of a building.

Never use a zoom as a function of a camera, especially when living creatures are in it and multiple objects are supposed to give the illusion of depth within that picture. Zooms are synthetic and lifeless. They work best as a means to convey an object's magnification or size in relation to the objects around it. They should never be used to close in on a person or object where depth perception is important. Avoid using multiple objects for zoom effects. Instead, use single-file symbols and keep your other layers empty or hidden during the tween. This allows your zoom to continue looking synthetic and mechanical, like a real zoom. In most cases, a cut to or dolly shot is preferred over a zoom.

Dolly Shot

Rather than the camera adjusting the lens to increase the magnification of a picture, in a *dolly shot* the camera is physically grabbed and moved toward or away from the object. The dolly shot is the preferred way of closing in and backing away from a character, object, or scenic elements in a film. Always use a dolly shot instead of a zoom if your object is something other than a flat surface. It gives the illusion of three-dimensional space and provides a more cinematic quality to your animation.

To perform a dolly shot in Flash, you must tween all the elements in your sequence at different speeds. The closer objects come toward the camera, the faster their speed increases. Look at this sequence from a deleted scene in my film *The Adventures of Krut and Mojo.*

The sequence begins with the camera focused on the overhead lights above the arena.

As the camera is carried down and pulled back, you see the ring is revealed.

To enhance the effect, the background is drawn in Perspective view. As we continue to pull the camera back, we pass right through the glass in a nearby announcers' booth.

Soon, after passing through the window, we also pass by the announcers, where the camera finally stops.

Crane Shot

A *crane shot* is performed when the camera is mounted on a crane. As the crane ascends or descends, the camera focuses on a target or pans to another area of the scene at the same time the crane is moving. It's a breathtaking shot and much more difficult to perform in Flash because much of it depends on how you draw the graphical elements in the sequence. To perform this shot in Flash, you first need to create a background in a way that may be distorted to conform to the movement of the camera, so when it's seen through the camera lens, it appears natural.

During the introduction sequence in my feature-length Flash film, *Without You,* we begin with a view of the Houston skyline as seen directly from below. The "camera," which is supposedly mounted on a crate, spins around in a 360-degree circle while at the same time ascending toward the night sky.

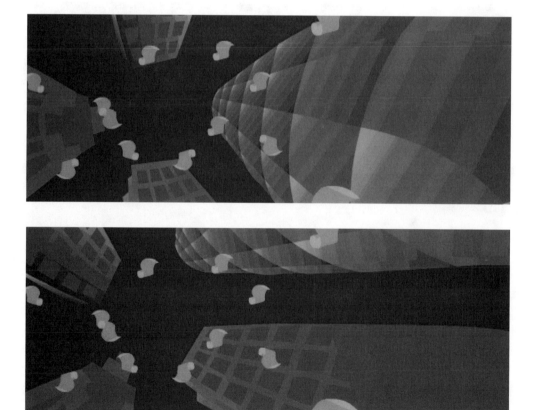

The crane continues to ascend and the camera continues to turn.

Once I complete a 360-degree turn, the camera begins to pan downward while, at the same time, the crane continues to rise higher.

At the end of the shot, the crane is way up in the air and the camera is pointing directly toward the city streets. We are so high up in the air that all we see is the building fading into the dark void and the lights from the cars far below.

So, how exactly is such a complicated shot created in Flash? If you look at the background in its entirety, you'll notice it's not so much a matter of the shot being complicated, but rather a clever use of perspective and distortion techniques within a single drawing.

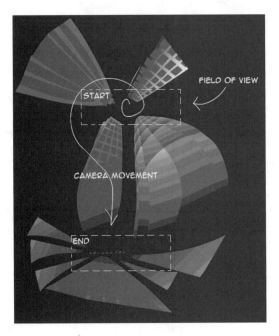

The Tilt

The *tilt* is performed when the camera is placed on a single location and tilted to shoot what lies to the sides without the camera actually being moved anywhere. Suppose you have a sequence where your character walks from one end of a hall to the other end.

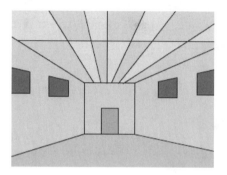

The tilt in Flash is done in a similar way to that of the crane shot, but the way you draw the background is far more extreme. For a tilt, you're literally warping a flat object to the point where it's bent and the two extremes are parallel to each other.

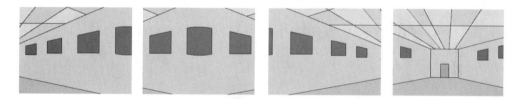

Here's the background as it was drawn. In fact, because this background has the same proportions on one side as it does on the other, it can be tweened and looped in a way that will make the camera appear to be rotating in full 360-degree cycles.

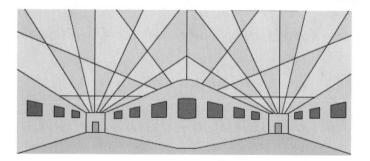

Tracking Shot

A *tracking shot* is when the camera is focused and locked on a moving element. In this sequence, the camera is tracking Angie's movements as she walks down along the sidewalk. This shot mimics that of a camera mounted on a dolly and dragged along as the characters walk by. In reality, what's going on here is that the animation cycle of Angie walking has been centered in the FOV and is being allowed to loop over and over at the same spot while the background is tweened from one side to the other.

Depth of Field

Depth of field (DOF) is the sense of a three-dimensional environment given through a motion picture. Because Flash is vector-based, it's harder to create the sense of depth created with raster-based tools. One of the most common ways animators create a sense of depth is to export their backgrounds and apply a Gaussian blur to it, and then reimport that image as a bitmap. This can be done through Fireworks, Photoshop, or any other raster-based graphic design software. The blurred background gives the illusion of the camera lens going out of focus the farther away it is.

Shown here is a sequence from Vaughn Anderson's brilliant experiment in camera manipulation, titled *Spaceman Bob*.

Gaussian-blurring an image isn't the only way to create the out-of-focus, DOF effect performed by Anderson in *Spaceman Bob*. In fact, by doing it using the vector images, you might save yourself a few KB of file size created by the bitmaps.

1. To blur a vector graphic, begin by converting the image into a symbol in Flash. In this case, it's the background.

2. Give the symbol a certain degree of alpha. In this case, I'm applying a 50 percent alpha to the background.

3. Duplicate the symbol at least two extra times.

4. Align the superimposed symbols against each other, but keep them offset by approximately 1 or 2 pixels. This is what causes the image to appear blurred.

5. You can make the blur even more realistic by tweening each instance of the alpha symbol and moving side-to-side no more than three pixels. This makes the blur appear unstable and mimics the effect generated by a real camera quite efficiently.

DOF doesn't necessarily have to involve any form of blurring effects. It may also be achieved through lighting or color balance. This particular sample was created by adding a new layer in between each preexisting layer. The new layer contains a blue rectangle painted with a blue fill set to 15 percent alpha. This causes the elements to become harder to see the further down they are in the stacking order. And, this creates a sense of depth close to what occurs naturally when various acetate cels are stacked on top of one another.

Cuts

The *cut to* transition is nearly the most preferable transition device in filmmaking, but it isn't only a transition technique. The cut to is an essential element in filmmaking that will keep your film from quickly becoming boring and monotonous.

It's essential to keep your audience's eyes refreshed with new images and angles every three to five seconds. Can you imagine ever watching your favorite television show through the eyes of a single camera mounted on a tripod? How boring would that be? People need to see the action from various angles and distances. If a shot is held for too long, it becomes boring. How long is too long? Most TV and film directors will tell you three seconds or five seconds at the most.

Although it's easier to draw your characters and actions performing through a single steady shot, get into the habit of changing to a new camera angle every three to five seconds of film. Your audience will love you for it.

Wide Screen and Cinemascope

Literally hundreds of wide-screen formats exist in the world. All wide-screen formats are based around the technical aspects of the cameras used to shoot the films.

Wide screen in Flash is done more as a novelty item than with the actual intent of showcasing the film on the big screen (although anything is possible). A wide-screen format has the same aspect ratio of many actual theatrical formats and tends to look excellent when presented through a web browser. Look at the Cinemascope-formatted movie in Figure 15-4.

Cinemascope, which is basically twice as wide as a standard 4×3 formatted movie, looks absolutely beautiful even at a 640×480 screen resolution. Wide-screen field

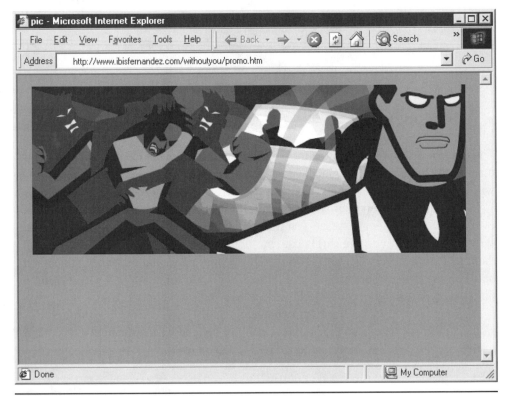

Figure 15-4   Without You *uses the same formatting as a Cinemascope movie.*

sizes, however, are as varied as are the cameras to shoot the films. HDTV, for example, is less wide than Cinemascope, but a bit taller. It measures 16×9 units. The theatrical Panavision format is even wider than that.

In short, wide screen is anything wider than 4×3. No set standard exists for it, just whatever looks good to you. Many people currently animate specifically for an HDTV-file size because the format looks just as nice on the big screen as it does on television.

Wide-screen formatting for the Web lets you create a movie that conforms itself more naturally to human vision. People sit about 1.5 feet away from their monitors, so anything that can aid their vision will greatly enhance the experience.

Wide screen has a theatrical feel to it. If the Flash film is of a dramatic nature or, perhaps, even satirical, the wide-screen effect will enhance the overall feel of it.

One thing you should know is wide screen doesn't always work and sometimes it might hurt your film rather than enhance it. People have come to expect a certain type of genre to be more theatrical in nature, while other genres are strictly for the small screen. Many cartoons that are fun and quirky rely, for the most part, on a small cast of characters—maybe one or two people on screen at the same time—and fairly basic backgrounds would look terrible and empty if shown on wide screen because the animation and scenery aren't as involved. These types of movies are perfectly fine using the small 4×3-viewing field.

But, if the film's purpose is to draw in the audience and immerse them in large, richly detailed landscapes and action that goes beyond a 4×3 screen, then wide screen is definitely for you. If your film will contain more than three characters on the same shot at once, then wide screen is definitely for you. The only thing you have to ask yourself is whether the backgrounds will be stunning enough or the action big enough to warrant a wide-screen presentation. If your answer it yes, then by all means go right ahead.

The next thing to ask is the infamous television question—will it fit? You can go about this by two routes. If you plan to have this film ported to video, then how will the film be presented: letter-boxed or full screen at 4×3?

Most people will go with the 4×3 presentation, even though this means the film will have to be panned and scanned, and much of the work outside the 4×3 area will get cut off. This doesn't have to be too big an issue. If this is the case for you, then you have to make sure that when you animate and produce the film, you plan ahead and keep your most important details confined within a 4×3 area.

Summary

Talking heads are boring. Shots that are held for too long tend to become boring quickly. Zooming in and out of an object is a terrible filmmaking technique. In this chapter, you learned about the use of cinematic elements within the Flash environment. You learned about field sizes and how animators go about preparing a shot using a graticule. And, you also learned how to use a 12-field graticule to format your Flash films, so they maintain academic standard field sizes. Here are a few more things to remember to help you become a better Flash filmmaker.

▶ Zoom shots should be used only when the object in question is a static image and no depth of field is to be implied.

▶ Dolly shots are the preferred way of moving toward an object or away from it. Dolly shots involve making the sequence appear as if you're physically carrying the camera and moving it across three-dimensional spaces.

▶ Camera shots, such as tilts and crane shots, can be shot the same way as a pan shot is, by tweening them from side-to-side. To give the illusion of a complex shot, however, the background elements must be drawn warped, in such a way that they conform to the path of the camera.

▶ TV cut-off and title-safe areas aren't a given because televisions are different in how much of the picture they cut off. By academic standards, the image cut-off area is three fields smaller than the actual field size (1.5 inches on the left and right, while conforming to the NTSC aspect ratio). The title-safe area is .5 inches inside the image cut-off zone.

▶ No camera exists in Flash so, rather than animating the camera across the stage, you have to animate the elements across the stage itself, which in Flash acts as the camera.

Index

NOTE: Page numbers in *italics* refer to illustrations or charts.

INTERNATIONAL CONTACT INFORMATION

AUSTRALIA
McGraw-Hill Book Company Australia Pty. Ltd.
TEL +61-2-9417-9899
FAX +61-2-9417-5687
http://www.mcgraw-hill.com.au
books-it_sydney@mcgraw-hill.com

CANADA
McGraw-Hill Ryerson Ltd.
TEL +905-430-5000
FAX +905-430-5020
http://www.mcgrawhill.ca

**GREECE, MIDDLE EAST,
NORTHERN AFRICA**
McGraw-Hill Hellas
TEL +30-1-656-0990-3-4
FAX +30-1-654-5525

MEXICO (Also serving Latin America)
McGraw-Hill Interamericana Editores S.A. de C.V.
TEL +525-117-1583
FAX +525-117-1589
http://www.mcgraw-hill.com.mx
fernando_castellanos@mcgraw-hill.com

SINGAPORE (Serving Asia)
McGraw-Hill Book Company
TEL +65-863-1580
FAX +65-862-3354
http://www.mcgraw-hill.com.sg
mghasia@mcgraw-hill.com

SOUTH AFRICA
McGraw-Hill South Africa
TEL +27-11-622-7512
FAX +27-11-622-9045
robyn_swanepoel@mcgraw-hill.com

**UNITED KINGDOM & EUROPE
(Excluding Southern Europe)**
McGraw-Hill Education Europe
TEL +44-1-628-502500
FAX +44-1-628-770224
http://www.mcgraw-hill.co.uk
computing_neurope@mcgraw-hill.com

ALL OTHER INQUIRIES Contact:
Osborne/McGraw-Hill
TEL +1-510-549-6600
FAX +1-510-883-7600
http://www.osborne.com
omg_international@mcgraw-hill.com